Arthur Crump

A Short Enquiry into the Formation of Political Opinion

From the Reign of the Great Families to the Advent of Democracy. Second Edition

Arthur Crump

A Short Enquiry into the Formation of Political Opinion
From the Reign of the Great Families to the Advent of Democracy. Second Edition

ISBN/EAN: 9783337070618

Printed in Europe, USA, Canada, Australia, Japan

Cover: Foto ©Suzi / pixelio.de

More available books at **www.hansebooks.com**

A SHORT ENQUIRY

INTO THE

FORMATION OF POLITICAL OPINION

FROM THE

REIGN OF THE GREAT FAMILIES

TO THE

ADVENT OF DEMOCRACY.

BY

ARTHUR CRUMP.

\SECOND EDITION.

LONDON   .

LONGMANS, GREEN, AND CO.

AND NEW YORK: 15 EAST 16th STREET

1888

PREFACE TO THE SECOND EDITION.

The first edition of this volume being exhausted the occasion presents itself for me to pass in very brief review the reception with which it has been favoured in various quarters. The main body of the work being made up of statements which anyone can verify for himself, the book must, as in all similar cases, stand or fall by testing their accuracy. This being unassailable, there would be little else left for the critic favouring the Tory side in politics to carp at but the deductions drawn from these facts. Many of my friends who have read the book said to me, " Yes, I have read it, but I do not agree with you." " Do not agree with what ?" was my interrogative reply. To this I could never get any satisfactory answer. The statements of fact on which the book is built up cannot, as far as I know, be gainsaid, which secures at least the premises from assault. There remain, then, first the deductions and then what is ventured on in the way of prophecy. No one can prove that the principles of the Liberal party will so successfully predominate over those of the Conservative party in the future as they have in the past, therefore it is only wasting time in arguing that point with an opponent. But, on the other hand, the Liberal can point out that, as in the development in other branches of human affairs, the predominance of Liberal principles in politics

has in the past been strengthened and extended by that
kind of irresistible force which orders the course of
the development of civilisation itself; and there is good
reason to believe that principles which are supported, I
say deliberately by, by far the greater number of impartial minds, will continue to gather strength, will
attract not only new adherents who come into being,
but will in course of time bring more converts, who will
be able, as many have done in the past, to shake off
their prejudices.

The Liberal party has on many previous occasions had
to regain its temporarily exhausted strength in the cold
shades of opposition, which is no doubt beneficial to the
party in the long run; and it has been chiefly owing to
the leaders of the Liberal party being thrust from office
through the timid weakness of a portion of their following when some new reform was being combated, that
their opponents have been able to get into power. Such
is the position of the Conservatives at the present
time. A Liberal was conversing the other day with the
editor of a Conservative journal, and as their talk proceeded the Liberal was unable to conceal what it was
that made him warm towards his whilom opponent in a
way that he had never until then been able to do. After
beating about the bush the Liberal, who was a large
owner of property, had the courage to make the confes-
sion, of which he wished to unburden himself, that " He
really, after very mature consideration, could not divest
himself of the idea that Home Rule for Ireland, in however limited a sense, *would disturb the foundations* of
property." That, of course, was a plain intelligible
reason to give why he did not approve of Home Rule in
any form, but the declaration stamped the man. How
the proposed measure was in his view likely to affect

him personally was all he cared about, and he transferred his allegiance on that ground alone. No very
prolonged search into the records of history is necessary
to show the inquirer how the transformation of Liberals
through Whiggism to Toryism was accomplished in times
gone by, when similar fears seized hold upon their minds ;
and this is the great difficulty the Liberal party in their
prolonged struggle to introduce such political reforms
as the advance of civilisation imperatively demands, has
always had to deal with, viz. the desertion by its supporters through fear of their property, or their privileges
being undermined by some proposed new reform. We
can all understand how easily apprehension of that kind
grows with some people in proportion as new property
or privileges are acquired ; but what would become of
the weaker section of the community if the stronger
were, in attaining the upper hand, to be allowed for
ever to band themselves together for the purpose of
governing the country in their own exclusive interests ?
The far-seeing politician, however, cannot fail to perceive, if he only carries his investigations into the past
far enough, that in politics, as in other sciences, there
is a resistless volume of force pushing on the development of civilisation to a goal at which each individual
will get his deserts and no more, and at which each
distinct race, if it has vitality and character enough to
be able to survive the dying-out of the lust of conquest,
will be allowed by their stronger neighbours to govern
themselves.

With these few remarks, suggested by the great Home
Rule fight which is still being waged, we come to the
way this book has been received by some of our friends
the critics. Politicians of Liberal persuasion have been
just, recognising that the object was to collect the facts

and from them to draw plain deductions.   For one bitter attack there have been a dozen reviews emanating from the best quarters expressing approval.   In such circumstances the bitterness we are justified in assuming is proved to be merely the venom which is the only weapon left to the crushed serpent.

	Date	Foreign Secretary.
C. .	Dec. 23rd	Grenville.
C. .	Mar. 17th	Hawkesbury.
C. .	May 15th	{ Harrowby. { Mulgrave.
L. .	Feb. 11th	{ Charles J. Fox. { Visct. Howick.
C. .	Mar. 31st	G. Canning.
C. .	Dec. 2nd	{ Bathurst. { Wellesley.
C. .	June 9th	Castlereagh. G. Canning.
L. .	Apr. 24th	Dudley.
C. .	Sept. 5th	Dudley.
C. .	Jan. 25th	{ Dudley. { Aberdeen.
L. .	Nov. 22nd	Palmerston.
L. .	July 18th	Palmerston.
C. .	Dec. 26th	Wellington.
L. .	Apr. 18th	Palmerston.
C. .	Sept. 6th	Aberdeen.
L. .	July 6th,	{ Palmerston. { Granville.
C. .	Feb. 27th	Malmesbury.
L. .	Dec. 28th	{ Lord J. Russell. { Clarendon.
L. .	Feb. 10th	Clarendon.
C. .	Feb. 25th	Malmesbury.
L. .	June 18th	Russell.
L. .	Nov. 6th,	Clarendon.
C. .	July 6th,	Stanley.
C. .	Feb. 27th	Stanley.
L. .	Dec. 9th,	Clarendon. Granville.
C. .	Feb. 21st,	{ Derby. { Salisbury.
L. .	Apr. 28th	Granville.
C. .	June 23rd	Salisbury.

CONTENTS.

Diagram showing the Duration of Liberal and Conservative Governments during the Present Century.

List of Administrations in the Present Century.

	PAGE
INTRODUCTION . . .	vii—xxxii

CHAPTER I.

The Transfer of the Government of the Country from the Great Families to the People of England . . . . 1—40

CHAPTER II.

The Value of Individual Political Opinion . . . . 41—70

CHAPTER III.

The Formation of Political Opinion under the Guidance of the Press . . . . 71—109

CHAPTER IV.

How Political Opinions are Formed by Members of Corporate Bodies . . . . 110—131

CHAPTER V.

Sequel to Chapter IV . . . . 132—141

CHAPTER VI.

The Loss of Power and Time caused by the Efforts of both Political Parties to Damage each other's Credit . . 142—149

CHAPTER VII.

PAGE

The Formation of Political Opinion in Times of Depression of
    Trade   .   .   .   . 150—159

CHAPTER VIII.

"One-Man Power"   .   .   .   .   .   . 160—164

CHAPTER IX.

Liberal Converts .   .   .   . 165—252
List of Bills Rejected by the House of Lords, with Particulars
    from Original Sources   .   .   .   . 217—225

CHAPTER X.

The Composition of the House of Commons since the Transfer
    of Power from the Great Families to the People, and its
    Capacity for Discharging its Duties   .   .   .   . 253—273

CHAPTER XI.

Bicamerism   .   .   .   . 274—279

CHAPTER XII.

Conclusion   .   .   .   .   .   . 280—291

INTRODUCTION.

POLITICIANS are divided for all practical purposes into two parties, Liberals and Conservatives. There may be Tories, Radicals, and moderate and ultra adherents of both sets, but it will be sufficient for our purpose to adopt one dividing line, since every politician of whatever degree must on all great questions throw in his lot with one side or the other. We propose to assume that we are addressing ourselves to people whose minds are open to conviction on the subject of politics, and that they will be made up, like those of the average honest juryman, after a fair and impartial consideration of the merits of the evidence laid before them. It matters not under what influences a man has grown up,—whether his father has been a large landed proprietor who has imbued him with the spirit and creed of politicians in that sphere of life, or whether he began life with nothing, and has studied politics with his mind unfettered by the various influences which Conservatives are well known to inherit in a more marked degree than Liberals equally well off do, he always knows in his heart what justice means. Every man knows under any and all circumstances whether in any particular case the verdict is as near just as it can be, or whether it is against the weight of evidence. All men of fairly developed reasoning power, whatever they may profess, know in their secret hearts whether the broad policy pursued by a political party is a just and righteous one, or whether it is a selfish and unrighteous one. No matter what a man's previous opinions may have been, owing to the circumstances in which he has been placed, or to the ignorance which is the mother of so much lamentable error; whether he admits it or not, he cannot persuade the world that he does not see that black is not white, or that he does not understand plain facts when they are presented to him; or again, that he is not arguing against his real convictions when he refuses to admit that those facts carry with them incontrovertible evidence in favour of the soundness of the course pursued by the party in whose support they are adduced.

One of the reasons, and we believe the main reason, why there are so many new Conservatives is, that the new generations of politicians, at the time when their opinions begin to crystallize, have neither taken the trouble to study the development of the science during the last fifty years, nor have even mastered the alphabet of their creed. This being the case, we now propose, to the best of our ability, to begin with the alphabet.

We have said already that politicians are divided roughly into two sections—Liberals, and Tories or Conservatives. The first thing the political student naturally asks himself on approaching the subject with an unbiased mind is, what do these two classes of politicians respectively profess? In other words, what is a Conservative and what is a Liberal? Each, roughly speaking, desires, in the first place, something for himself. Let us take the Conservative first, if for no other reason than because he belongs to the oldest order.

Conservative literally means preserver, guardian. It is a term by which, between 1825 and 1835, the political nickname Tory was superseded. Parties were originally divided into Whig and Tory. They are known now as Liberal and Conservative.

The head and top of the Tory, and afterwards of the Conservative system of politics, was the monarch, and the bottom or base of the system was the small landed proprietor, whose vassalage the monarch desired at all times to secure for his own safety. How this system was originally built up is easily understood if we go back to the time of the Conquest, after which the whole territory of England was regarded as the property of the Conqueror. Since he could not manage it all by himself, and be the only Tory in existence, he was compelled to associate other Tories with himself. He accordingly divided the land among his barons, who in their turn divided portions among their dependents. Although the feudal system has not been alike all over Europe there has not been much difference. Each lucky individual who lived early enough in the history of the world to become practically a little sovereign in his own dominions would naturally enjoy a good time of it, and his descendants might be expected to die hard, as regards the abandonment of their special privileges.

If these small feudal sovereigns had large holdings, they lived in castles which, notwithstanding the liberal views of Charlemagne, the owners wished to fortify, not only for purposes of defence, but for those of rapine, which, in the good old Tory days, was not looked upon at all as lawless or interfering with other people's interests.

The traveller who has enjoyed a trip up the Rhine has seen for himself the still solid evidence of castellic Toryism, which shows at convenient intervals, from Bonn to Bingen, how well the riparian owners understood to

" conserve " their baronial residences, from which they ever and anon descended to plunder and despoil their weaker brethren. The Tory king lived on the heights in his castle, and nestling, as it were, at the foot of the throne dwelt his vassal marauders in the village, under the shelter of the castle walls.

The owners of these castles may be said to have formed the " Upper House " of those feudal times, being in relation to each other as peers or equals.

The system pursued in most countries was much the same, the rights at a very early stage assuming the hereditary character, the feu, fief or feoff passing from father to son on condition of his paying the dues exacted.

Here then we have in a greater or less degree in all countries the root of the Tory aristocracy. Human nature is much the same all the world over. Rights or property once acquired, for which there was the slightest justification at the time of the acquisition, have been in the past, and always will be in the future, clung to with that tenacity which is a characteristic of brute as well as of human nature. It has only been by the institution of laws, the growth of a higher standard of justice, and the building up of resistless " resources of civilization " that such proprietary rights, long enjoyed almost exclusively by a privileged class, have been made gradually to yield up, if not the proprietorial rights themselves, at least some of the benefits to be derived from them for the public good.

It is but natural that all new acquirers of property, in whatever form, desire to enjoy its advantages just as much as the hereditary barons we have referred to, and they have, acting under the impulse of the same instincts, joined the " Conservative " ranks. A Conservative father, in ninety-nine cases out of a hundred, has Conservative sons and daughters, and precisely the same may be said of the Liberal father. The transmission in due course of the parental political creed is nothing more than is to be expected. If we find large numbers of well-to-do men of business knowing little or nothing of the history of politics, and being guided in the side they take by what affects their own personal interests, in whatever sphere of life they may happen to be thrown, there is no cause for surprise that the child who apes the father from his earliest years in most other things, should move also in precisely the same political groove. From the hour he can prattle, the boy repeats the well-worn parental maxims as if he understood and believed them; he thinks as the parent does for lack of being able to think for himself, and at last perceives that he has gone too far to change, if perchance he sees the error of his ways, and moreover perceives that he would lose his character for consistency, which many think too great a sacrifice even for the truth.

Such is the method on which political creeds are grafted from the parent tree to the youthful sapling.

These remarks bring us briefly as far as what we may call the exposition of Conservatism, as it originated with kings and their retinue of dukes, marquises, earls, and barons. From the monarch down to his noble dependents there was the same motive. Each order desired to enjoy all the wealth, honour, and dignity that was to be derived from the position of vantage which birth or accident might have afforded them. Once acquired, the inherent selfishness of the man was ever present to resent any suggestion of the privileges being shared with anyone else, unless under circumstances of imminent danger of the person chiefly interested being himself

despoiled. Only under such a pressure would he enlist
the aid of new blood to swell the number of those who
fortified him against attack. So has it ever been even
down to the present day, subject, however, to the very
important modifications which the following pages will
show have been introduced through the agency of the
great Liberal reformers, who have by constitutional
measures compelled the original inheritors of the soil
and of the privileges attaching to wealth, place, and
power, to share the benefits derived from them with the
community as a whole.

Next in order to the monarch and his noble dependents
we have the landed gentry, the squirearchy, and all
their dependents. A great Tory landlord of course
would prefer a Tory farmer as a tenant to a Liberal
farmer, and when a farm becomes vacant, due care is
taken to make sure, if possible, that a Tory farmer rents
it. The farmer in his turn will take care that his dependents, as far as possible, shall support the same cause. If
his wages depend upon his politics and he has nothing to
eat, the poor man must pretend he is a Tory, if he be
not one in reality. Hence the great majority of landowners will be Conservative.

Although the House of Commons contains a larger
number of Liberals than Conservatives, the proportion
of the former is not greater than that of two to one.
' Whitaker's Almanack ' gives the number of Members for
England and Wales in the present Parliament at 489;
for Scotland 60; and for Ireland 103. Of these the
same authority tells us 336 were Liberals; 241 Conservatives; and 61 Home Rulers.

*The English House of Commons, at the time of
the Union with Scotland, in 1707, consisted of 513

* ' Whitaker's Almanack.'

Members; 45 were then added for Scotland, and in
1801, 100 for Ireland, making the total of 658. This
total number was preserved by the first Reform Act
(1832), as well as by the recent one (30 and 31 Vict.
cap. 102), but in each case the apportionment was
altered, and it now stands — England and Wales
493 Members, Scotland 60, and Ireland 105. By the
Reform Act of 1867, 11 English boroughs were totally
disfranchised, and 23 others lost 1 Member each; but
25 seats were bestowed on new boroughs and universities, and 28 on counties. Four boroughs, with 6 seats,
have since been disfranchised for corrupt practices, viz.
Beverley, Bridgewater, Sligo, and Cashel, and in 8
others, representing 13 seats, the writs are suspended,
making the present number of sitting Members 639.

Total number of electors in England and Wales,
2,591,402; Scotland, 315,121; Ireland, 228,278.

. Under the new Act every man occupying a tenement
or land in a borough or county in the United Kingdom
of a clear yearly value of £10 is entitled to be registered
as a voter. The 1884 Act will admit to the franchise
more individuals than any previous measure. The 1832
Reform Bill added less than 500,000 voters, the 1867
Act rather more than 1,300,000, and the 1884 Bill, it is
estimated, will increase the number by 2,000,000. Of
these, 1,300,000 will be added to the register in England
and Wales, more than 400,000 in Ireland, and the
remainder in Scotland. Those having a direct voice
in political affairs will thus be raised to the total of
5,000,000, of whom four fifths will be qualified as householders.

It is a noteworthy circumstance that just as the representative system of government was being improved by
the addition of 2,000,000 to the electoral roll, which

extends the area of reform so as to include for the present probably all competent voters, the Conservative section of the House of Lords under the guidance of Lord Salisbury made the most hopeless of all their efforts at obstruction to prevent the Reform Bill of 1884 from passing.

The 2,000,000 who will be invested with the new dignity and responsibility of a voter will be interested to know briefly something of the history of Parliamentary Reform. Sir Erskine May says, *" The theory of an equal representation, at no time very perfect, had, in the course of ages, been entirely subverted. Decayed boroughs without inhabitants, the absolute property of noblemen, and populous towns without electors, returned Members to the House of Commons, but great manufacturing cities, distinguished by their industry, wealth, and intelligence, were without representatives."

In looking through the history of Parliamentary. Reform, that which at once strikes the impartial mind is, that the intellectually great people of the earliest times were all in favour of reform, but that their efforts were invariably frustrated by the ignorant and selfish.

Sir Erskine May again tells us that " schemes for partially rectifying these (the above) inequalities were proposed at various times, by statesmen of very different opinions." Lord Chatham was the first to advocate reform. Speaking in 1766 of the borough representation he called it " the rotten part of our Constitution ;" and said, "It cannot continue a century. If it does not drop, it must be amputated." In 1770 he suggested that a third Member should be added to every county, "in order to counterbalance the weight of corrupt and venal

* P. 393, vol. i, ' Const. Hist.'

boroughs." Such was his opinion of the necessity of a measure of this character, that he said : " Before the end of this century either the Parliament will reform itself from within, or be reformed with a vengeance from without." His prediction has been slowly verified. The reform has come from without, for time has conclusively shown that in the absence of that pressure from without which has been due to the growing enlightenment of the people, all the efforts of the wisest of men within would have been put forth in vain.

What then is the consummation which that persistent pressure has at length achieved? The curtain rises on the stage of politics in the year 1885, and England finds herself with a democratic Government, which means that the sovereign power resides in the collective body of the people. The accidental transfer of power nominally to the Conservatives does not alter the case. It is, all the same, the Democracy that governs. In other words, the political system on which the nation is governed has been in less than a century completely and entirely reversed. At the beginning of the hundred years of which we are now in the fourth quarter, the Government was aristocratic, that is to say, representing the interests of the minority. Now it is democratic, that is to say, representing the interests of the majority. The descendants of the Anglo-Saxon race have gone through the same experience under different circumstances which led to democracies among the ancients. The difference is, that our larger communities cannot govern directly, but it must be done by chosen representatives, which is a modern idea. As communities grow in numbers, representation through delegates has to be resorted to. In Switzerland, in North America, and in France in 1848 the system was adopted. It is comforting to know that the conditions under which new countries are opened up and peopled in modern times preclude the possibility, for example, of the dependencies of Great Britain having to do over again what the Anglo-Saxon race has done. We have arrived at democratic institutions by much the same process as the Greeks did, owing to the majority having fallen into a more or less abject state of dependence upon a privileged minority. In other words, we have had gradually to overthrow a feudal system. The opposition to the dominant class, who based their rights on their exclusive occupation in war and the possessions they acquired for those services, was gradually strengthened by the growth of cities whose communities acquired wealth and contingent rights that the aristocracy could not ignore. As early as the Anglo-Saxon times any merchant, for instance, who had made three voyages ranked with a thane; and shortly after the Norman Conquest the cities obtained an equal footing in Parliament with the warlike aristocracy. A new departure was taken after the Norman Conquest, when the cities were represented in Parliament on the same footing as the aristocracy. It is instructive to note the fact, that in their turn the citizens who are now being enfranchised are only making the same demand as the trades and guilds clamoured for until they obtained a share in the municipal government of the towns. Thus is the basis of democracy being continually widened.

The problem which is now presented to the country is —how can the people effectually govern themselves? How can they delegate the execution of that stupendous function without at the same time sacrificing some of the power which it is the great object of democracy shall reside in the collective body of the people? It is certain that the

same force which renders Communism impossible outside
the domain of theory, will exert itself to deprive a democratic form of government of some of the power which it
is the intention of reformers it shall exercise. In other
words, the great men will rise to the top and try to
assert their own wills, and endeavour to exercise a too
personal influence in carrying on the affairs of the
nation.

Aristotle and Xenophon are agreed that the art of
government should be exercised by the best men in the
State for the benefit of the nation. But can the people
exercise such a control over the best men that they shall
be contented to subordinate their personal wills to the
collective will of the people? Great men love power,
and the weakness of human nature is, if we only knew
it, as weak in great men as it is in little men. It is
easy enough to govern downwards from the apex of the
cone to the base, if the ruler has the physical power at
his disposal. That we have seen. That is the aristocratic system of government. Now we are going to
govern from the base upwards, which is a much more
difficult task, unless we can institute a system of controlling committees, as we have suggested farther on.
In our opinion there should be a system of checks, or
the weakness of human nature will assuredly drift in the
direction of " one-man power," which will rob the last
reform carried of its most precious fruits. It is often
maintained that the Government must be trusted to
negotiate international treaties, &c., but it should always
be subject to the ratification of Parliament. We do not
live in a Roman age when great party leaders acquired
popularity by their military successes and great wealth,
by which means they could enlist adherents to their
cause, decide who were to be elected as magistrates, and

how the popular assembly were to vote. The Tories, even of our day, cannot apparently dissociate their ideas from a state of things in which men like Cæsar, Pompey, Marius, and Sylla had large personal followings, owing to the powerful influence which their heroic deeds exercised over the popular mind. In those days it was not a great cause that the people advocated as they do in our time; it was a purely personal attraction, as in the case of Napoleon Bonaparte. In the same way that one-man government is gone and it is henceforth to be the voice of the people that rules, so it is not the merits of one man that will attract the support of the country, but the cause, if a right one, which he upholds.

The Tories are very fond of telling us that the " man in the gutter" has not the same right to a vote as the rich man of education, and that this is an argument in favour of the government of the country continuing to be carried on by the aristocracy. Our reply to that allegation is a twofold argument. It is an old Tory fallacy that the same theory of government holds good in these days as it did in those of the ancient societies. The fallacy lies in the fact that whereas ancient societies consisted largely of serfs who had no political rights, modern societies are composed entirely of freemen. Not only are they freemen, but down to the £10 householder, and including the service franchise, are they very many of them indeed as capable of forming a sound opinion upon the politics of the day, when they are properly explained to them, as many of their richer and better educated fellow-citizens. Our second argument is that the aristocratic form of government has been tried quite long enough, and has been found in some respects most lamentably wanting. We require no better proof of this than the fact that the aristocratic rulers have been defeated in a hundred fights in which they had to stand always on the defensive; and that after fighting for a hundred years for supremacy, their tenure of power as a Government has, until the short revival of the Disraeli period in 1874, been precarious, not to say feeble. In fact, it is hardly too much to say that their political existence has been purchased at the expense of handing the government of the country, with brief intervals, practically over to their opponents. Formerly they were the dominant political power; now they are a diminishing minority whose chances of regaining the ground they have, as a party, lost, must depend upon their willingness to follow the path, when returning to power, that is marked out by the great reforms which the Liberal party have carried with the consent and approval of the majority of the nation.

The reason why the aristocratic system of government ought in justice to be permanently superseded by the democratic is plain to a thinker who is under no influences which divert him from the straight path to the truth. A minority of a nation, entrenched as it were against the demands of the majority, cannot be impartial judges, and not being that, are unfitted to govern a nation. Moreover, even if a Government representing a minority of the nation could prove that in all cases the exercise of their judgment was impartial, the highest moral standard set up for his personal guidance by the most conscientious statesman cannot guarantee such just administration of the affairs of a nation as will be secured by allowing the whole nation to act as a jury. Sir George Cornewall Lewis says, *" The mere aggregation of incompetent judges will not produce a right judgment, more than the aggregation of persons who have no know-

* 'Influence of Authority on Matters of Opinion,' p. 111.

ledge of a matter of fact will supply credible testimony to its existence." This argument is supported by stating that the people at large formerly believed in the Ptolemaic system that the sun moves round the earth, and that now they are quite as satisfied to believe in the Newtonian system, which entirely reversed the principle. A good deal of the force, however, is taken out of that argument in the same way as we showed just now in the difference between society being constituted in ancient times mostly of serfs, and in modern times of free men, and moreover of free men who are far better able to judge of political questions than a good proportion of those who were not serfs in ancient societies. The Ptolemaic system was, moreover, believed in in the same way that the ignorant and superstitious believed in wizards and necromancers; but the human mind of our day is enlightened on general subjects to a much greater degree than at any former period. There are hundreds who can prove the Newtonian system to be a sound one, whereas the Ptolemaic system was with almost everyone at that period a belief on a par with the spiritualistic theories entertained by some silly people even in our time. In brief, we have at length arrived at the democratic stage of government, owing chiefly to our having emerged from a state of existence in which one portion of society was able to use the rest for their own purposes. The governing power under such circumstances would naturally protect themselves by trying to make it appear that they exercised supernatural powers, and by keeping the rest of the community in such a state of ignorance that they would not discover the fraud that was being palmed off upon them. This, in fact, is precisely what has been done, more particularly by the Church, and this is the great blot upon its history and traditions that will without a shadow of doubt lead ultimately to its disestablishment.

The theory that statecraft is a business demanding special experience and training is not inconsistent with the theory of democratic government. All institutions require a captain and lieutenants, just as the organ gives out its sound at the direction of one pair of hands, but to ensure perfect harmony every pipe must be accurately tuned and connected with the keyboard. So with the units of the nation. Each one, when sufficiently educated, is entitled to be connected with the delegates they may collectively appoint as their mouthpiece and is entitled collectively to control them. As time goes on, and other nations perfect their machinery so as to render it as fit as ours is to work on a democratic basis, there will no longer be the necessity for so much secret negotiation with other Powers as is the custom in the present day. Secret negotiations always suggest more or less of Machiavelism which belongs to the age of aristocratic government. The one system as well as the other accords, in fact, with a state of society which is dissolving, while new outlines are already strongly marked indicating a new departure, which means that if nations, like individuals, want anything of each other the better way is to speak out in an audible voice so that both sides to the bargain are under no possible misapprehension as to what it is that is really proposed to be done. In support of the contention that the time is ripe for the introduction of the democratic form of government, it may be remarked that the argument, sound in itself, that every man is to a certain extent limited as regards judgment to his own subject or class of subjects, is not inconsistent with the view that, upon subjects connected with the government of the

country, when raised for discussion in these times and
fully expounded for the benefit of all, every man of
average intelligence is capable of forming a sound
opinion. Unless that position can be proved to be
untenable, which we maintain that it cannot, we hold
that not only is the country ripe for the democratic
form of government, but that no other includes all the
elements of which modern societies like ours are entitled
to demand that it shall be composed. This argument is
supported by the following remarks of Sir George
Cornewall Lewis:—*" There is no one body of persons
who are competent judges on all subjects, and who are
qualified to guide all sorts of opinion; there is no intellectual aristocracy separated from the rest of the community and predominating over them indiscriminately.
Every subject in turn has its own peculiar set of competent judges, which vary for each; and he who belongs
to this select body for one science or art, or other practical department of knowledge, is confounded with the
crowd in all others. Again, a person whose opinion is
without authority on this and that and the other subject,
at last arrives at some branch of knowledge or some
portion of the business of life on which his opinion has
a claim to attention."

The Greeks evidently were of opinion at one period
that the people were entitled to decide matters relating
to their own welfare, for Plutarch reports that Anacharsis
expressed his wonder that in the legislative assemblies of
the Greeks the wise spoke and the ignorant decided.
Ignorant is a relative term, and it may fairly be argued
that their ignorance could not have been very profound,
or the wise men could not have been contented to abide
by their decision. Laplace in his work, ' Essai Philoso-

* ' Influence of Authority,' &c., p. 115.

phique sur les Probabilités,' lays it down as a general maxim that if the question is of such a nature that it is more than an even chance that each member of the assembly will form an erroneous opinion upon it, then the decision of the assembly will probably be wrong. But he leaves apparently out of his calculation the fact that the members of an assembly can inform themselves by consulting those on whose judgment they may rely. Moreover, the comparatively short period that has elapsed since Laplace wrote has made such a great difference in the means at people's disposal for inform- ing themselves upon almost every subject, that what he claims then to have established as a general maxim is no longer entitled to that dignity. The position taken up by Xenophon in his tract upon the Athenian State is only a sound one when examined in the light of the circumstances which obtained when he wrote it. The aristocracy and the popular party, he says, were symbolical of good and bad respectively; but those who found their political opinions upon authority like that, forget that Xenophon was probably born about 2,300 years ago. The difference between modern societies and those of that period is in many respects very great. He then wrote: "In every country the best portion of the citizens is hostile to democracy; for among the best citizens there is the least dishonesty and irregularity of conduct, and the greatest strictness of principle, while among the people there is the greatest want of intelli- gence and of good conduct, and the least virtue." The most ordinary reader of that statement would admit at once that it could not for a moment be held to apply to modern society, except as regards the dislike of the best portion of the citizens to the democracy; and even then it is not true, because in our day the Tories, who are hostile to democracy, are not in the higher sense the best portion of the community. Our society includes a great middle class of citizens, probably much better informed and having infinitely better means of obtaining information on political affairs than was the case with the middle classes in Grecian democracies; and who besides are neither prejudiced by the selfishness of the stratum immediately above them, nor the comparative ignorance of that below them. The society which furnished Xenophon with the material for his tract possessed no such social ballast as that which is to be found in the democracy of our time. He saw little besides two extremes, and therefore his argument loses its force when applied to the state of society which exists 2,000 years after he lived. Plato thought that a perfect State could be founded only on the intelligence of the ruling body, neither family nor wealth being sufficient in the absence of the former. Aristotle considered that aristocracy was the government of the best men in all respects tested by the standard of moral virtue, and not by some arbitrary standard of excellence. Xenophon again dilates upon four heads, viz. honesty, principle, intelligence, and virtue, and as regards all four he holds that the aristocratic party is entitled to govern on the ground of their being more richly endowed with those characteristics. In Xenophon's time an investigation might have established the soundness of his affirmation, but it most certainly would not at this period of the world's history. Cicero says in his 'De Republica' that no form of government can be worse than that in which the richest people are considered the best. Time has again proved the soundness of this maxim, the government of the greatest empire the world has ever seen having been, in our time, taken out of the hands of the great families and the greatest land proprietors, and handed over to the people to be discharged through their appointed delegates.

The moderate constitution which this country has now arrived at, which duly regards the rights of all the citizens, and is founded mainly on the support of the middle class, but inclining to democracy, Aristotle calls πολιτεία. He speaks of the danger of a Government being too democratic or too oligarchical, but at the same time he remarks that of the two extremes, the oligarchical is the most dangerous, since the excesses indulged in by rich people destroy the State oftener than those of the classes beneath them. It is important also to remember that there is a great difference between democratic England and democratic America. England and her institutions have gone through the purifying furnace of time. Her people move more slowly from a political point of view; they possess much more coherence as a society, and are much better fitted to practise a system of government in which so large a number have a voice than a people composed of many nationalities, loosely knit together and caring much more for their own personal comfort and advancement than for the political figure they cut in the eyes of the world. The American nation does not possess in its society, nor will it possess for hundreds of years, the political material which enables England to create the most perfect democracy the world has yet seen. The various qualities demanded by the highest standard of government can only be very slowly grown and matured. It may be said by Tories that such a standard has existed in the aristocratic government the Radicals have overturned. The reply is, an aristocratic government has amply proved itself to be an institution destined, comparatively speaking, to last but a few years. It has always been overtuned, and always will be wherever it exists. In Russia and Germany, for example, it rests on rapidly decaying foundations. What has been the process? A dominant class has always, up to the time when the English colonies started on a democratic system to begin with, oppressed and thrown into political bondage those under them, until they were able successfully to assert their participation in rights which a privileged class endeavoured to retain for themselves. The development of the principle has, however, always left still a class below those who, by acquiring wealth, land, and power to form one aristocracy under another, imitated in their turn their superiors and sought to protect their own position by continuing in force the aristocratic principle of feudal society. The merchants banded together; the guilds, with their privileged industries, the landowners and agriculturists all formed a subsidiary aristocratic development, always leaving a greater or less residuum to protest against the injustice of their not having had a fair start in the race, and of their being left out in the cold. The upholders of the democratic principle, however, maintain that the government of the country of right belongs to them, on the ground that they are the majority; and being the majority, have the same right to decide all political questions as a majority does in a division on any question in the Imperial Legislature. That the people of a country have a perfect right to assume that attitude and maintain it if they can is beyond question. They have now wrested the power after a protracted struggle from their opponents; and it may well be that the Tories are somewhat apprehensive of the use they intend to make of it in the sense of reprisals.

We have heard a good deal lately of people's "natural rights," and a certain number of men have banded themselves together with the avowed object of dividing the wealth of the world on what they conceive to be a more equitable basis. The cry for the nationalisation of the land is, however, one which no statesman possessing any sound views on political economy could for a moment entertain. The hero of this modern crusade is Mr. Henry George, a man having nothing worth speaking of of his own, and whose knowledge of political economy has been shown to be very imperfect, since the opinions set forth in his book, ' Progress and Poverty,' are so ludicrously absurd that none but the most ignorant people could be taken in by his doctrines. The land is but a portion of the property owned by the community, and what applies to one part must with equal force apply to all others. By limiting his proposal to the land and not to other things, such, for example, as he owns himself, Mr. George shows he does not really believe in the soundness of his own theory; and it deserves, therefore, only to be dismissed with the remark, that it is but a vulgar Socialistic device, on a par with those which have on so many previous occasions been propounded by adventurers who have seen their way to a cheap notoriety by deluding the poor and raising false hopes in the minds of the ignorant.

There are no doubt many reforms of a more or less radical nature which have yet to be carried before the people have entered upon their full and just share of the rights and privileges which are their due ; but much as we desire to see further progress made in that direction, no encouragement should be given to such wild and im-practicable schemes as the nationalisation of the land. The measures by which we have been able to arrive at our present political development have been passed with due deliberation and on constitutional lines, and the same caution should be exercised in the future as has been observed in the past. Such brilliant success as has been achieved always more or less intoxicates a certain order of unballasted intelligence, but it is quite as much the duty of those who have secured for the people the great benefits which they now enjoy, owing to liberal reforms, to check a tendency to license, which, if uncontrolled, is productive of much mischief and injurious to the reputation of the political party to which these unsound Socialistic extremists profess to belong.

The reputation of M. de Tocqueville, as everybody knows, is a great one ; and yet it is curious how a man, whose book on ' Democracy in America ' has earned for him such fame, could commit himself to such strange conclusions as are to be found therein. The unsoundness of some of those conclusions seems to be due to the fact that he thinks that the democratic characteristics of the Americans are peculiar to all democracies. Such erroneous deductions would appear to be due to the circumstance that M. de Tocqueville did not allow for the fact that the ancient democracies arrived at that form of government by a process of evolution, while the Americans formed themselves into a nation with a democratic government to start with. M. de Tocqueville observed certain peculiarities in the mode of life, &c., of the Americans, and he jumped to the conclusion that all democracies manifested the same tendencies. Among the general propositions he laid down are the following :—
(1) A desire to possess inferior works of art. (2) A taste for showy ornamental architecture of a cheap and perishable nature. (3) A natural inclination for Pantheism. (4) A passion for abstract and generic terms.

(5) The production of poets possessing a turgid style, rising superior to the classic forms and academic limits which artists of the first order recognise as their best guide and master. (6) An inability to appreciate the refined and intellectual modes of recreation which form the amusements of aristocratic societies. (7) A fondness for rapid and easy successes. These are peculiar inductions which a Frenchman is more likely to be the author of than one of any other European nation. As a race, we know they are hasty in drawing conclusions, and are apt to be narrow-minded through their stay-at-home tendencies. It requires, however, no profound knowledge of human nature to enable a man of the most ordinary intelligence to perceive that the few propositions we have enumerated, which are only some of those contained in M. de Tocqueville's book, are not peculiar to democracies, but are characteristic of the *nouveaux riches* as a class, wherever found. All the problems in fact are susceptible of one solution, which is contained in the well-known proverb, "Imitation is the sincerest form of flattery." The main object which most people in the world have in view is to get as much as they can for themselves of everything that is worth having. If they cannot afford diamonds they will sport paste. If they cannot afford marble facings to their dwellings they will, as M. de Tocqueville saw in the row of small palaces in the Grecian style of architecture near the shore at New York, have them painted in imitation of that costly material, with coloured wooden columns in imitation of the same. The Pantheism may be traced to the diffusion among a people with unsettled ideas and habits of the modern German philosophy. Their crude and untutored ideas about art were easily satisfied with the cheap productions of modern mechanical

invention. The lower classes of the ancient republics no doubt had similar tastes to those of the offshoots from our race who formed the foundation of the American democracy; and the educated Greeks and Romans retained, as our educated classes undoubtedly will, that refined appreciation in all matters relating to art, which makes those who cannot afford to possess the master-pieces of painters or sculptors, or to live in marble halls, satisfied with occasional sights of such treasures, without descending to the vulgarity of surrounding themselves 'with the poor and empty imitations which can alone afford satisfaction to the uneducated eye and the untutored judgment.

The English nation makes now a fresh start on the broadest political basis it has so far been able to mark out for itself. In what direction will the new forces com-bined with the old exert their influence? We venture to predict that the democratic power will at first over-reach itself, for extreme Liberal politicians, unless restrained by the moderating influence of that high sense of justice and political propriety which can always be relied on as the inheritance of the sober, thoughtful, undemon-strative middle section of society in the hour of their great triumph, are sure to attempt to push their success beyond legitimate bounds. There are already signs of this among those who lead the extreme Radical section. The probabilities, therefore, are in favour of a Conser-vative reaction, if not at the next general election, not long after it, which will give again a check to Liberal reforms. If this happens, and the Conservatives come into power and decline to continue to carry out the Liberal programme by reforming the land laws, &c., it would be a national disaster because such reforms are urgently needed. A powerful party of Conservative

" middlemen," especially lawyers, will, of course, oppose a reform of the land laws, and the Radicals will be exceedingly ill-advised if they indulge in excesses to an extent that will force the moderate section of their own party to check the pace by putting their opponents into office.

The last Ministry of Mr. Gladstone essayed to, and in many respects did, reach the highest standard of statesmanship, which only those possessing a long range of political sight can thoroughly appreciate at first. Shallow thinkers call it weakness, and they contrast it with what they thought was the strength of Lord Beaconsfield; but those who think thus will change their minds if they live long enough to overcome their prejudices. The ' Pall Mall Gazette ' of the 17th January, 1884, had the following paragraph on this subject which is worth preserving because it is the truth :

" There is another line of cleavage which seems to us probable enough, although if it should come to be the real division it would make such havoc among existing parties that we are not surprised that men have shrunk from facing it. Yet it is an old division, and one which is eternal. It is the division upon which parties joined issue at the last general election, and it may well be the division on which they will join issue again hereafter. That issue is the old question between Duty and Selfishness, between ' I ought ' and ' I want.' Lord Beaconsfield was shipwrecked upon the national conscience. Mr. Gladstone triumphed because he appealed to duty. The great issue fought out in ever-varying fields from 1876 to 1880 was whether or not a nation had a right to make self-interests the single and supreme law of its action. ' British interests ' was the rallying cry of Lord Beaconsfield ; ' British duties ' the watchword of Mr. Gladstone. The essential infamy of

Jingoism was its assertion as the first law of its being that might was right, and that because we were strong this alone was mandate enough to warrant us in taking what we wanted. With the Jingoes the measure of our strength was the charter of our authority over the interests, the property, and the liberties of our neighbours. Mr. Gladstone boldly challenged all this as detestable and even infernal. He asserted, even in the crucial case of the Russian advance on the Bosphorus and on Afghanistan, that we must subordinate our wants to our duties. He confronted the doctrine of everlasting grab by the doctrine of the categorical imperative, the absolute Must of Duty and of Right, and he achieved the most signal triumph that our annals record. Is it too much to believe that the same principles, the same ideal of life and conduct, will inspire the new electorate as they inspired the old?"

The above, we may say, is the text upon which we have attempted to found the discourse which follows, and with it we close our Introduction.

CHAPTER I.

THE TRANSFER OF THE GOVERNMENT OF THE COUNTRY FROM
THE GREAT FAMILIES TO THE PEOPLE OF ENGLAND.

THE circumstances connected with the political reign
of the Tory party, and the means by which they secured
their tenure of power up to the passing of the 1832*
Reform Act, we need not, except for purposes of inci-
dental reference, include in our present survey. Up to
that period there can be said, strictly speaking, to have
been no formation of political opinion at all. All voices
but those of Tory politicians were drowned, and their
mouths gagged by open violence. The rule, in fact, of
the Tory party, until their ranks were broken and routed
by the first Reform Act, may be likened, in most of its
details, to the despotism of the French Catholic Church,
which was countenanced, protected, assisted, and in
every way favoured by the State. But how did such an
unnatural, inequitable, and unjust rule in both cases
end? We will quote Sir George Cornewall Lewis's†
account of the French Catholic Church. " It was established by law;" but it is important to remark here that,
in both cases, the law was made by the oligarchy whose
special privileges it was designed to protect and maintain.
"It was exclusively and richly endowed; its clergy were

---

* The Reform Bill was rejected October 7th, 1831, by a majority of 199
peers to 158; 21 bishops voting in the majority, and 1 on the other side.

† 'The Influence of Authority in Matters of Opinion,' p. 208.

1

numerous, held a high social position, and enjoyed important political privileges.   Dissidents were discountenanced, oppressed, and scarcely tolerated. Everything
that the State could do, or could give—exclusive favour,
rank, wealth, consideration, political power, persecution
of rivals and enemies—was done for and given to the
French Church." Then he proceeds to describe the
consequences of that ecclesiastical policy, which resemble
in so many respects the political revolution whose upheaval gave birth to the first Reform Act. " It nursed
up within its bosom a body of writers who attacked not
only Catholicism, but Christianity, with every weapon of
argument, irony, ridicule, and invective, and whose
attacks circulated throughout Europe, and gave the
tone to all aristocratic society and literature. And when
the Revolution broke out, and the old French Government was destroyed, the whole ecclesiastical system of
France—establishment, endowment, and all their appen-
dages—was swept away, as being a part of the political
abuses against which the popular frenzy was directed ;
and it was found that whatever religious feeling survived
owed its continuance to causes wholly independent of
the State endowment." The one revolution was a bloody,
and the other, happily, a bloodless one. Both were
equally necessary for the permanent destruction of a
system born of greed, both of wealth and power; and
both mark a boundary where the few, inheriting power
and riches, sought for ever to entrench themselves,
barring out their fellow-creatures from privileges which
they had a right to, in violation of the first principles of
justice and humanity. The Tories, Sir Erskine May
tells us,* " forgetting their recent differences, were suddenly reunited by the sense of a common danger." What

* ' Const. Hist. Eng.,' vol. ii, p. 197.

they were chiefly in fear of was the loss of their own power and privileges, which was a danger not so "common" as specially affecting themselves. He continues, "The utter annihilation of their power was threatened ; and they boldly strove to maintain their ground. But they were routed and overthrown. The ascendancy of landlords in counties, the local influence of patrons in boroughs, were overborne by the determined cry for reform ; and the dissolution of 1831, when none of the old electoral abuses had been corrected, secured a large majority for Ministers in the House of Commons. The dissolution of 1832, under the new franchises of the Reform Acts, completed their triumph. Our author ends up that memorable episode in the history of the Tory party with the melancholy remark : " Sad was the present downfall of the Tories." Sad, indeed, for them was the decline in their numbers and prestige ; for, it appears from statistics of the old and new Parliaments that, in the Courts and Cabinets of William IV and Queen Victoria, there were 149 Conservatives against 509 Reformers of all descriptions.

How did the Whigs use the opportunity which the growing intelligence and enlightenment of the nation had afforded the majority? The long period of slavery was at an end. The principles of the Whigs had not only prevailed in theory, but they had placed themselves in a position to teach their rivals a lesson which they would never forget. As our political diagram shows, they had wrested the helm of the State from the Tories, who were doomed henceforth to govern only about one year to their opponents' two, and then only on condition that they trod very much in the footsteps of the Liberal party, in confirmation of which we may mention Mr. Disraeli's Reform Act of 1867. This was a measure of

far less importance to the people than the Act of 1884,
for the enfranchisement of 2,000,000 of Englishmen ; yet
the Conservatives in the House of Lords rejected it, and
thereby upset the principal legislative work of the session.
Seeing no hope of being able to retain power unless
they brought in a Reform Bill in 1867, they thought the
constituencies in a fit of caprice might again put their
party in power if they could only, by hook or by crook,
force a dissolution. It is difficult to feel the respect one
would wish to for a party that thus jumps first one way
and then the other to get into office, no matter how, so
long as they succeed. As a bid for the support of those
who always approve of taking whatever one can get,
they annexed Cyprus, which we did not want, while the
move into Afghanistan has been shown to have been a
blunder, occupying the attention and incurring the cost
of an army of 40,000 men, without adequate return,
and justified by no political exigencies. Subsequent
events in that part of the world are pointed to now by
Conservatives as justifying Lord Beaconsfield's political
foresight and the course he pursued regarding Afghanistan when he was in power. The reply to that argument is, that no subsequent events justify the annexation
of territory belonging to alien races unless they expressly
petition a foreign Government to that effect.

How did the Whigs proceed to use their newly-
acquired power ?*   " They forwarded the noblest legislative measures which had ever done honour to the
British Parliament. Slavery was abolished; the commerce of the East was thrown open; the Church of
Ireland reformed ; the social peril of the poor-laws
averted." The Liberal party had, however, no sooner
secured for themselves this great prize than the dregs,

* Erskine May, vol. ii, p. 198.

which are to be found at the bottom of every cup, showed
themselves in the demands of the Radicals, who thus
for the first time gained a footing in the House of
Commons. Democracy was now represented in Parliament, and as Dissenters were jealous of their Church of
England social superiors, the Radical politicians combined
against the Government they had helped to bring
into power, for the purpose of securing what they considered to be their share of the results of reform. In a
word, one of man's prominent weaknesses showed itself
in this band of about fifty Radicals clamouring for the
fruits of a better system of representation. There were
more particularly the grievances of the Nonconformist
element; the jealousy and envy arising out of the
monopoly of the best offices in the State by the better
classes of the Whigs; while the Irish party, under O'Connell, by throwing their influence first to one side and
then to the other as they saw a chance by so doing of
gaining some special privilege for their own country,
did for that epoch what Mr. Parnell and his band have
done for this, which reminds us that they have apparently made no progress in removing the feeling of indifference to the general interests of the Empire which has
always characterised them, and probably always will.
It was hardly to be expected that the members of the
Whig aristocracy could mix on equal terms with the
rich, but comparatively uneducated manufacturers of the
northern counties. The Reform Bill effected a political
union, but only time and education could fill up the gulf
which socially must for a period separate them.

The difficulties which thus beset the Liberal party,
notwithstanding the strides they had made in the direction of reform, were not unseen by their opponents, who
were writhing under the sharpest defeat they had ever

sustained. Internal discord was hushed, and under the
stimulus of hatred of the Whigs and jealous fear of the
Radicals, they closed up their ranks to enable them to
take advantage of the reaction which inevitably follows
the greatest success.   As far as their political prospects were concerned they had indeed been despoiled.
" *Their nomination boroughs were lost.   The close and
corrupt organisation by which they had formerly maintained their supremacy was broken up; but the great
confederation of rank, property, influence, and numbers
was in full vigour.   The land, the Church, the law, were
still the strongholds of the party; but having lost the
means of controlling the representation, they were forced
to appeal to the people for support.   They readily
responded to the spirit of the times."   Then follows a
significant sentence.   " It was now too late to rely upon
the distinctive principles of their party, which had been
renounced by themselves, or repudiated by the people."
" It was," as this political historian continues, " a period
of intelligence and progress, and the Tories were prepared to contend with their rivals in the race for
improvement;" but he might with much force have
added, that they had never shown a desire to contend in
any such race until they discovered that they had been
for ever ousted from a position, only maintainable while
those below them in the social scale were forcibly excluded from the advantages which gave them the knowledge and power adequate to the task.

The altered circumstances of the party made it necessary to cast about for a new title.   That of Tory was
under a cloud.   It was associated with defeat and
obloquy.   The Tories may perhaps retort that if they
had changed the name of their party, so did the Whigs

* Erskine May, vol. ii, p. 203.

change theirs; but with this material difference, that the change from Tory to Conservative meant retrogression as compared with progression which the term Liberal implied. The change alone in the title was an acknowledgment that they had been on the wrong tack; that they wished to conciliate those whom they had wronged; to share privileges with others whom they had unjustly deprived of them; and to extend liberties to those whom they had tried to enslave. The only question was how to do it so as to preserve a semblance of consistency and yet at the same time to make it appear like such an offer of friendship as should give them a chance of recovering their old supremacy. But the hour had struck; the knell of the parting day, which had witnessed their discomfiture, had tolled. Its lingering and despondent sounds had died out and were for ever smothered and drowned in the chorus of rejoicing that heralded the great emancipation which was begun in 1831, and may be said to have entered its penultimate stage of development in 1884. "It was a name of reproach, as it had been 150 years before; and they renounced it."* Why not now change the title of Conservative to Quasi-Liberal or Semi-Liberal? By such progression there might be in the end such a smoothing away of factitious differences of opinion, as well as of titles, that although there still existed an Opposition, all that miserable " obstruction" which has wasted so much precious time, might be for ever banished and the work of the Houses of Parliament be done in a sensible and business-like manner.

The title of Conservative we are told was intended to proclaim a mission for "the maintenance of the Constitution against the inroads of democracy."† How far

* Erskine May, vol. ii, p. 203.
† Ibid.

that title was justified has been shown by the fact that
ever since those, so calling themselves, have been losing
ground and have been entrusted with the administration
of the affairs of the nation, as we have said, one year to
the Liberals' two. Moreover, their opposition to the
reforms successively introduced and passed by the
Liberals has also been shown to be merely factitious,
a circumstance which is confirmed by the fact that
powerful former adherents have subsequently left their
ranks for the opposite camp, while experience has
further amply proved that the legislative measures of
the Liberals have been of incalculable benefit to the
people. The activity, it is true, of the Radicals, caused
naturally some dismay among the more cautious of the
Whigs, who were not at all prepared to do at a gallop
what could not be safely done beyond the pace of a walk.
There were in consequence some cases of secession on
the breaking up of Earl Grey's Ministry. Of the four
thus retiring Mr. Stanley, Sir James Graham, and a few
followers changed to the benches below the gangway.
Although the latter took this step and joined the party
headed by Sir Robert Peel, on which he himself was destined to turn his back, there is no doubt that he was a
true Liberal at heart. Changing from one side of the
House of Commons to the other once in a lifetime is as
much as the reputation of any man can stand.

In July, 1834, the Ministry that had done so much for
the English people had ceased to exist, but only to allow
their successors under Sir Robert Peel to enjoy a brief
reign. The spell of lengthened Conservative government had been broken, and remained so down to 1874,
when Lord Beaconsfield maintained his party in power
for six years till 1880,* supported, however, it is impor-

* 'Times,' 18th August, 1884.

tant to remember, by a minority of the votes actually polled.* Now that the representation of the people has been perfected up to the present point, including the measure of Mr. Gladstone's Ministry of 1884, it remains to be seen whether or not by adapting themselves more to the times in which they live, and by striving, when they get the chance, to govern the country on the principles which the Liberal party have established, they can sufficiently regain the favour of the constituencies to enable them to enjoy a fair share of office.

No sooner had the Conservatives grasped the reins of office than fortune seemed to be displeased at the fall of a party which had planned, fought, and won such a memorable political battle as that which had caused riots in the streets of Bristol, the burning of Nottingham Castle, and very nearly a march of the men of Birmingham to London to compel the Peers to listen to reason. The King, apparently over excited by events which were no doubt well calculated to stimulate the nerves of all highly-placed individuals who perceived that the outer works of their political stronghold had been razed to the ground, precipitately dismissed his Ministers. This arbitrary act revived in a moment the flagging energies of the recently much enlarged Liberal party, and all sections rallied to a common centre to renew the battle which one individual, albeit a monarch, had dared to challenge them to. The Liberal instincts of Sir Robert Peel, combined with a rare intelligence, soon enabled him to perceive the true drift of events, and from that moment he had taken the resolution to throw in his lot with the Liberals. His promises, however, availed nothing. They would not trust even one

---

* This statement has been challenged by Mr. Shaw-Lefevre in the 'Fortnightly Review' for Feb., 1885.

of the best of those who had for so long trampled on
them, and resisted to the very utmost the extension of
the privileges which had now been wrung from them
by nothing short of force.   Sir Robert Peel's brief reign,
with the number of his followers raised from 150 to
250 by a dissolution, was followed by the restoration to
power of Lord Melbourne.

We have spoken of the alteration in the title of Tory
to that of Conservative, which marked a change of
feeling such as that party had not experienced since it
was a party at all.   We come now to the period at
which their opponents were witnessing the introduction of new elements which were to give them such
important new blood, new intelligence and energies
which were destined to carry their fortunes to a limit
of success little dreamed of at the time.   Like the sub-
terranean force which lifts the mountain peak into the
heavens, an outraged and oppressed people burst the
political bonds which confined them, and rising, joined
hands with those, who though socially higher than themselves, shared their sentiments and sympathised with
their aspirations for political freedom.   In so short a
time the differences which separated Whigs and Radicals
could hardly have been entirely adjusted ; but an understanding had been so far arrived at, that they were
able to co-operate for their mutual benefit under the
title of the " Liberal Party."

Here then, it may be said, Her Majesty's Government
and Her Majesty's Opposition represented two newly-
constituted political bodies who were to divide the
country between them, with the exception of a few
free-lance, neutral, or independent members of society.
The opposing political armies may be said to have been
reorganised, redrilled, and rearmed ; but to what a

ory party. Ministers laboured earnestly to reform political and social abuses. They strengthened the Church both in England and Ireland by the commutation of tithes; they conciliated the Dissenters by a liberal settlement of their claims to religious liberty; they established municipal self-government throughout the United Kingdom. But, placed between the Radicals on one side and the

* Erskine May, vol. ii, p. 207.

Conservatives on the other, their position was one of continual embarrassment." There were thus three elements to mix instead of two; the Tories at the top, and the Whigs in the middle, trying to prevent a mortal conflict between the newly-represented Radicals and their avowed enemies. It was evident that time and the most judicious management could alone prevent the smouldering embers from bursting into a flame, the object of which was to consume the House of Lords, the bishops, the Church, and all parts of the political and social fabric of society which was tainted with opposition to the new order of things. In a word, there is no denying that a section of the community had been quite justifiably forced into a position for which, however, they were not as yet fully qualified. The mission of the Whigs, in these circumstances, was to act as a buffer between Tories and Radicals, while the latter by study, observation, and experience, realised the nature of the responsibilities their own efforts had thrown upon them, and in addition perceived that, however much they might feel exasperated at their long exclusion from their just rights and privileges, their further success depended upon their using with moderation and wisdom the power they had acquired.

Meanwhile the Conservatives, encouraged by the attitude of the Radicals, whose ambition was so overweening that even the new measures of reform proposed by their own friends did not satisfy their too great pretensions, were actively reconstructing their party. If the Liberal party was composed of more or less heterogeneous materials, much the same was true of the Conservatives. Anxious to enlist as many as they could persuade to join their ranks, which was made up of ultra-Tories, Orangemen, ultra-Protestants, &c., some of the Tory leaders of that day gave the same advice as Lord Randolph Churchill in our time, viz. " appeal to the people." But, unfortunately for them, the appeal to the people, both then as now, related to a question about which the mind of the people had been made up. Tories appealing to the people, in such circumstances, was something like the lamb which the lion had devoured appealing for mercy. The Reform Bill of 1832 had swept away a portion, at least, of the system by which they had continued their abuses. All the Tories could hope for, as the result of an appeal to the people, was that the interval between that and the next Reform Bill might be long enough to enable them so to set their house in order that they could withstand, without destruction as a political body, a further loss of power and privileges.

But it was obviously not in the interests of the country or of the Whigs that the Radical element should be more for the present than a subordinate section of the party into which they had been recently admitted, and all moderate men would, in the interests of order and social stability, adjust the balance of parties the moment they had reason to believe that the new element was inclined to be grasping and unreasonable. With a brief interval of Conservative reign, during the ten years from 1830, the Liberals had been in office. All Administrations wear themselves out. The Ministers exhaust their energies, and their own and their supporters' ingenuity, after which it is right that others with fresh ideas and plans and recruited strength should take office; but in connection with this subject the fact is a deplorable one that the age of enlightenment in which we live should not ere this have witnessed such a ripening of human wisdom, good sense, and toleration, that two political parties can face each other in the Houses of Parliament

of England to transact the business of this empire without their discussions being so often characterised by a
degree of acrimony and irascibility that would disgrace
a debate at a parochial vestry meeting. The answer to
this always is, " We are but human." But surely humanity
is not such a poor thing after all that no better result
than we see is to be achieved after hundreds of years of
training. Are more empires and nations and languages
to disappear and be forgotten before the light dawns
upon an age when man can control his temper, and the
Legislatures of the leading races in the world are able to
discharge their functions without an amount of heated
discussion and a display of ungovernable anger which
belongs to the dark ages of civilisation ?

Sir Robert Peel's advice to the managers of the party
to which he still nominally belonged, " Register, register,
register," was acted upon, and the diversities of opinion,
which under the circumstances would have estranged
many of the adherents of the party, were for the time,
at all events, sunk, in order that an undivided stand
might be made against the increasing power and influence
of the Liberals. There is always a number of persons
ready to follow any party which holds out the faintest
hope of being able to forward their material interests in
any way, and unusual activity may always be observed
in the ranks of this politically invertebrate section when a
change of Government is impending. When a party
that has been out of office for years has fair hopes of
coming into power they are very prone to make liberal
promises to trusted supporters who will put their shoulders
to the wheel at the critical moment. Such is the ambition of aspirants to these high places.

Having scarcely tasted the sweets of office for ten
years, it is no matter for surprise that the most strenuous

efforts should have been made to retrieve a position which many of the party had come almost to look upon as an hereditary right. These efforts were successful, and Sir Robert Peel commenced his second period of office as Prime Minister in 1841, being joined by the Ministers who had deserted the Reform Ministry of Earl Grey.

There is no more remarkable incident in the history of the Liberal party than the impetus given to their cause by the events which were now to precede, and to culminate in, the repeal of the Corn Laws. The composition of Peel's Ministry was a peculiar one. While there were to be found there men of the true old Tory type, there were also gathered round the same table men of advanced Liberal tendencies, of the possession of which they seemed to be hardly aware themselves. And, singularly enough, the one whose Liberal proclivities were the most pronounced was the head of the Government himself. Never was the trite saying, that a house divided against itself must fall, more signally exemplified. The old instincts of the Tories soon began to assert themselves when it became evident that Free Trade principles were in the ascendant and what must be the effect of their general adoption upon the interests of landlords, agriculturists, and others who were fattening on Protection. The Conservatives, of course, in a body opposed these measures, without, however, being able or caring to perceive that by so doing they were only hastening the destruction of privileges which had been too long enjoyed, and which the advance of political science had shown could only be retained at the expense of a revolution, in a much more severe form than that which succeeded in establishing the needed reforms. But the Prime Minister had to sacrifice himself, his principles, and his colleagues to a course which in his heart he knew was just. All honour to a man who could retrace steps in his political career, which he was started upon by those whose understanding was feebler than his own, and whose views were as unsound as their pretensions were extravagant. Whether the true light had dawned upon his mind before or not, no matter. Now, at all events, he saw the truth, and he had to change his course without unnecessarily sacrificing his dignity as a statesman. " *The dangers of his path were shown by the resignation of the Duke of Buckingham, the representative of the agricultural interest, before the new policy had been announced. In 1842 the Minister maintained the sliding scale of duties upon corn, but relaxed its prohibitory operation. His bold revision of the Customs tariff, in the same year, and the passing of the Canada Corn Bill in 1843, showed how little his views were in harmony with the sentiments of his party. They already distrusted his fidelity to Protectionist principles, while they viewed with alarm the rapid progress of the Anti-Corn Law League and the successful agitation for the repeal of the Corn Laws, to which he offered a dubious resistance. In 1845 the policy of Free Trade was again advanced by a further revision of the tariff, and the suspicions of the Protectionists were then expressed more loudly. Mr. Disraeli declared Protection to be in ' the same condition that Protestantism was in 1828 ;' and expressed his belief ' that a Conservative Government was an organised hypocrisy.' " This latter was a strange remark coming from a man who was afterwards to lay over his shoulders the Conservative mantle, which Sir Robert Peel found it in his conscience impossible to continue to wear ; and it is

* Erskine May, vol. ii, p. 211.

still stranger when we remember that Lord Beaconsfield commenced his career as a Liberal.

Sir Robert Peel soon perceived that to attempt to stem the tide of public opinion, which was every day becoming stronger in favour of Free Trade, was hopeless. In fact, as we show elsewhere in the chapter on Liberal converts, the period of his real conversion to Liberal principles dated some fifteen years before he proposed, to his colleagues' dismay, the repeal of the Corn Laws. He had, however, made up his mind, and on their refusal to adopt his views he resigned. Thus ended practically a career which from the point of view of Liberal principles, the vindication of which is our principal object, should receive the close attention of the political student. However much Sir Robert Peel is deserving of blame for his infidelity to his party, and for breaking his pledges, to our mind it is clear that his action was amply condoned by the motives which determined his course of action. He felt he had been wrong and that Liberal principles were right. He had come to see that Protection was a fallacy, and that in principle Free Trade was the truth ; that if Tory selfishness and greed continued to prevail, it must in the end plunge the country into revolution and anarchy, and that if he sacrificed himself and trailed in the eyes of the Tories his reputation in the dust, which he did, no matter, so long as his country's real interests were promoted, even if his friends and supporters had to share the obloquy which was heaped upon him by the party he had deserted.

Before we proceed to trace, in brief outline, the tortuous course of politics which was to follow the downfall of Peel and the commencement of Lord John Russell's Government on July 6th, 1846, we should

2

pause here for a moment to take note of the momentous crisis which had been reached not only in the political, but in the industrial history of this country. We arrive here at a point at which the nation had to make a choice, either to remain Protectionist under the erroneous guidance of a few pursuing their own ends, and continue to try and develop its resources and extend its commerce upon a principle which every intelligent man of sound opinions admits is fallacious, or to declare for Free Trade and let the Tories and their Protectionist friends do their worst. One section of the nation—representing the inherited wealth, honours, distinction, and superior intelligence, as far as higher education can give it, which raise the patrician in social status above the plebeian—stood at one point of departure, and the Liberals at the other. There were only two courses to pursue; one that was right, or one that was wrong. The Conservatives invented Protection, the Liberals Free Trade. The man who, by passing a measure for the repeal of the Corn Laws, had sacrificed himself and, by his noble conduct in the interests of truth and justice, "all future claim to govern," as one historian says, had disappeared from the political arena as in a transformation scene, and a man of another stamp appeared in the breach—one Richard Cobden. Educated in a different atmosphere, in which from the first he had an opportunity of studying practically the working of the commerce of his country, his mind had realised at an early age what were the true principles upon which the trade of this country could be best fostered. In other words, he was the apostle of Free Trade, and had been opposed by the very man — the first statesman of his age — who in the closing years of his life renounced his old faith, and, more eloquently than he could do by any words, acknowledged by acts that he had been in the wrong.

Even as recently, historically speaking, as some thirty years ago the term Free Trade may be said to have been a proposition which was the subject of active disputes. There are now people, woefully, it must be admitted, in the dark, who still believe in the principle of Protection; but from year to year, as these unsound thinkers die out, this tinge of error in the politico-economical atmosphere becomes perceptibly fainter, and, moreover, is confined chiefly to those not endowed with a very strong understanding.

The term Free Trade, which was once the badge of a political party, is now the most important fundamental truth in political economy. How has this position been established ? By experience on the one side of failure, through a deviation from the principle, and on the other by the measure of its success, which has placed the commerce of this country where it is—the most gigantic in volume that was ever known.

"Under a system of perfectly free commerce each country naturally devotes its capital and labour to such employments as are most beneficial to each. This pursuit of individual advantage is admirably connected with the universal good of the whole. By stimulating industry, by rewarding ingenuity, and by using most efficaciously the peculiar powers bestowed by nature, it distributes labour most effectively and most economically; while, by increasing the general mass of productions, it diffuses general benefit, and binds together, by one common tie of interest and intercourse, the universal society of nations throughout the civilised world. It is this principle which determines that wine shall be made in France and Portugal; that corn shall be grown in America and

Poland; and that hardware and other goods shall be manufactured in England."*

Had the Tories succeeded in compelling this country to follow their advice and adhere to the principles of Protection, what would have been the result? The material and intellectual development of not only our country, but that of all countries, would have been indefinitely retarded, with what injurious consequences to civilisation may be imagined compared with the general state of comparative wellbeing which we see to-day. On this particular point a great authority speaks as follows :†

" Finally, commerce first taught nations to see with good will the wealth and prosperity of one another. Before, the patriot, unless sufficiently advanced in culture to feel the world his country, wished all countries weak, poor, and ill-governed but his own; he now sees in their wealth and progress a direct source of wealth and progress to his own country. It is commerce which is rapidly rendering war obsolete, by strengthening and multiplying the personal interests which are in natural opposition to it. And it may be said without exaggeration that the greater extent and rapid increase of international trade, in being the principal guarantee of the peace of the world, is the great permanent security for the uninterrupted progress of the ideas, the institutions, and the character of the human race."

Considering the enormous development of the commerce of this country since 1846, when the deathblow was given to Protection, we are able to realise what we have lost in a material as well as in an intellectual sense by the country not having been able at an earlier date to overthrow the opposition of the Protectionists.

---

* Ricardo, p. 76.
† J. S. Mill, 'Pol. Econ.,' vol. ii, p. 122.

To show how strong was the feeling of our merchants in favour of Free Trade as far back as 1820, we may refer to a petition " to the Honorable the Commons, &c., the Petition of the Merchants of the City of London," which will be found in full in the ' Wealth of Nations,' note xv, p. 547, of McCulloch's edition. It is there spoken of as forming " an era in the commercial history of the country." Similar petitions were subsequently presented from all the great trading and manufacturing towns. What, we may ask, are the political students of our time to think of the principles of a party which could be allowed to oppose an appeal from all quarters of the realm to abolish all prohibitions and regulations for the protection of domestic industry, and for the abolition of all duties on importation not imposed for the sake of revenue ? Here was a just demand from the section of the community which represented the pillars of its physical wealth, the sound pioneers of its industry, the most enlightened of its traders ; and yet from 1820 —*for twenty-six long years !*—to 1846 did the Government of this country—as regards commerce the foremost in civilisation—turn a deaf ear; and all for what reason ? To protect those who, so far, had been able to wield the powers of Government for their own and their immediate supporters' selfish· ends.

The progress made by this country between 1846 and 1874 showed that in round numbers the value of the exports had tripled, from 40 to 120 millions. Now the combined total of the imports and exports of Great Britain and Ireland reaches some 700 millions. This development is the result of Free Trade, and the removal of every possible trade restriction and impost which could hamper trade. The clearing of the ground from all such objectionable barriers to the full development of the nation's trading energies has been accomplished by the party who took up the work initiated by Sir Robert Peel when he passed the Bill for the Repeal of the Corn Laws. Free Trade to the individual means giving him the right to do as he likes in the best way he can for his own interests. The Tory principles opposed this, and we have seen by experience how wrong they were in thinking that the welfare of a nation was not best secured by affording the freest scope and the greatest encouragement to the abilities and enterprise of the units composing it.

Here is so complete a demonstration of a deplorably erroneous course having been pursued for all that long period in the face of reason and justice that, if nothing more could be adduced, the position of the Conservatives as regards their principles of action would be so irretrievably discredited that one not only does not wonder at their having been in office only one year to the Liberals' two for the last fifty years, but one is astonished that a party with such traditions can be allowed to govern at all. In fact, it is quite clear that they could not have been allowed to enjoy that privilege in the absence of such an effective controlling influence as that which is applied in the form of the public opinion of the country.

In resuming the thread of our political narrative we come upon the remark that the repeal of the Corn Laws was passed " *amid the reproaches and execrations of Sir Robert Peel's party." This was natural enough. People who have become unjustifiably accustomed to the idea that certain privileges and emoluments are exclusively their own, instead of being the inherited rights of the community as a whole, are not likely to relinquish their grasp of them without a struggle. The way in

* Erskine May, vol. ii, p. 213.

which the interests of the community had been played with for hundreds of years, and had been made to support a few in luxury at the expense of the many, is signally illustrated in the case before us. The Corn Laws was a term given to certain statutory enactments the object of which was to restrict the trade in grain. These enactments date back as far as 1360, in the reign of Edward III. From 1360 to 1846, when the Corn Laws were repealed, is 486 years, or nearly five centuries. During the whole of that period the people of these islands were suffering in one way or another through the operation of unjust laws. First the exportation of grain was prohibited and then the importation. Before 1360* " there seems to have been a general rule carried into effect by the Crown against the exportation of any grain; and the Act of 1360 enacts the prohibition, but at the same time excepts Calais and Gascoïgne, with any other places which the King may appoint by license from its operation. In 1393 the arrangement was reversed, and the right to export was made general, unless to those places to which it was prohibited by Royal Proclamation. An Act of 1436 permitted exportation when the price of wheat did not exceed 6s. 8d. per quarter. Hitherto there seems to have been no prohibitions against importation; but in 1463 an Act was passed prohibiting it so long as the price at home was below the 6s. 8d., after which there was free exportation. The next change was in the reign of Henry VIII, when an Act of 1534 prohibited all exportation, except by license specially granted under the Great Seal." There were further changes backwards and forwards until the Restoration, when the system of imposing duties on importation to protect agriculture

* ' Chambers' Encyclopædia,' vol. iii, p. 241.

and the landed interest at home, began to take permanent root. The Union of 1707 ended the grain contests
which had for so long embittered the feeling between
England and Scotland, owing to the war of reprisals
which was waged up to that period. The agricultural
interest shaped the laws affecting their own property
and the produce derived from it pretty much as they
liked. They, however, overreached themselves in 1670.
They passed a law prohibiting importation while the
price of a quarter was below 53s. 4d., and imposing a
heavy duty above that figure. Their design was, however, frustrated by the circumstance that the country
produced more than it consumed. That was followed
by offering a bounty on exportation at the Revolution.
Thus for a century there was a shifting about in accordance with the views adopted by the landed interest, of
what best suited their own interests. The consumer
was not invited to say what was in accordance with his
interests. He was nobody, and only to be considered as
just a grade above the oxen that pulled his plough, or
the horse who took the grain to market. The argument
was that maintaining the prohibition to import grain
would give an impulse to production in the country, and
no doubt it would if the demand increased. The basis
of that argument was, however, a very transparent one,
as anybody could see. To increase home production by
prohibiting imports would obviously benefit the landlords, their tenants, the clergy, and all others gaining
their living from such sources. In 1814, however, the
bounty system was abandoned as useless, and the "sliding scale" of duties on importation was perfected by
1828. But the dawn of brighter days for the people was
at hand. They had been humbugged long enough by
Governments whose members were drawn almost exclu-

sively from the classes who owned the land, and enacted
laws to suit their own puposes, and regardless of other
people's interests. Education was spreading, and intelligent men of the middle classes were making enough
money to enable them to give their attention to deeper
subjects than the mere marketing of their manufactures,
and there arose agitators bold enough to denounce the
injustice of the course which the Tories had been so
long pursuing ; but, it was only after a long while that
the people could be sufficiently educated to induce them
so to move in the matter themselves, that the old fabric
of Government was made to totter and tremble. As an
example of the attempts that were made to deceive them,
we are told that* "there was a powerful party who
defended the Corn Laws, and represented with wonderful
plausibility that these restrictive statutes were identified
with the best interests of the country. Their arguments might be thus summed up :—1. Protection was
necessary in order to keep certain poor lands in cultivation. 2. It was desirable to cultivate as much land
as possible in order to improve the country. 3. If
improvement by that means were to cease, we should be
dependent on foreigners for a large portion of the food
of the people. 4. Such dependence might in the event
of war lead to the stoppage of supplies, resulting in
famine, disease, and civil war. 5. The advantage gained
by Protection enabled the landlords and their tenants to
encourage manufactures and trade ; so much so, that if
the Corn Laws were abolished half the country shopkeepers would be ruined ; mills and factories would be
stopped, the workpeople thrown out of employment,
capital withdrawn, and disturbances ensue. It cannot
be uninstructive to put on record that these arguments

* 'Chambers' Encyclopædia,' vol. iii, p. 244.

exercised a commanding influence over the labouring
classes, the small shopkeepers, almost all the members of
the learned professions, and a considerable section of
both Houses of Parliament."

Readers of the above sentence may some of them
wonder how the intelligent section of society should
have been so influenced; but the answer is obvious.   The
members of the learned professions, the law, the Church,
medicine, diplomacy, art, were brought into more or less
close contact with those who used the above arguments.
They were mostly their servants, depending upon their
favour and countenance for their living, just as a vicar
is bound to agree with the political views of the rector
who pays him his stipend, and the tenant with the landlord from whom he hires his farm.   How is it the
political bias of universities is nearly always Conservative? 1. Because they were founded by Tories and have
consequently fixed Tory traditions; and (2) because the
students who attend them are drawn mostly from the
wealthier classes, who are Conservative by instinct.

That the small shopkeepers should have been influenced by such pessimist views as the above is not to be
wondered at; but surprise is naturally felt that the
learned professions and many Members of Parliament should have been equally alarmed.   It can only be
accounted for by the fact that, out of a hundred people
so influenced, scarcely one took the trouble seriously to
reason out such questions for himself; and if he did, his
habits of thought were so foreign to the subject, and he
was so little posted in the views of the sound authorities, that there was very little chance of even the zealous
exercise of his faculties enabling him to see through the
fallacies of those who wished to influence his judgment,
by expounding them in their own favour.

Fortunately there were at hand men who saw the truth, who were not bound hand and foot by the chains which the repeal of the Corn Laws broke, and were determined, like true statesmen, to direct the gathering forces of public opinion into one channel, and so sweep away a scandalous state of things for ever. We may sum up this brief reference to a turning-point in the fortunes of the British people, which was to blossom and flower into growing prosperity and freedom from the political tyranny of the upper classes, by repeating what was written twenty years ago, viz. " Every evil prognostication has been falsified." Sir Robert Peel in 1843 tried modifications of the sliding scale, but his efforts were useless to mitigate the hostility to the Corn Laws, the injurious effects of which were then beginning to be better understood by the light of the teachings of Mr. Cobden, Mr. Bright, and others. Petitions poured into Parliament, Sir Robert Peel himself was converted, and a system false in theory and conception was destroyed for ever. The full benefits of Free Trade were reserved, however, for a later period. The price of bread did not fall then or for years after to the extent anticipated. The next generation were destined to reap the great benefits of the memorable reforms which Sir Robert Peel was to aid in initiating.

The position of the Conservatives was at this period— July, 1846, when Lord John Russell took office—one, to say the least, of extreme embarrassment. " *Suddenly deprived of their leaders, and committed to the hopeless cause of Protection, they were for the present powerless." The party was now led by Lord Stanley, who succeeded to the earldom in 1851, a man who was as famous for shifting his political principles as his son.

* Erskine May, vol. ii, p. 215.

For all that, he was a great orator. While they were
lacking in courage and without organization, and more
disgusted with the past than hopeful of the future, the
Whig Ministry suffered from a want of cohesion, which
they sought to remedy by giving hopes that the franchise
might be further extended. Lord John Russell's Government lasted till February, 1852, when Lord Palmerston,
the ablest disciple of Canning, rashly, and without consulting his colleagues in the Cabinet, supported the
coup d'état by which Louis Napoleon made himself ruler
of the French people; in consequence of which he had
to resign. He was out of office, however, for but a
brief period. The Whig Ministry, which broke up in
twelve months, was succeeded by the Derby Ministry,
and that almost immediately by the Coalition Ministry
of Lord Aberdeen, in which Lord Palmerston was Home
Secretary. The dissatisfaction, however, caused by the
mismanagement of the Crimean War brought about a
dissolution of this Government, and Lord Palmerston
succeeded to the highest office in the State on the 10th
of February, 1855. Had other circumstances not arisen
to prevent the Conservative party from retaining their
grasp of office, the memory of their late disastrous
defeats in another arena was sufficient to ensure their
exclusion until they had been able to do something to
condone the evil consequences of their unjust treatment
of the middle and lower classes. The Earl of Derby,
we are willing to admit, was in his way a grand statesman, and inspired his party with the confidence of which
they were sadly in want; but Free Trade was flourishing,
and the very hint at a revival of Protection was sufficient to arouse a storm of disapprobation. While most
of the prominent members of his party were still in
favour of Protection he could not abandon it, and he

knew that to attempt openly to advocate a return to
those principles meant the certain destruction of his
Government. The party, in fact, were a generation
behind in their ideas. Spoiled in the lap of luxury, they
had not kept pace with the times, and they suffered in
prestige, as is usual with those who are hopelessly dis-
tanced in the race. They tried one device and then
another by which to endeavour to rehabilitate their
credit with their own followers and outwit their opponents. But warfare of that kind, resembling somewhat
the desultory, ill-organised, spiritless efforts of the
French, in another sphere, to retrieve the disastrous
consequences of the capitulation of Sedan, availed
nothing against the solid onslaught of a foe which had
right and might on their side. The Conservative leaders
proposed Protection in counties as a counterweight to
Free Trade in towns. " * In vain did many ' Liberal-
Conservatives' outbid their Whig opponents in popular
professions; in vain did others avoid perilous pledges,
by declaring themselves followers of Lord Derby, where-
ever he might lead them. They were defeated at the
elections; they were constrained to renounce the policy
of Protection; they could do little to gratify their own
friends; and they had again united all sections of their
opponents."

While the Conservative party had been tossed about
in the shallows into which their want of foresight and
selfishness had drifted them, since the fall of Sir Robert
Peel, the followers of that statesman had held aloof for
six years, there being no possibility of their again joining
the Conservatives. Their sympathies, in fact, were
naturally with the other party. So hopeless indeed was
the prospect of the Conservatives that all who decently

* Erskine May, vol. ii, p. 217.

could went over to the other side, thus depriving the opponents of the Liberals of their best men. The tremendous strides made by the popular party during the first half of this century is seen again from the following. "*Five-and-twenty years before, the foremost men among the Tories had joined Earl Grey; and now again, the first minds of another generation were won over, from the same party, to the popular side; a fusion of parties had become the law of our political system. The great principles of legislation, which had divided parties, had now been settled. Public opinion had accepted and ratified them; and the disruption of party ties which their adoption had occasioned brought into close connection the persons as well as principles of various schools of politicians." There was still, however, a want of cohesion among the men, whose views had in many cases been made to converge towards a common centre, more by circumstances than through conviction, and the discord naturally arising therefrom, added to the disasters of the Crimean War, brought about a dissolution of the Aberdeen Ministry two years after it was formed. The new adherents retired and the Liberal party had to work upon the narrower basis of its old connection. This division raised the spirits of the Conservatives, who watched their opportunity, but circumstances were for a time in favour of Lord Palmerston, the chief of which was the conclusion of peace with Russia. The Peace party opposed the operations against China. His friends the Peelites turned on him, supported by the whole force of the Conservatives. But such a man was not to be cowed by a coalition which he knew well enough was composed of elements which could hold together but for a brief period, and he

* Erskine May, vol. ii, p. 218.

appealed to the country. The result was an over-whelming defeat of his opponents. The parties which had previously combined against him again overthrew his Cabinet by a majority of nineteen, and the Earl of Derby, whose Ministry in 1852 lasted for 305 days, was destined on this occasion not to endure longer than one year and 103 days. It is thus seen how little real confidence was felt by the country in a party which had since 1846 suffered so many successive defeats and such discredit as a consequence of their radically wrong policy, and their obstinate determination as far as possible to adhere to it. If reference be now made to the political diagram showing the duration of the Liberal and Conservative Governments respectively, it will be seen that the repeal of the Corn Laws dealt such a blow to the party which opposed it, and who, at the same time, showed such determination to adhere to the principles which it was designed to overturn, that the Conservatives lost their hold of the power of governing this country practically from the date of the passing of that measure in 1846, down to the 21st February, 1874, when Benjamin Disraeli commenced his six years' tenure. In 1852, it will be seen, the Earl of Derby was in office for 305 days, again in 1858 for one year and 103 days, and lastly, for one year and 236 days in 1866. Mr. Disraeli succeeded to the office of Prime Minister on the 27th February, 1868, and held it for 286 days, when he gave way to Mr. Gladstone. With the exception of these comparatively brief periods during which the Conservatives managed to retain power, the Liberals kept the government of the country in their hands for a period rather exceeding one quarter of a century. This fact, looked at by the light of all the circumstances to which we have drawn attention in this chapter, and which is, as we have remarked, but a brief outline of the events which changed the whole aspect for ever of the political affairs of this country, is one which forms and ought to form the principal study of every student of politics. He here sees on the one hand the policy of the Tories first discredited and then abandoned, while on the other he may observe the triumph of the policy of truth, and of liberality in its literal meaning, which was henceforth to resist all further attempts to replace it for that policy which means the propagation of fallacies and the advocacy of such doctrines as Protection. Moreover, the basis on which it now stood was to be strengthened and solidified, and that in their own interests, by the very party who, so long as they dared, had opposed the successive reforms with the most violent and uncompromising resistance.

Chastened by practically twenty-eight years' exclusion from office, the Conservative party began to show signs of being able to bend their hitherto inflexible wills to the inevitable. The only chance of their obtaining any lengthened lease of power was by avowed penitence and an open renunciation of the unsound doctrines which they had attempted to teach and practise at the expense of the people. Lord Beaconsfield understood how to make his party swallow the leek and keep the Conservatives in power, by adopting very much the same line as had proved so successful with the Liberals and so disastrous to his own adherents.

Meanwhile we return to the period just prior to the second advent of Lord Palmerston to power, and we may already perceive from the following passage the change that had been wrought in the minds of the Conservatives by the various reforms which had followed the repeal of the Corn Laws. " *The Conservatives as

* Erskine May, vol. ii, p. 221.

the strongest party, were restored to power under the Earl of Derby. The events of the last few years had exemplified the fusion of parties in the Government, and their combination on particular occasions in Opposition. The relations of all parties were disturbed and unsettled. It was now to be seen that their principles were no less undermined. The broad distinctions between them had been almost effaced; and all alike deferred to public opinion rather than to any distinctive policy of their own. The Conservatives were in a minority of not less than one hundred, as compared with all sections of the Liberal party; and their only hopes were in the divided councils of the Opposition, and in a policy which should satisfy public expectations. Accordingly, although it had been their characteristic principle to resist constitutional changes, they accepted Parliamentary Reform as a political necessity, and otherwise endeavoured to conform to public opinion. For the first session they were maintained solely by the disunion of their opponents." By the infusion of new blood, not committed in the same way as their predecessors to pursuing the old errors, and also under the influence of a gradual process of enlightenment, the Conservatives very slowly regained a little of the confidence which had been lost, and they tried to accelerate the pace of their re-entry into public favour by themselves advocating reform. A Reform Bill was introduced; but the Liberal party composed their differences and attacked the measure. The Conservatives appealed to the country, hoping this time they would be successful and secure a firmer hold of the reins of government. They were, however, doomed to disappointment. The country could not believe that the recantation of their old faith was genuine, and, moreover, were of opinion

3

that there was too much danger that the good the
Liberals had done might be undone if their opponents
were allowed to govern until a new generation of Conservatives had at least been educated in a reformed and
purified political atmosphere. Their opponents outbid
them, and they fell, Lord Palmerston returning to power
on June 18th, 1859. Thus for the second time the
Conservatives were again allowed only to taste power
when they saw a popular Liberal Minister again assume
the reins of government, supported by all shades of
Liberal opinion. Now came a period of calm. The
Conservatives, in fact, for a time threw up the game.
To attempt to cope with adversaries who were so im-
measurably superior, not only as regards the justice of
the principles of their cause, but in the men who had
come to the front to fight the battle of the people against
a foe whose power had been built up on a basis of error
and fallacy, was seen to be hopeless, and so Lord
Palmerston remained at the head of affairs for over six
years. " * Thirty years of change in legislation and in
social progress had brought the sentiments of all parties
into closer approximation. Fundamental principles had
been settled; grave defects in the laws and Constitution
had been corrected. The great battlefields of party
were now peaceful domains, held by all parties in common.
To accommodate themselves to public opinion, Conservatives had become Liberal; not to outstrip public opinion,
ultra-Liberals were forced to maintain silence or profess
moderation. Among the leaders of the Conservatives
and the leaders of the Ministerial Liberals there was
little difference of policy and professions. But between
their .respective adherents there were still essential
diversities of political sentiment. The greater number

* Erskine May, vol. ii, p. 223.

of Conservatives had viewed the progress of legislation, which they could not resist, as a hard necessity; they had accepted it grudgingly and in an unfriendly spirit, as defendants submitting to the adverse judgment of a court when there is no appeal. It had been repugnant to the principles and traditions of their party; and they had yielded to it without conviction. The true Conservative, silenced but not convinced by the arguments of his opponents and the assent of his leaders, still believed that the world was going very wrong, and regretted the good old times when it was less headstrong and perverse."

The question of what were the principles upon which the country was to be governed may be said to have been settled when Lord Palmerston returned to power. The fight had lasted for more than a dozen years after it had assumed the acute form which meant the more or less permanent ascendancy of one or other of the parties to the conflict. The Liberals had won and the Conservatives were nowhere. Their return to office would depend to a large extent upon the energies put forth by their opponents and upon the blunders they might commit. However sound may be the principles of a party, and to whatever extent they may employ their powers in the direction of reforming obvious abuses and passing measures which are plainly for the benefit of the whole community, they will not be tolerated any longer in office if they begin to show signs of being exhausted both in mind and body. The use, in fact, of two parties is, that the one which is out of office shall recruit its energies and formulate new and useful measures to be introduced and, if approved, carried in due course. Although we do the Conservatives no injustice in saying that their party is as a rule much feebler in nearly all respects for legislative purposes than the Liberals, at the same time it cannot be denied that their ranks include men quite capable of governing, and they have been placed in office when the country was satisfied that they would use aright the powers entrusted to them.

At this period a free election of Members had been secured, and the House of Commons was now composed of men representing more completely the varied interests of the people than had ever been seen before. Party fights they were no longer interested in. The crew of the ship had been got together, the captain appointed, and now the passengers desired all attention to be given to the navigation, that they might have a speedy and prosperous voyage to new havens of prosperity, comfort, and repose.

What the country had been saved from is clearly seen in a cutting from 'Blackwood's Magazine,'* which Sir Erskine May gives in his 'Constitutional History of England,' vol. ii, p. 226. Speaking of the former association of great families who divided the Government patronage among them, and distributed offices, honours, and pensions to their own friends, we read: "No game of whist in one of the lordly clubs of St. James's Square was more exclusively played. It was simply a question whether his Grace of Bedford would be content with a quarter or half of the Cabinet; or whether the Marquis of Rockingham would be satisfied with two fifths; or whether the Earl of Shelburne would have all, or share his power with the Duke of Portland. In those barterings and borrowings we never hear the name of the nation; no whisper announces that there is such a thing as the people; nor is there any allusion, in

* No. 350, p. 754.

its embroidered conclave, to its interests, feelings, and necessities. All was done as in an assemblage of a higher race of beings, calmly carving out the world for themselves—a tribe of epicurean deities, with the Cabinet for their Olympus." It is very refreshing, as no doubt many others will think, to read such a sensible paragraph cut from a periodical which has since distinguished itself by printing sentiments so very different and so much less worthy of the pages in which they have appeared.

The great families which had been practically deposed from their position as exclusive rulers of the nation retained much of their influence, as they naturally would, on account of their great wealth and the prestige which the highest position in society would give them ; but for all this the change in their position from a political point of view was a move from the top to the bottom. While they and their friends governed, the people were their servants. By the establishment of a free representation, the people governed through their appointed Ministers. If the ennobled families were represented at all henceforth in the Cabinet, it must be on the condition that they acknowledged this change to be irrevocable, that they were satisfied to fill those high offices in the interests of the people, and that they were otherwise qualified to administer the affairs of the State. The imperfections which demoralisation had introduced into government as carried on by the great families afforded ample scope to the reformer, and the question which presented itself to a reformed Parliament was more how to eradicate the vices of the system than what to eradicate. The transfer must of necessity be a slow one. To turn out the whole Executive, as the Americans do when a new President comes into office, is admittedly fraught with the greatest inconvenience, and causes infinite trouble even in a country where the people are accustomed to a loose and rough-and-ready way of doing things compared with the bureaucratic decorum of the English system of government. Whatever the cause of change might be with us, the objectionable elements must therefore be eliminated without unduly straining the machine, and without exciting such hostility between the two parties as would entail mischievous and injurious results. The rulers who were to be displaced knew in what they were deficient, and that their subordinates were, many of them, wanting in zeal and competence. To make up for these deficiencies attempts were made to introduce into public life promising young men from the great seats of learning, and many thus found their way into lucrative public offices who in our time have to compete with any who choose to fit themselves to be candidates for such a position.

The House of Commons has thus been gradually transformed, from a collection of gentlemen representing nomination boroughs, and the educated and polished dependents of families who could afford to pay for such a distinction, into an assembly which demands qualities of a more business-like nature from those who aspire to enter its portals. In our day the kind of speech which was listened to with such pleasure by the admirers of Curran and Sheridan would excite but little interest. The literary curiosities which Mr. P. J. Smyth, for example, occasionally delivered fall distinctly flat, and are evidently looked upon by an assembly which cannot get through half the work it has to do, as mere academic displays which are more or less out of place and a waste of precious time. The late Mr. Bernal Osborne tried hard to deserve the mantle which the two first-named Parliamentary wits so ably wore. But, even in his time, oratory of the *jeu d'esprit* order was going out of fashion.

Our object in this chapter has been to show, more by a bold outline than by reference to details, the course of events subsequent to the passing of the great Re'form Bill of 1832, which led to the transfer of the government from the great families to the people of England. In the succeeding chapters the successive reforms which were the motive force used to drive the great families from a position which they had been allowed much too long to retain, will be referred to in detail, the part played by the Upper Chamber being significantly recorded in the form of a list of the legislative measures which they rejected in their desire to continue an exclusive aristocratic rule.

" In the multitude of counsellors there is safety."

The cabinet of counsellors always know now that they have to arrive at decisions subject to the ratification of a larger body of counsellors—the nation. To this is no doubt due the delay, the apparent hesitation and vacillation which the Conservatives loudly complained of during the Egyptian difficulties which the Gladstone Ministry had to deal with. Although there may be delay, and we admit there may very possibly be sometimes injurious delay, under this system, is it not certain that under an oligarchy much greater mistakes and far more unjustifiable courses have been pursued, leaving the balance of advantages immensely in favour of a system of government founded on the observation of a greater number of observers ? When each capable citizen feels that he assists in moulding opinion he will take greater interest in studying all questions as they severally come up for discussion.

Finally, it is no small satisfaction to have lived to witness the government of the country forced from the vicious circle which fostered the growth of political inequality into the natural orbit which is productive of political equality ; while we may rest assured that those whose convictions prompted them to take a part in promoting the reforms which led up to this most desirable consummation, have felt a just pride in being so fortunate as to have had a hand in such a glorious work, which is the crowning triumph of civilisation in the nineteenth century.

CHAPTER II.

A DISTINCTION must always be drawn between home and foreign politics in estimating the worth of individual opinion. We have endeavoured elsewhere to show that such a distinction should always be kept in view for obvious reasons. Every man of average instructed intelligence is capable of forming more or less of a sound political opinion on home affairs, because he is himself more or less conversant with the circumstances arising from day to day which demand the attention of the Legislature. With foreign politics, regarding which, curiously enough, people as a rule seem to think that a sound opinion can be formed on the most superficial data, the case is very different. The very fact that the Executive Government often think it of paramount importance to maintain the strictest secrecy regarding the negotiations that are being carried on, proves that the material on which the public so often form dogmatic opinions is quite insufficient for the purpose. This is one of the reasons why we suggest in another place that the interests of this great empire demand that a larger body of delegates than a Cabinet Council, for they are but the delegates of the nation, should sit permanently to discuss all the bearings of the propositions which this country may make to or receive from foreign Powers. When Mr. Gladstone is ill, for example, some people go

into paroxysms of fear and write leading articles in
their papers as if the future of this country depended
entirely upon the life of one man.   Experienced persons,
it is true, know that such alarmist articles are often
born of motives other than real apprehension, which
justifies the rebuke, in passing, that high-class journalism
should aim at leading the public straight along the right
path, and not at deluding the unwary to serve party
purposes.   The old saying that there are as good fish in
the sea as ever came out applies to Cabinet Ministers quite
as much as to other professions.   When Lord Palmerston
was ill the same dismal predictions appeared in the
alarmist organs of the press of that period.   He died,
and as in other walks in life, given the opportunity, a
successor was soon found equal to the occasion.   So it
will be again, the difference between the past and the
future being, that there will be many more capable
candidates for high office in the future than there have
been in the past.   The political nursery is for ever being
enlarged, and the result will no doubt be an increasing
number of capable politicians who only require opportunities to prove, that in some cases at least, the Prime
Ministers that must in the natural course of things be
removed from the political stage can be replaced without
damage to imperial interests.   Even if we are unable to
produce such first-class men as some of those who have
served their country and run their course, we are happy
in the knowledge that the great body of the nation,
from whom the second and third ranks of politicians are
drawn, is much more capable of coming to a sound
decision than it used to be on important questions, and
moreover possesses the most perfect organisation yet
devised for rapidly making known its views and for
having them carried into effect.

Sir George Cornewall Lewis made some pertinent remarks in his time on the formation of political opinion,
and adorned them with some good quotations bearing on
the subject which are worth reproducing.

It is well known that whatever course any Government may adopt under given circumstances, there is a
large number of persons who, having ranged themselves
in opposition to the political principles professed by
the Government, will without hesitation pronounce the
course adopted to be a wrong one. If, for instance, one
pays a visit to the Stock Exchange, to a Conservative
club, a bank, an assembly of clergymen, or of liverymen, a convocation of bishops, a meeting of country
landlords, or squires ; any corporation in fact, the interests of whose members are bound up with the maintenance of the *status quo* of the corporation in question,
there will be perhaps 1 or 2 per cent. of the number
who will allow that a Liberal Government has done the
best that could be done under the circumstances. The
entire body, minus this small proportion, will unhesitat-
ingly denounce the Liberal Government as incompetent,
and accuse them of bringing the country to ruin. If a
Conservative Government is in office, Liberals, we admit,
do very much the same thing ; but they do not do it to
the same extent, because Liberal associations include as
a rule fewer bigoted politicians and a larger proportion
of men possessed of sounder political instinct than is to
be found among the same number of Conservatives, or
they would not be Liberals. This is the opinion we have
formed after a long and close observation of the conduct
of different sets of both Liberals and Conservatives, and
we maintain that the proposition can be proved and is
proved in this book. The power of mind of men of the
average stamp differs but in a small degree. Occasion-

ally a generation produces among philosophers a Bacon; among dramatists a Shakespere; among musicians a Beethoven; among scientists a Newton; and in politics a Pitt, a Peel, a Bright, a Cobden, or a Gladstone. Occasionally there is one, perhaps two, three, or even more possessing original minds who may exercise great influence in their time over those with whom they associate in proportion to the energy and originality of their characters. In other words, the individuals constituting a political association are guided more by the views of the leading men among them than they are by their own judgment. The great bulk of the members of an association are in fact simply guided by what they conceive to be in support and furtherance of their own interests. If the measure proposed threatens, however remotely, those interests, that is sufficient without further inquiry for them to denounce it and the authors of it.

But we will suppose, for the sake of argument, that the units of which such a corporation is made up did really desire to open their minds to the truth, and were brought into such a frame of mind in which they were entirely unprejudiced and unbiassed, what proportion of them would be found competent to form unaided an opinion worth anything upon any one of the more difficult foreign questions, for example, which are from time to time brought forward for their consideration and approval by Government?

Regarding incompetent judges Sir G. C. Lewis remarks: "Now, whether the opinion be sound or unsound, it is in general received without any adequate process of examination or verification, *and is held merely upon trust;* so that the concurrence of the multitude adds little or no weight to the judgment of the competent judges." Then he gives us a very apt quotation from the posthumous work of Helvétius, ' De l'Homme,' sect. xi, ch. 8, as follows: "Les hommes, en général, approuvent ou condamnent au hazard, et la vérité même est, par la plupart d'entre eux, rêçue comme l'erreur, sans examen et par préjugé." In a word the translation of this is, that men as a rule judge of things at random with their minds made up before they have made any examination.

There is another passage which all amateur politicians should ponder before hastily uttering crude and ill-considered opinions :—" The authority of every scientific or professional man, every man having a special aptitude of judgment, *is limited to his own subject or class of subjects*. Out of this range his opinion is worthless, or, at all events, only on a par with that of any other man of sense and of practised habits of thought, having no special knowledge or experience of the matter. The opinion of an astronomer or a geologist upon a question of jurisprudence, of a lawyer upon medicine, of an agriculturist upon military or naval tactics, of a sailor upon chemistry or painting, of a botanist upon navigation, would certainly be of no more value than that of any other person taken at random from the midst of society. Every man, however highly endowed by nature, and however qualified by study, reflection, and experience, to pronounce on a particular subject, *is a mere undistinguished cipher*, only one of the great multitude, upon all other subjects. Upon these his opinion ranks with that of any ordinary person. A scientific or professional man may, therefore, be compared to a court of limited jurisdiction, which is competent to pronounce on one class of questions, but is without power of deciding on any others. On the other hand, there is scarcely any

man, however uncultivated his faculties, and however
limited his powers of observation, who is not qualified to
form an opinion upon some subject, if not of speculation,
at least of practice. An unskilled labourer, an artisan,
a domestic servant, or a petty trader, *each in his own
calling, becomes acquainted with certain facts and processes, acquires a certain experience, and is thus qualified
to form a judgment on that particular subject, confined
and comparatively simple as it may be.*" After more to
the same effect Sir G. C. Lewis remarks :—" It follows,
from these remarks, that there is no one body of persons
who are competent judges on all subjects, and who are
qualified to guide all sorts of opinion ; that there is no
one intellectual aristocracy, separated from the rest of
the community and predominating over them indiscriminately. *Every subject in turn has its own peculiar set of
competent judges, which vary for each.*" In a word, each
person has his own special department, and should, to
put it in the mildest form, be diffident in expressing
his views on subjects which are outside that special
department.

The foregoing is the soundest of common sense,
as every sensible person will allow whose judgment
is not warped by fears for his own personal interests.
But, unfortunately, all political action directly or indirectly affects people's personal interests. Politics is
the science of government. The duty of all Governments is to legislate for the many and not for the few.
The greatest happiness for the greatest number is the
guiding principle. This has been the principle, as
opposed to the Tory principle which favours the few at
the expense of the many, which all Governments of the
truly Liberal type have followed for many years past,
and it has been under the guidance of that principle

that so many beneficial reforms have been initiated and carried by Liberal Governments.

These reforms being in the very nature of them changes by which the many would benefit at the expense of the few, who up to the time of that change had, in very many cases, enjoyed an undue share of the good things of this world, owing in very many cases to accidental circumstances, it is quite natural that the few should, as far as they could, try to prevent such reforms from passing; but their reasons have always been too transparent for any sensible person to be deceived as to the motive for the opposition shown.

The judgment then of say 98 per cent. of the persons in a privileged position, such as a member of any of the corporations to which we have referred, regarding any proposed reform affecting their interests would be worthless. Even the more enlightened among the Conservatives who perceived the justice of the several reforms proposed for the extension of the franchise, would in many cases have voted against the measure if they could have done it without being seen. "We should be glad," they have said, "to help other people if we were sure it would not hurt us;" but the difficulty always has been, that the extension of the vote might bring about such reforms in the end as to cause, as Mr. Bright once said, landlords to cut and run for their lives. Some such vague fear has no doubt always actuated the Conservatives in the opposition they have shown, and neither time nor experience of the working of previous reforms enables them to shake it off.

Every man of intelligence, as well as vast numbers of people whose standard of intelligence is low, follows the course of political events, when he is able to see the daily papers, with the same, if not sometimes greater,

regularity than he takes his meals. He who thus reads
as he runs, not only knows what political reforms are
the fruit of each session, but he knows also everything
that has been said *pro* and *con* during their passage
through the fiery ordeal of debate. He also watches
the operations of the Government by the light, often
very partial, which is afforded him in respect of their
foreign policy. If the opinion of one amateur politician
is no more worth having than that of any other ordinary
man when all the materials necessary to enable him to
form a right judgment have been threshed out in broad
daylight by competent critics, he can hardly be expected
to have anything to say worth hearing on points where
he is not only deprived of light " in the public interests,"
but is often purposely mystified during the process of
incubation.

And yet we should think there are few who will deny
that if there is one department of the Government's
action more than another about which the most heated,
dogmatic opinions are uttered according to the political
bias of the individual, it is in that of foreign affairs.
Nothing for years has so amused and astonished us as
the expressions we have heard applied to Mr. Gladstone
with reference to the policy of the Government in
Egypt immediately following upon the overthrow of
Arabi. Numbers of people one has been accustomed
to meet in one's daily walks, no one of whom was
either known to fame, or had risen higher in the
intellectual scale than the performance of that mechanical work which when done to perfection is rightly
described by the poet Heine as characteristic of cultivated mediocrity, have soundly denounced the Prime
Minister as a lunatic, and good for nothing. These individuals have displayed a degree of heat and indigna-

tion that would seem to argue on the surface that they
had got up the whole case from the top to the bottom,
and had evolved from the most mature and rightly-
informed reflections an opinion, of the soundness of
which they never paused for a moment to entertain a
doubt. This heat and indignation has, to our certain
knowledge, been generated entirely and solely, time after
time, by "news" printed in big type one morning and
contradicted absolutely the next. The worst of it is
that much of the impression created by that false news
remains after it has been contradicted. The mind of
the recipient of that false news was, in very many cases,
eager for some fresh evidence that would justify him in
further denouncing the Government of the day. He
goes about his work charged with material for argument
which is absolutely untrue. He never thinks for a
moment that he ought to wait, or to search elsewhere
to see if it be confirmed. Very likely it is reproduced
in big letters on the bills of the evening papers, which
causes his memory so tenaciously to retain it, that its
absolute denial the next morning is quite insufficient to
undeceive him. Political opinion is continually being
formed in this way on erroneous data, and the unfortunate part of it is, that this is an evil which the
growing competition in journalism intensifies.

Every individual who takes any interest in politics at
all may be said to start a creed—how, we shall endeavour to show hereafter—and light a fire under it. He
gathers his fuel according to his creed, as a rule. If he
be a Liberal or a Tory of a very low standard of understanding he can only see along one straight line at a
time. If there are any branch lines which it is necessary to include in his view he becomes confused, and so
his only chance is to have one single groove in which to

4

run his reflections. This, as a matter of course, involves the selection of only just that political fuel for his fire which he recognises, or is told belongs to his party. This applies much more to Conservatives than it does to Liberals, because Liberals who are not converts, as a rule are Liberals by conviction from the beginning, whereas very many Conservatives are converts because they think it is more respectable to attach themselves to the fringes of a party which includes the greater number of the aristocracy. Moreover, the worth of the individual opinions of a party who have steadily opposed almost every reform which the Liberals have carried, shows on the face of it an entire absence of that one valuable element, viz. independence of view, which alone gives value to an opinion.

As an example of the way in which some Conservatives will argue blindly in their own interests, take a letter of Mr. Henry H. Howorth, in the 'Times,' of July 7th, 1884, on the Franchise Bill and the House of Lords. He says, *inter alia:* "When the eager champions of woman suffrage vote against it, while they concede a vote to criminals and paupers, we still feel the cold air of the same cloudy realm. When we are continually told that education and wealth and social position should have no more weight in deciding the fortunes of a great empire than ignorance, poverty, and obscurity, Utopia is still in sight. Utopia supported by sophistry has not hitherto been a congenial aim in the politics of the English crowd."

If we analyse closely this paragraph, are we not justified in asking if there are not criminals and paupers in all classes of society; and if the upper classes do not include quite as great a proportion of abandoned profligates who are now entitled to vote, as the stratum which

includes the 2,000,000 which the new Bill proposes to
enfranchise?

The blind way in which one party will attack the proposed legislation of another is here conspicuously shown.
The Prime Minister, during the passage of the measure
through the House of Commons, pointed out that the
extension of the franchise to householders in the counties
gave the Conservatives a better chance of increasing
the number of their supporters than it did the Liberals.
This statement was accepted as the truth; but, says
Mr. Howorth, that does not matter: it is wrong because
the Liberals propose it.   Such is a by no means isolated
sample of the arguments which Tories advance.

Mr. Howorth sets " education, wealth, and social
position " against " ignorance, poverty, and obscurity."
The one, as a social force, sounds no doubt very formidable when compared with the other; but its formidable-
ness consists a good deal more in the sound than in the
reality.   Mr. Howorth will not deny, we apprehend,
that this country is no longer governed by the Upper
Ten, but by the nation.   Facts cannot be ignored, however liberally we may be prepared to view differences
of opinion.   That being an undisputed fact, on what
show of justice can so large a number of the nation as
2,000,000 be excluded from the number entitled to
vote?

Mr. Goschen was at first of opinion that these 2,000,000
were not fit to be voters; but when the House of Commons by a large majority agreed to the extension, he
gave way at once.   But there is a much stronger ground
to be taken up against Mr. Howorth's pretensions than
that which rests upon those 2,000,000 of voters being
sufficiently educated to justify their being enfranchised.
The fact of the nation, as the real Government of the

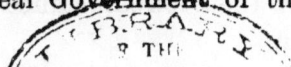

country, having been substituted for the representatives
of an ancient oligarchy, a system long swept away,
notwithstanding its being supposed to include all the
educated, wealthy, and those in the best social position,
proves that the growing enlightenment and civilisation
of the people declined to tolerate any longer a system
of government which was uniformly carried on in the
exclusive interests of that oligarchy and its dependents.

It may be argued, and with justice, that in the early
years of this century, when the aristocratic families
ruled this nation, they sowed the seed of the greatness
to which the empire has developed. We do not deny
that; but what we do deny is, that the system on which
the government of this country was carried on in those
times would be tolerated now, either by the people
of this country or by the other nations of Europe.
The romantic feudal style of annexation which characterised that epoch in our history, and which was sought
to be continued under the Beaconsfield Ministry, is opposed to the unwritten code of international law which
keeps in check the Governments of our time. Decent
respect for the national rights of all peoples is the
maxim which does and should form the guiding principle
with the great Powers of Europe.

The claim of the Conservatives that they have a right
to govern on the ground of superior education, wealth,
and social position is one long since disallowed. The
right on such grounds claimed by that class has been
proved over and over again, beyond a shadow of a doubt,
to have been acquired and exercised exclusively in their
own interests, without a hope of the classes under them
having a chance of getting voluntarily from them any
concession at all as regards political privileges. How,
in these circumstances, is it possible that any man can

pretend to claim, in the altered times in which we live, any prescriptive right to govern for a class which has for the best part of half a century so abused its privileged position as seriously to jeopardise by its selfish obstruction the very existence of the only fighting ship of their whole fleet that is left to them—the House of of Lords ?

It would appear from the letter of Mr. Howorth, from which we have quoted the foregoing paragraph, that, if he be a Tory—which we presume he is, or he could not adopt such a line of argument—the natural endowment of his mind, from the point of view of political justice, consists of the very qualities which he thinks disqualifies other people for having conferred upon them the franchise, viz. "ignorance," "poverty" of imagination, and that class of "obscurity" which keeps a man's mind from being penetrated by the light of truth.

The conclusion of Mr. Howorth's reasoning is amusing if not edifying.   He says, " Utopia is still in sight ;" but it is a Utopia of his own invention.   He continues, " Utopia supported by sophistry has not hitherto been a congenial aim in the politics of the English crowd ;" what the meaning of this sentence as a whole is we fail to understand.   Mr. Howorth evidently does not appreciate the aim of the English crowd because they keep the Liberals in power two years to the Tories' one. That may not seem to be fair to the Tories, but the nation, which is the Government, is evidently of that opinion or it would not be so.

It may perhaps be said that the Liberals as a party produce better men, and that it is owing to the "English crowd" being guided by these better men that the Liberals have enjoyed for many years past two years of office to the Tories' one. We should rather say the

reason of it was that the nation by the superior enlightenment which has been given to it during the last fifty
years, has perceived slowly and surely, as one reform has
followed another, that the true friends of the whole
community were those who introduced and carried those
reforms. Nearly all those reforms which we shall refer
to later on have not only been the work of the Liberals,
but they are the result of work done in the teeth of
bitter Conservative obstruction.

Now, it seems to us quite impossible that so many
reforms could have been passed by one party against the
will of the other without it being quite evident on the
face of all of them that they were for the good of the
community as a whole. Had these reforms been destructive of what the Conservatives, according to their
creed, think should have remained unchanged in the
interests of the community as a whole, surely the
" crowd " must long ere this have realised the fact that
the party they had kept in office two years to the other
party's one, was altogether on the wrong tack. No
amount of argument diminishes the force of the fact
that the proof of the pudding is in the eating. Mr.
Howorth's crowd has for a long period partaken of the
Liberal pabulum and no subtlety of reasoning or array of
facts will enable him or anyone else to prove that the
English crowd, that is, the great majority of the English
nation, exclusive of its democratic offshoots all over, the
world, prefer a Tory to a Liberal fare. To attribute their
choice to want of education or ignorance or obscurity
will not either bear the test of analysis.

Even supposing that the Conservatives as a body possessed a monopoly of the superior qualities claimed for
them, their title on that account to have a larger share
of voting power would be forfeited in the eyes of any

just judge, if for no other reason than that the whole history of the party is redolent of but one principle, and that is, to wall round for themselves and their exclusive benefit all the good things the country produces, and to preserve for themselves and their descendants the great privileges acquired by force in the feudal times when the strong were permitted to beat down and rob the weak, with no power in existence whose business was the administration of justice to stand between and protect the community against the tyrant and the robber.

We hold that it is not a matter of opinion whether or not such are the traditions of the Tory party. The pages of history bristle with facts which not only support that view, but leave no room for doubt as to the deliberate intentions of Conservatives. From the beginning they occupied the vantage-ground, and their ranks have always been recruited, not from converted Liberals who have become convinced that Liberal principles were unsound, but from those whose personal interests, having for their mainspring the riches they had acquired, gave life to Conservative instincts. It is no doubt the duty of every member of the community to endeavour so to fortify his own position in the world as to render himself as far as possible independent. So long as this can be done by legitimate means no one has any right to interfere. But as soon as it becomes evident that individual interests are to be protected and fostered by sweeping legislative measures, or, which is the same thing, people are to be deprived of the fruits of their labour by refusing them such measures of reform as the changed circumstances in which they live shall show them to be entitled to, then all who are in a position to judge impartially, all who are free from the obliquity of political vision which comes from being trammelled by

deep-rooted hereditary selfishness; all who can recognise
and understand what the advance of civilisation and
enlightenment means, and are intelligent enough to
admit that these elements constitute a gathering force
that no human power can withstand, must admit that
professed Conservatives represent a power which they
fondly hoped at one time might conserve for ever their
privileges, but which has been for a long time only too
palpably crumbling into the dust, which is fast being
levelled with the Liberal plane.

Many observers have no doubt frequently remarked
that the Conservatives of our day in giving expression to
their opinions of particular acts of Liberal Governments,
whether in the press or on the platform, do not show
any particular anxiety to enlighten their followers, by
reminding them of all the circumstances which caused
their downfall and practical exclusion from office from
1846 to 1874. Does one ever see in Conservative
journals or periodicals as much as a hint at these
momentous events, which are the shining glory of a
political history which records the triumph of justice,
the sure advance of sound government as a science, and
the relegation to obscurity and disgrace of a system
which was only just destroyed in time to save the nation
from falling into the rank of a secondrate, if not a third-
rate Power ? As all Governments know too well, prosperous finance forms the sinews of war and the sure foundation upon which the welfare and happiness of a people
rests. There could have been no lasting and healthy
financial development under a system of protected industry ; under one of Free Trade the development has
been enormous. The Conservatives likewise are very
fond of twitting their too successful opponents with a
want of spirit in their foreign policy. What is easier

than to be spirited, may we ask? With the resources of such an empire as ours, it requires no statesmanship to qualify a Government to go "empiring it about the world" as the Yankee said. Lord Beaconsfield was just the man to emulate the enterprise of Napoleon the Third, who in his political career, as the Swedes say, "went up like the sun and came down like a pancake." Statesmanship does not mean only spirit,—it means as a rule a little spirit diluted with a great deal of prudence and discretion. In a word, a statesman who is to manage successfully an empire like the British Empire of to-day must be a man of business. When you have an empire to make out of nothing, to shut one's eyes and pursue a filibustering policy, ousting by main force, without any parleying, anyone who stands in your way, may be considered legitimate enough in an age when morality and right were scarcely recognised. The Tory Jingo party were very useful for that kind of statesmanship, and being, like the rest of us, true Britishers, could hold their own against all comers. But our empire is made; we have now too much to lose to continue the practice of that kind of statesmanship. If Lord Beaconsfield had continued in power he would probably have gone "empiring it all over the world," until other nations would have been exasperated into combining against him; and being spread out as we are in these days, a serious disaster to the fleet might have half ruined us before we recovered the lost ground. No. The true policy of a British statesman of our time is to do all he can to uphold respect for international law; to scrupulously respect the rights of other nations, and to annex no territory anywhere unless the circumstances of the case imperatively demand the protection of what we already possess.

Again, ordinary folks do not perceive that the cry
for a spirited policy comes as a rule from those whose
business is inactive, and whose fortunes are either not
increasing or are dwindling through the fall of prices.
Merchants whose trade is standing still, owing to political troubles in any part of the world, cry out for the
Government to do something—it matters little what, so
long as an end is put to the stagnation. Much of Lord
Beaconsfield's popularity was achieved in this way. The
mere announcement that the Mediterranean fleet had
been ordered to pass through the Dardanelles, before
the short-lived treaty of St. Stephano was signed by the
Plenipotentiaries of Russia and Turkey, caused a rise in
the stock markets of Europe at once. What was the
result? Invertebrate Liberals, the prices of whose bonds
had been falling in the market, declared themselves
thoroughgoing Tories on the spot, and began to sing
on the Stock Exchange the popular Jingo song of the
hour.

We do not recall this circumstance with the object
of finding fault with that particular decision of the
British Government. If the policy of keeping Russia
out of Constantinople was a sound one at the time—
which we believe it was—to thus frustrate her design
was a right move. We are trying to show how political
opinion is formed. The act of sending the fleet to the
Dardanelles was decided on when the stock markets
were inactive and stockbrokers were making no money.
That particular act of Government revived business for
awhile and the stockbrokers made money; therefore,
all Liberal or most Liberal stockbrokers declared themselves Conservatives, and Conservatives they have
remained. This is the way Conservative ranks are
recruited. Politicians of that stamp are no more guided

by any principle in their decision than a horse who elects which of two water-troughs he shall drink out of. Political recruits are gained in other departments of business in the same way. People advocate a spirited policy because it puts money into their pockets. There is not one in a hundred who expresses an opinion upon such an act as that of sending the fleet through the Dardanelles on that particular occasion who understands at the time all the bearings of the case, for the simple reason that nobody but the Government is in possession of *all* the facts which enable them to arrive at a decision. It is, in fact, one of the curiosities of life, the remarkable confidence which each person who takes an interest in politics feels in the infallibility of his own judgment, when it is tolerably certain that in a large number of cases, as we have said, they have neither the capacity nor the necessary data to enable them to arrive at a sound judgment. This view, as we remarked at the opening of this chapter, has reference more to the complicated questions of foreign policy than to matters of home reform. The rapid and accurate formation of public opinion regarding the principles of all the great domestic reforms which begun, for instance, with the repeal of the Corn Laws, proves on the contrary that those particular measures proposed changes the beneficial effects of which appealed to the natural instincts and common sense of every person of ordinary powers of judgment. The rapidity, in fact, with which the various measures followed each other shows how the people had advanced in education and enlightenment at that period.

It is instructive to note, regarding the introduction and discussion of the successive measures of domestic reform which have been introduced by the House of

Commons, what a rapid change takes place in the formation of political opinion when those interested are brought
face to face with the proposals, and have them explained
by competent Ministers, so that they really understand
what the proposed reform means. Take for instance,
the Reform Bill, which received the Royal assent on
June 7th, 1832. That Bill, which was Lord John
Russell's first scheme of reform, passed the second
reading by a majority of only one. It showed that there
were a number of Liberals even, who did not fully
realize the nature of the benefits which that measure
proposed to confer upon the people. But the animated
discussions which secured its passage even by that one
single vote, threw a flood of light upon the important
question of reforming the system of representation,
which had the effect of rapidly dispersing the darkness
in which many politicians of both sides were enveloped.
When the Bill was reintroduced after a dissolution of
Parliament, it passed the third reading by a majority of
113. The Upper House, of course, threw it out by a
majority of forty-one, and Parliament was prorogued,
just as Mr. Gladstone prorogued it in 1884, when the
Peers rejected the extension of the Franchise Bill of
that year. The proposal of Lord John Russell not to
diminish the number of Members, as the former two
Bills had done, was accepted by the Opposition, who,
after the agitation they had passed through, were no
doubt glad of this as an excuse to escape from an
untenable position, and on the 12th of December the
third reading was passed by a majority of 116. That
was not bad progress. The Bill begun in the Commons
with a majority of one ; that rose to 113, and from that
to 116. On this occasion the Peers also had learned
wisdom, and the Bill was carried by them by a majority

of nine. But at that period of our history an incident occurred something like the agitation caused by the objection of the House of Lords to pass the Franchise Bill of 1884 without the Redistribution Bill. In 1832, Lord Lyndhurst carried by a majority of thirty-five a Motion proposing the postponement of the disfranchising clause until that for enfranchisement had first been considered. Whether or not this was a stratagem for trying to defeat the Bill altogether, as it is pretty evident was the case when Lord Salisbury and the Peers threw out the Bill of 1884, because it was unaccompanied by the Redistribution Bill, Lord Lyndhurst's proposal was carried by a majority of thirty-five. The Ministry proposed to create new Peers to enable them to overcome the opposition in the Upper House; but the King declined and they resigned. Intense agitation followed, as was also again the case in 1884, more particularly at Birmingham, where Lord Randolph Churchill and Sir Stafford Northcote ventured to invade the Radical stronghold, and disgraceful scenes followed, which, however, were at the same time a clear indication that the majority of the inhabitants of Birmingham disapproved of the Conservative tactics and of the position they had taken up in opposition to the will of the great majority of the people. In 1832, however, occurred what has frequently happened since : the Lords gave way. In a word, they dared not precipitate a renewal of the agitation, and stayed away from the House in sufficient number to leave the Ministry a majority of eighty-four, and the Bill received the Royal assent on the 7th of June, 1832.

Those who are forming their political opinions, whether old or young, before they attempt to judge of particular contemporary reforms or acts of the party in power, should study the history of past reforms. They will thus gain some insight into the difficulties which have to be encountered by the inexperienced in endeavouring to form an opinion upon proposed reforms; they will learn how very erroneous have been the opinions held by large numbers of those in the past who were opposed to reform, and also how very unfounded have been the fears entertained regarding the action of the newly-enfranchised voters. Those even who forced on the Reform Bill of 1832 were themselves not without fears that the democratic element might dangerously predominate; but the sluice gates had been opened and nothing could arrest the force of the people's will. They had come to see and to understand that what was proposed was an extension of their rights, and having once clearly perceived that what was offered to them by the leaders of the Whigs was but bare justice, of which a minority strenuously endeavoured to deprive them, if the Tories wished to escape annihilation as a part of the political fabric of the realm, they must cease to oppose and stand on one side while the measure was passed into law, and took its place on the statute-book. What was the result? A reaction immediately followed upon the cessation of the contest, by which the hopes of those who supported the Bill, and also those who opposed it, were equally falsified. The consequence of this has been that the Liberals have learned by experience that there is no danger in admitting to electoral rights those below them who are sufficiently educated, and Bills for the further extension of the franchise have from time to time been proposed in Parliament and passed into law. But there is this curious feature in the case as regards the Tory party, that notwithstanding the fact that their own leaders have themselves proposed a Bill for the extension of the franchise, yet the Tory party as a party is now at this moment as

much opposed to such reforms in their hearts as ever
they were.   To say that is no calumny upon the party.
The history of their tactics, both in and out of office,
shows conclusively that what little the few members of
their party have done, more in a negative than a positive sense, to forward the reform of the system of representation has been yielded by way of purchasing their
own escape from effacement.   Without the support of the
people, they soon saw that their opposition was hopeless, and hence Mr. Disraeli, as was his wont, turned
right round, throwing all the principles of the party to
the winds, and brought in a Reform Bill himself.   We
remember very well how violently incensed were the
Tories with Sir Robert Peel for doing in his day much
the same thing, when he proposed to, and did sweep
away hundreds of vexatious imposts.   We are told that
his party then virtually abandoned him with disgust.
But the Tories did not abandon Mr. Disraeli for introducing his Reform Bill in 1867 ; on the contrary, they
were so delighted at the idea of regaining a lease of
power, however short, and moreover were many of them
so aware by this time of the damage their prestige as a
party had suffered by their persistent opposition to all
reform, that they were more or less callous what their
leaders did so long as the party could keep in power.

There is no doubt that that particular act of the
Government, the passing of the Reform Bill of 1832,
assisted very materially the great mass of the people,
who were not experts on the subject, in the formation of
sound opinion regarding the justice of an extension of
electoral rights.

Another circumstance worthy of remark here is, that
the teaching of history is not lost upon some of the
younger members of the Conservative party, and that

they are not by any means prepared to run in the narrow
groove which the Tory party has hitherto followed.
Lord Randolph Churchill broke away from his allegiance
on a memorable occasion, because he saw clearly enough
that Lord Salisbury and the more obstinate of his followers had learnt nothing by their experience of the
past forty years. Lord Randolph saw, and openly declared, that he understood that successful opposition
to any measure proposed by their opponents was not to
be looked for unless a majority of the people were with
them. The light of the truth penetrated, at least in his
case, the darkness with which the rancour of partisan
hatred had so thickly encrusted the understanding of
his older associates. At that moment that young and
able politician had taken a step in the direction in which
Sir Robert Peel fled, late in his career, when the truth
had come thoroughly home to him ; but Lord Randolph
Churchill was snatched back. He had a great career
before him among the Tories, if they could get into
office, whereas among the Liberals his chances were
small, comparatively speaking ; this circumstance may
not have been without some influence in inducing him to
retrace that step which he took in the direction of
Liberalism.

The third Reform Bill, which was the first actually
passed, was a particular act of Government which there
can be no doubt made a permanent breach in the ignorance which had up to that period prevailed regarding
the benefits to be derived from enlarging the franchise ;
and let us go further and see if still more of the darkness in which the Tories were so anxious to keep the
question enveloped, was not dispersed by the discussions
and agitation over the second Reform Bill.

The eyes of the people had been opened to what was

in store for them, if they only knew how to make use of
their power. They had already amply proved that the
Peers and the Tories generally were afraid of them, and
all they had to do now was to follow up their success
by renewed agitation, as soon as events showed that the
country was ripe for the extension of those privileges
which had been in part granted by the House of Commons. The measure of 1850 extended the borough
franchise and made additions to the county franchise,
and from that date Tories and Liberals were more or
less to vie with each other in their attempts to continue
to reform the House of Commons. In thus exerting
themselves some of the Tories were no doubt wise, and
nobody wished to question the motives of the party
whose political opinions had undergone so remarkable a
change, at least in the persons of some of their leaders.
Many onlookers no doubt thought, although they openly
said nothing, that the sincerity of that section of the
political community would have been more fully believed
in, had it been manifested before the determined obstruction of the Peers and the Tories in the Commons
to the three separate Bills which culminated in that of
June, 1832. Having been utterly routed, they must, if
they were to regain any of the lost confidence, at least
make a show of being in sympathy with the political
opinions of the people, and nobody better could be found
to turn the Tory stream into the Liberal channel than a
man whose early career and associations had accustomed
him to look at Government, the advancement of civilisation, and the good of the people, from the standpoint of Liberal principles; and it is a great pity that
a round man so evidently in a square political hole as
Mr. Benjamin Disraeli was, had, more by accident than
design, to throw in his lot with the Tories. He no doubt

5

admired the tinsel and the gaudy trappings of a peerage, and was drawn to its fineries and glitter like a moth to the candle, because his mind was of the inventive order and he loved romance; but, he was no more in his heart one of the grim Tory-bred despots of the Lord Salisbury type than was his great antagonist, Mr. William Ewart Gladstone.

A more comprehensive measure than that of 1832 was proposed by Lord John Russell in 1854, but the breaking out of the Crimean War caused it to be abandoned; and the next attempt was made by the Government of the Earl of Derby, the Bill being explained by Mr. Disraeli, the object of which was to secure identity of franchise between the county and the town, by which means the Tories hoped to place themselves on a level with the Liberals, whose strength lay in the towns, while theirs was more in the counties. Two influential Cabinet Ministers took alarm and resigned, and the opposition of the opponents of the Government, led by Lord John Russell, caused them to be defeated by a majority of thirty-nine, when they dissolved, but failed to secure a majority, and gave way to a Palmerston Administration, in which Lord John Russell once more took up the question of reform, and introduced a Bill in 1860 which, however, came to nothing, and was withdrawn. Then commenced an agitation which very materially aided in ripening public opinion upon the subject. In 1864, 1865, and 1866 there were active discussions on the question of reform, and no doubt the experience which Mr. Gladstone then gained decided the question in his mind in 1884, that the Franchise Bill should be introduced first and the Redistribution of Seats Bill afterwards. Although the Tories have tried hard to make party capital out of a sentence of Mr.

Bright on this question, detached from its context, if they look back to 1866 they will find that he it was who first tabled a Bill to deal with the franchise *alone*. Whatever, therefore, they may be able otherwise to show, here is recorded evidence that as a question of procedure he thought it advisable to pass the measures separately.   How hopelessly a party must be driven into a corner by their opponents when they are compelled to raise subscriptions to placard towns, and in other ways to make such a fuss about one sentence!   Mr. Bright, at all events, has been associated with the winning side from the commencement, while many of his opponents have seen the error of their ways and have gone over to the Liberal camp, much, be it said, to their credit.

Whether it was due to the two Bills brought in by the Liberal Government of that day being combined or not, the Government failed to get them through Committee; and being defeated by seven gave up their places to the Conservatives.   Nothing in the end, however, was lost by the failure of the Liberals to carry their measure.   The formation of sound political opinion was going on apace.   The Liberals could well afford to allow their opponents to put their shoulders to the wheel of the vehicle which was conveying to the Liberal goal what they had striven so long to bring there in the face of Conservative opposition and obstruction.   Whether Lord Derby and Mr. Disraeli knew it or not, the country was " giving them rope " when they went into office in 1866.   The working classes had been educated up to the point of understanding what reform really meant for them, and from opposition to the wishes of the people the Conservatives had, after a hard struggle, first changed their attitude for one of more or less

passive assent; and now it had become a question of
who was to outstrip the other in the race for a further
extension of the franchise.   What a triumph for the
Liberals ! Who can read the history of the events connected with Parliamentary reform from 1831 to 1866,
to go no further, without realising how radically wrong
were the principles of the Tories, and how fundamentally
right have been those of the Liberals ; and yet with all
this overwhelming evidence against them, journals and
politicians re-expound and reiterate their fossilised but
exploded arguments against all the great reforms by
which the Liberals have transformed the industries and
political status of the country from a crawling ante-
diluvian sluggishness into the most flourishing and
prosperous nation that the world has ever seen.   What
a glory to have been actively associated with such a
work ! What a shame to have been an active and
persistent obstructor of it; and what a still greater
shame to continue to obstruct the progress of a work
which no one with a really healthy understanding would
hinder, if he were not hardened in a course of action
which it is now impossible to forsake without sacrificing
everything that for a politician of any position is worth
living for.

Then we come to a memorable period in the history
of Parliamentary reform.   The Tories did not see why
they should not get some of the credit for improving the
House of Commons as well as the Liberals.   Mr. Disraeli
was no doubt the chief mover in the matter.   He and
his party had prevented the Liberals from carrying their
Bill, and now that they were in office there was no
escape ; they must deal with the question themselves.
After much discussion and many attempts to overcome
the opposition raised by dissentients, who were opposed

to all reform, the difficulties in the way of introducing
the Bill of 1867 were got rid of by three members of
the Government resigning. Mr. Disraeli was never a
man for half measures. If he had anything to do with
reform at all, he would show how radically Liberal he
could be, and the consequence was the country was surprised. In fact if he had gone over to the other side of
the House and declared himself a Liberal, as other Tories
had done, he could not have created more surprise.
Difficulties raised by the House in matters of detail were
met by threats of resignation which had the desired
effect, for after their long exclusion from office the party
was kept in hand by the leaders by a wholesome dread
of being outvoted, which the Government were on the
Minority clause by a majority of 141. But in spite of
this the Bill was passed by the exertions of Mr. Disraeli,
who succeeded to the Premiership, Lord Derby resigning, owing to ill-health. Other measures effecting
changes in the electoral system followed what Lord
Derby, who still laboured under the misgivings which
had made the Tories oppose all reform from the commencement, called " a leap in the dark." The fears both
he and those who thought with him entertained were as
groundless as those which worried his predecessors.
The real mischief in such circumstances is caused by
such men as Mr. Walpole, who, as Home Secretary, refused permission to the people to hold public meetings
in Hyde Park. Such an act was part and parcel of a
policy which has from time to time brought the Conservatives into so much trouble; but experience has
taught them very slowly the error of their ways.

With the passing of that Bill of 1867 the Tory party
may be said to have been at length converted to a faith
they had so long and persistently declined to embrace.

Political opinion with them had in fact undergone such a radical change that they had not only turned reformers, but had pushed the principle even farther in their own Bill than probably the Liberals would have done themselves. This was indeed a deep acknowledgment of their past errors and an attempt to condone the wrong they had done the country, by standing so long in the way of granting electoral rights. In a word they tried to make amends by literally showering favours upon the people. Although the Conservative reign was but brief, after that Bill became law, Mr. Disraeli showed that if he was not a farseeing politician he was on that occasion at least a good man of business. He waited patiently, and the next time he got a chance the constituencies did not forget the liberality of 1867, and he enjoyed a longer lease of power—from February, 1874, till April, 1880— than any Conservative Government had experienced since the repeal of the Corn Laws. In a word, he had sprung from the people, and knew well enough how to meet their wishes if he could only have his own way. In his heart he was no more a Tory than William Pitt, and both cases are a warning to rising politicians not to take sides until they understand politics sufficiently to know and feel sure that in forming their political opinions they stand on neutral ground to begin with, and are unfettered either by hereditary principles, by the opinions and doctrines of unsound thinkers, or by the biassed views of people who are guided in forming their judgment purely by self-interest.

CHAPTER III.

ON the subject of the growing influence of the
press as the mouthpiece of the public, Mr. Sheldon
Amos* remarks :—" There is no doubt that a number
of social and political circumstances, to which it is
needless particularly to allude, have combined to im-
part to the general public habits of keen attention to
politics, and even of acute political discrimination in
matters involving a very comprehensive survey of the
whole political field—foreign and colonial, as well as
domestic—which is wholly unprecedented in former
times. Side by side with this new development, the
operation of the Reform Bill of 1832 has been on the
whole, as is generally admitted, to introduce into the
House of Commons a larger number of Members whose
sole qualification is their wealth, and to exclude the
small class of persons who under the older system were,
in spite of all its gross shortcomings in other respects,
frequently admitted on the sole ground of their purely
political qualifications. The removal of the Paper Duty,
and the extraordinary growth and improvement of the
newspaper press, as well as the lately invented facilities
for locomotion and rapid communication of news, have
all conspired to render the public nerves susceptible in
the highest degree to the slightest indication of any

* ' Fifty Years English Constitution,' p. 464.

unexpected political movement in the Houses of Parliament, or in the counsels of the Executive Government. The result is, that the aggregate popular force, will, and intelligence outside the Houses of Parliament has become, as it were, incorporated into a potent political organ, which not only competes with the recognised Legislature, but threatens at times—even where there is no immediate prospect of an appeal to the constituencies—to overpower and drown its voice. The more normal operation of this popular factor is to give increased weight to the mere fact of debate and discussion in the Houses of Parliament, as compared with the weight due to a preponderance of voting power."

" In a recent paper on Modern Parliaments, Professor Pearson, of Melbourne, has drawn attention to other consequences of the same general tendency. He has shown that not only as above indicated is the aggregate popular force outside Parliament being increased at the expense of the Legislature, properly so called, but that in democratically constituted communities, to the type of which all progressive communities must approach, some of the most influential politicians, and the most skilled specialists in different departments of political science, must, by the nature of the case, be outside the walls of Parliament, and yet none the less exercise the strongest direct influence on its counsels and resolutions."

We are of opinion that Mr. Amos overstates the case when he says that the House of Commons has suffered in quality through the 1832 Reform Bill. Even if the argument were well founded the skilled specialists referred to at the close of the quotation would not be prevented from contributing their knowledge through some other channel by the mere fact of their being excluded from Parliament. As a rule, the mental and physical qualities which enable a man to acquire wealth are just those which, combined with the qualifications, without which a man stands little chance of gaining a seat at all in the House of Commons, make the best administrator. It was the absence of those politico-business qualifications that led Mr. Disraeli into some of his romantic adventures during his period of rule. Men who are admitted as members of a Government " on the sole ground of their purely political qualifications," are just those persons who get a country into scrapes through their " spirited foreign policy." They are not accustomed to weigh the cost of personal in-dulgence, and they carry the same habits into the service of the State. Nothing is easier than to initiate the spirited policy that is advocated by Tory merchants and stockbrokers when trade is dull. The profit they individually make by it renders them quite indifferent to the amount they have to pay for extra income-tax. On this particular point we may pertinently quote the following passage from Mr. L. Courtney's speech at Liskeard which is reported in the 'Times' of the 10th Oct., 1884 :—

" There is one great danger of the future to which I wish to direct your attention, and yet I do so with some hesitation, because there is a time when calling attention to a danger may precipitate it. But we are undoubtedly exposed to a risk of serious demands being made on the national Government and Treasury for incurring great works at the public expense. These attempts are made on all sorts of pretences—philanthropy, trade, or the restoration of an exhausted and impoverished people. You know well how frequently demands are made in behalf of Ireland for public money in aid of this and that

scheme for putting people on their legs. Demands of
the same kind come from other parts of the country for
loans or grants in aid of fishing harbours, harbours of
refuge, &c., all of which are made to represent speciously
enough plans for the improvement of the condition of
the people, and all of which would, for the time being,
be attended with a good deal of popularity. Suppose
the Government of the day could be persuaded into re-
solving to advance a hundred millions of money, consider how many persons would be delighted—capitalists
with money to invest and workmen in want of employment. If you are going to spend 100 millions on your
navy, your coast defences, on harbours and piers, on
improving and fostering this and that industry, if you
do that you will for a certain number of years give a
good deal of occupation to a large number of people, you
will give a great stimulus to trade, and you can imagine
how pleased and prosperous the country would look for
a time. But at the end of the time, when the 100 millions were gone, you would have the people left burdened
with debt and with nothing to set against it. Now,
that is a most popular programme—a programme which
has been played over and over again in the colonies, and
a programme which I would not trust some people who
are now aspiring to power to attempt to play over again
in this country. (Hear.) It is most desirable, then—
in view of that kind of programme which appeals, as it
does, to popular support, which would offer such tempting and alluring inducements to working men to vote
for the Tory candidate who would give him all these
means of obtaining employment and good wages—in
view of that programme I think it most desirable, if
possible, to insure in the House of Commons first of all,
but also in the second Chamber, a solid, steady, and

trustworthy basis of mature opinion which will resist
these fascinating schemes, these plans for getting happy
present times at the expense of future misery. (Cheers.)
How to get this House of Lords is the difficulty. At
all events, we may begin with a little reform of such
House as does exist. (Hear, hear.) Mr. Gladstone has
pointed out one plan of reform which would certainly
increase the facility of getting Bills through the House
of Lords. He pointed out that the Scotch and Irish
Representative Peers are elected in such a fashion that all
the Scotch and all but one of the Irish, without exception, are Tories. Call you that a representation of the
Irish and Scotch Peers ? Why, it gives a standing body
of fifty Tory Peers added to the House of Lords beyond
its natural number. If you had anything like proportional representation of the Scotch and Irish Peerage in
the House of Lords, and I am glad to think that
Mr. Gladstone insisted on the necessity, you would get
one cause of the present abnormal preponderance of
Conservative opposition in that body checked. (Hear.)
By-and-by it is possible that in the case of the English
Peers we may get some sort of sifting of them (cheers),
and by that method we may reduce their power, and
then if we can increase very much the number of life
Peers, of whom at present there are only two, by these
slow steps—and we must not be too impatient—we may
bit by bit transform the House of Lords from a house of
privilege to a house of endowments. We shall transform
it from a House which derives its main existence from
the fact of a certain number of men being the eldest
sons of their fathers to a House composed of men who
have each some title to honour, each of whom may say
that he has been put into the House because he has been
trusted by the nation, and that he has won his position

by services to the State. (Cheers.) In that way, by a
slow process of law and no other, without revolution,
without haste, without passion, without violence, we may
transform the House of Lords that now is into a House
of Lords that shall be a sure, steady, and useful assistance to the State, which shall keep our path straight
and not liable to vacillation, not liable to be running
now into one extreme and now into another, but going
on in the steady and regular path of progress which,
looking back upon the last fifty years, we may say we
have, on the whole, gone through since the great Reform
Bill of 1832. (Cheers.) This reform, which would do
for the House of Lords what we have been trying to do
over and over and over again for the House of Commons,
would bless the nation with a Legislature reflecting its
best qualities, doing its best work, and securing the
fulfilment of its highest aims. (Cheers.)"

No sensible man needs to be told, that people who
have been accustomed to spend freely what they have
not earned acquire habits of extravagance which they
can seldom or never shake off. Such persons, when
appointed to responsible positions under Government,
carry more or less their extravagant ideas into all the
departments which it may fall to their lot to administer.
The item of expense, in other words, is, with men of
their order of mind, quite a matter of secondary consideration. No one, knowing the facts, will dispute that,
as a rule, Tory Governments have been always cha- ·
racterised by a much looser regard for cost, and a
disinclination to view projected enterprises from a
strictly business point of view, than has been the case
with Liberal Administrations. Nothing is easier, for
instance, than to gain popularity among the shipping
and kindred interests by precipitating a war which will

involve the chartering of a number of vessels to carry troops. Factitious prosperity is easily fostered for a time by such methods; and it is, moreover, very tempting for a party which is continuously losing ground with the country to resort to such a mischievous device, with the object of regaining their waning popularity. There is no doubt this is one of the chief reasons of the Conservatives having lost the confidence not only of all sound Liberal politicians, but of a good many of their own party, who now take up a Liberal-Conservative attitude.

There are 180 daily papers in the United Kingdom. These are divided into 74 Liberal, 40 Conservative, 29 Neutral, 34 Independent, and the remaining three are undefined. Of these journals we find 27 Liberal were originally established as weekly, and subsequently published as daily papers, while the number of Conservative so originating is 21. Of 40 existing Conservative journals 21 are therefore seen to be the survival of weekly papers, while of the 74 Liberal the proportion is 27. From this we are justified in inferring that while there are 7 more weekly Liberal journals than there are Conservative the increase in the Liberal daily papers, started as such, is 47 as compared with 19 Conservative. Eight Conservative weekly papers were established during the last century and 6 Liberal. From these statistics it is seen that the spread of education and the advance of civilisation is accompanied, as regards the daily papers of the United Kingdom, with a loss to the Conservatives and a considerable gain to the Liberals. Curiously enough the oldest Conservative weekly journal, the 'Edinburgh Courant,' was started in 1705, at Edinburgh, and after an existence of 154 years it retained sufficient vitality to appear daily in 1860. The 'Bristol

Daily Times' was started as a weekly in 1735 on Conservative principles, and appeared for the first time as a
daily paper in 1865.   In 1737 the Conservatives started
the 'Belfast News Letter,' which appeared as a weekly for
118 years, when it was changed into a daily in 1855.   The
'Birmingham Daily Gazette' saw the light in the same
interest as a weekly paper in 1741, and after an existence of 121 years was continued as a daily in 1862.
The 'Aberdeen Journal' started as a Conservative paper
in 1748, and, like the 'Edinburgh Courant,' held its own
for a long period in Liberal Scotland.   It ran as a
weekly for 128 years, and then appeared as a daily in
1876.   The 'Leeds Yorkshire Post' commenced its
career in the Conservative interest in 1754.   As in the
case of others the more rapid march of events and the
increased facilities of communication necessitated its
appearance more frequently, and it was published as a
daily in 1866.   Lastly, the 'Exeter Daily Telegram,'
which indicated by its name the cause of so many conversions of weekly into daily papers, was transformed in
1863, after an existence of eighty-three years as a weekly.

As regards the earliest weekly journals established in
the interests of the Whigs, of which, as we have said,
there were fewer than Conservative, the 'Nottingham
Journal' started as an Independent-Liberal in 1710, five
years after the 'Edinburgh Courant' saw the light.
The word 'Independent' tacked on to the title suggests
the difficulties that lay in the path of commercial success.   Conservatives with Liberal tendencies were no
doubt thus angled for by the proprietors, and they could
in case of need shelter themselves behind this compromise in the title of the paper.   The 'Nottingham
Journal' appeared as a penny paper in 1863.   Next
comes the 'Leeds Mercury,' established in 1718 as a

weekly and appearing as a penny paper in 1861. It was
thus established seven years later than its contemporary
at Nottingham, but yielded to the exigencies of the
times two years before the less enterprising Nottingham
proprietors, who although nearer the capital supplied
news and wrote for a population in a less active business
centre. The ' Newcastle Daily Chronicle' was published
as a weekly in 1764, and was transformed into a daily
in 1858, three years again earlier than the ' Leeds Mercury.' So far then it is seen that the farther we get
north the greater appears to be the enlightenment and
the keener the appetite for news and Liberal teaching.
To some extent no doubt the extension of the telegraphic
system called for more frequent quotations for the different qualities of coal raised in this district. If this
were one of the causes, however, it seems strange that
the ' Newcastle Daily Journal,' which was started in
the Conservative interest in 1832, should have been behind its contemporary three years. There need be no
sacrifice of political principles, one would have thought,
in following the lead of a political opponent in introducing a reform, which must have been evident to persons
possessing any foresight at all could not be avoided if
the paper were to live. In 1790 both the ' Bristol Mercury' and ' Daily Post,' and the ' York Herald,' saw the
light in the Liberal interest, but the former was far in
advance of its contemporary in yielding to the pressure
of the times, having come out as a daily in 1860 while
the ' York Herald' delayed the step for thirteen years
subsequently to that date. Perhaps the proprietors of
the journal, which ventured to publish itself in the patriarchal stronghold of an archbishop, were so over-
awed by the shadow of the venerable Minster and the
frowns of the Episcopacy, that they dare not venture to

appear so frequently in the streets until they found themselves drifting into bankruptcy for their want of courage.

The journals devoted specially to furnishing news and information to the members of the army and navy are all either neutral or independent. The reasons why these journals take no side in politics are too obvious to need any mention. It is, however, well known, and, moreover, is very natural that the political views of men whose business it is to fight for their country should have more of a ring of war than of peace about them. It is at all times advisable that the editor of any journal should counsel moderation and the avoidance of anything approaching to an arrogant bearing on the part of his country towards an alien Government, no matter what the circumstances. As such a course would probably be distasteful to the great majority of his readers, a very little reflection and a very limited experience shows beyond question that opinions, one way or the other, had better not be expressed, and that the principles be announced from the outset as neutral or independent.

That there should be this necessity, however, calls for some remarks upon it. If the principles upon which a soldier or a sailor founds his opinions are laid upon foundations of justice and reason, what harm, it may be asked, can come from their ventilation or advocacy in a public journal? The danger of harm resulting arises from the well-known leaning of the men engaged in those professions towards opinions which under nearly all circumstances would advocate war. The reason why they advocate war is that they personally may have a better chance of obtaining quickly active service, which is what they entered the service for; and, secondly, that, as a consequence of that active service, they may have a better chance of distinction or promotion. If this argument be well founded, we are justified in drawing the conclusion that neither a soldier nor a sailor founds his opinions upon any principles at all. They cannot be founded on either justice or reason, when it is evident that, in the great majority of cases, all he thinks of or cares about is his own personal gain and advantage.

Further, since there is another political party besides the one to which the majority of soldiers and sailors are well known to belong, it would be highly injudicious for prominent members of either profession to make known their views in the same way that members of other professions do—such, more particularly, as Members of Parliament publish theirs. The violent expression of partisan opinions would diminish the chances of employment by a Liberal Government, and as Liberal Governments have for many years past been in office two years to the Conservatives' one, the impolicy of publicly avowing their opinions, whatever these officers may think, is evident.

With the exception of 'Bell's Messenger' and the 'Magnet,' the journals devoted to agriculture, appear, like the press of the army and navy, to find it in their interests to be colourless as regards their political views. That such an attitude is in accordance with their interests we may take it for granted. While the landed interest, embracing all their dependents from the tenant-farmers down to the lowest labourer in the field, were able by themselves to support journals openly and avowedly of their own political colour, we need entertain little doubt that refuge would not be taken in a neutral tint. We shall no doubt be told that the same argument applies

6

to the Liberals; but such is not the case. The Liberal
journalist has not had the same start as his Conservative
opponent. This is obvious to those who have read our
introduction. The Conservative was found in possession,
and armed to the teeth, by the Liberal, who has had to
fight an uphill game thus handicapped from the commencement. The time may come when there are so
many more Liberal supporters than there are Conservatives that the agricultural journals, which are now
afraid to run the risk of losing their Tory subscribers,
will find themselves strong enough to declare for Liberal
principles without introducing any compromise into the
titles, as 'Bell's Messenger' and the 'Magnet' have
done.

With one or two quite unimportant exceptions, all the
Commercial, Financial, Medical, Literary, Dramatic, &c.,
and Trade journals, are either neutral or independent.
Their pecuniary interests so obviously suggest to their
proprietors that they could not live under an avowal of
Conservative principles, inasmuch as their supporters
are Liberal as compared with Conservative in the proportion of ten to one at least, that journals of this type
could hardly be expected to take sides. If they avowed
Liberal tendencies, the few Conservatives who subscribe
would discontinue, and if Conservative it would mean
ruin. The only alternative, therefore, is neutrality, whatever may be the proprietorial or editorial views on politics. With this sweeping clearance of the journals
which do not profess to educate the public in the formation of political opinion, or in the science of government
at all, the task of judging to what extent the people are
reached by the political teachers of the press becomes
considerably narrowed.

Many and great as had been the attempts to gag the

press and prevent journalists from affording the great public that light by which alone they could form political opinions, the opening of the nineteenth century was to witness a material change in the influence which newspapers exercised. Even at that period the journals, as they have done ever since with increasing celerity, out-stripped official sources with their news. As they increased in power and financial resources higher intellects were attracted into journalistic ranks and trustworthy correspondents were appointed to transmit news regularly from all the capitals of Europe and from most other centres. Attempts to suppress Sunday papers were made for the same reasons that the Conservatives wished to block up every channel through which the truth might be disseminated, and by which their special privileges were in danger of being undermined. We readily admit that sixty years ago journalists were much less particular than the best of them are in our time as to the nature of the matter which appeared in their papers, the public taste being very different then from what it is now ; but that circumstance furnished the Tories with no excuse for endeavouring to crush out and destroy an institution which every one of them knew very well must inevitably become one of the greatest powers in the land. Their efforts, in fact, to prevent the growth of that power are the best proof of the magnitude of their fears, feeling and knowing as they did, that the ascendancy of the press meant the destruction of abuses and the annihilation of the power of those who had practised them. That this was the opinion of some at least of the sharpest intellects of that time is seen from the celebrated exclamation of Sheridan : " Give me but the liberty of the press, and I will give the Minister a venal House of Peers : I will give him a corrupt and servile

House of Commons; the full swing of the patronage of office; the whole host of Ministerial influence; all the power that place can confer upon him to purchase submission and overawe resistance; and yet, armed with the liberty of the press, I will go forth to meet him undismayed : I will attack the mighty fabric he has reared with that mightier engine; I will shake down from its height corruption, and lay it beneath the ruins of the abuses it was meant to shelter !"

The reign of Anne again witnessed the dawn of a new era in the history of the press. We are told that on assuming their present form the papers then were characterised by more enlightenment, and that for the first time political discussion was part of the programme. Although the influence of the press became greater from that period, it is evident from what we know of the jealousy with which the successive Governments, from 1702 up to the passing of the first Reform Bill, guarded their exclusive privileges, that the press during that period was more or less trampled upon. Ill able to support an independent existence, many journals would be unable to resist the offers made them to support rival factions. What was the rule then is the exception now, so far at least as the critical eye can detect. The institution in our day of " society " journals revived to some extent the scandals of the early period referred to, when Lord Mohun publicly chastised one Dyer, and Tutchin was beaten to death. Always characterised more or less by venomous onslaughts upon individuals or parties, there was no advance in real literary merit or decency of selection during a period which was famous for such men as Goldsmith, Johnson, and Pope. Journalists were in fact too often hired to ridicule successful opponents and injure their characters, an employment of their talents which finds many imitators in our own day. The *modus operandi* in these times may be less coarse on the surface, but the hidden sting is felt to be equally venomous. The influence, however, which the press was rapidly acquiring during the reign of the Georges, and especially in that of George III, may be seen from the following : * "A late nobleman, who had been a member of several Administrations," said Smollett, "observed to me that one good writer was of more importance to the Government than twenty placemen in the House of Commons." The celebrated case of the committal of John Wilkes to the Tower, for publishing an offensive libel in his paper, the 'North Briton,' shows how the power of such public organs was increasing as soon as the people understood what an instrument the press was in their hands.

In passing, it is interesting just to contrast the radically different position occupied by the press now as compared with a couple of hundred years ago by quoting the following :† "In 1641, the Long Parliament permitted the publication of its proceedings, which appeared under the title of ' Diurnal Occurrences in Parliament.' The printing of speeches, however, without leave of the House, was for the first time prohibited. In particular cases, indeed, where a speech was acceptable to the Parliament, it was ordered to be printed; but if any speech was published obnoxious to the dominant party, the vengeance of the House was speedily provoked. Sir E. Dering was expelled, and imprisoned in the Tower, for printing a collection of his speeches; and the book was ordered to be burned by the common hangman."

---

* Erskine May, vol. ii, p. 247.

† Erskine May, vol. i, p. 34.

The more or less rigorous censorship of the press in most foreign countries up to the present day contrasts very unfavorably with the almost complete freedom from such control which English journalists have enjoyed since the refusal of the House of Commons to renew the Licensing Act which expired in 1695. The case of our Government having suppressed a miserable German newspaper started in London in recent years by German Socialists with the object of publishing defamatory and insulting articles against that Government, which in addition advocated assassination of prominent persons, does not constitute a retrogressive policy in the matter of censorship of the press. It is the bounden duty of every civilised Government to crush out such nefarious attempts to preach a crusade against the Executive Government of foreign nations. In such cases *ut tibi sic alteri* is the guiding principle. Subject to the restrictions of the law of libel the English press has been free since the above date.

In the reign of Geo. III the press made great progress in the direction of freedom as well as in the development of its influence, the main cause of this being the passing of the Libel Bill of 1792, which placed the liberty of the press under the protection of juries. This was an enormous stride in the direction of affording facilities for a free and unfettered formation of political opinion, and at the same time it meant the destruction of another pillar among those which had for so long supported a system of rule whose object was to stifle all free thought and action, and make the community the slaves of the few whose superior wits, courage, and assurance enabled them to reach the highest places. There was, however, yet one other important step to take before the press could be said to be wholly free in the sense of being able to develop itself untrammelled by the prejudices of men or weighed down by taxes which were purposely levied to stifle its utterances and impede a progress which was felt to be highly dangerous to privileged interests. Mr. Milner Gibson led a movement to repeal all "taxes on knowledge." The duty on advertisements was done away with in 1853, and the final penny of the duty on newspapers was abolished in 1855. All that then remained was the paper duty. The total repeal of the stamp duty gave birth to the penny press, and it being almost essential to their existence that all burdens on the materials they required should be removed, they proceeded at once vigorously to assail the paper duty. Assisted even by all the friends of cheap literature and the liberal philanthropists who advocated popular education, it took six years of parliamentary contest before the opponents of the measure finally gave way. For six long years! did our friends the Tories keep their relentless heel upon the neck of one of the greatest powers for good which has exercised its influence in this country. What did Rousseau say? He said that, "To open the schools was to shut the prisons." Although some may object to the imputation, the inference is no more than a natural one that a party which did practically nothing to promote education among those below them were on the face of it indifferent to the question of whether or not the prisons were kept closed on their unhappy inmates. They apparently preferred to keep the ignorant in their ignorance; to obstruct the spread of knowledge, and the enlightenment and elevation of the lower strata of the nation. Such are, indeed, brilliant antecedents for a great political party.

The judges of that period, and the chief legal autho-

rities, naturally objected to the Law of Libel, as tending
to deprive them of some of the power which experience
has amply shown a good proportion of them have been
little fit to wield.*   If a record of the decisions reversed
by a Court of Appeal were collected, the public would
be amazed to see how very fallible have been the human
beings thus highly placed, and how necessary it was to
introduce a measure, such as the Law of Libel referred
to, which reflected so much honour upon Mr. Erskine,
Lord Camden, and Mr. Fox.   The iniquitous amount of
undeserved punishment that has been inflicted, even in
civilised countries, before the institution of trial by jury,
would make the blood run cold were it possible to
unearth and lay bare all the cases of miscarriage of
justice, which will ever be a standing reproach to ages
of enlightenment, whose unwritten records abound with
the black pages of despotic foul play and favouritism in
the matter of administering the laws of the country.†
The tremendous power which was placed in the hands
of a ruler to avenge imagined wrongs, or to trample
upon hated rivals, prior to the establishment of this
bulwark of our liberties, enables the imagination to
paint in sufficiently vivid colours the cruel injustice that
was suffered by hundreds of those among the generations which have long ago gone to their rest.

* Lord Braxfield was another specimen of the Tory of the period of
1793. He harangued the jury upon Parliamentary Reform at the trial of
Muir, and said, " The landed interest alone had a right to be represented ;
as for the rabble, who have nothing but personal property, what hold has
the nation of them ?"

† The trial of Muir, 1793. " Throughout the trial he was threatened
and brow-beaten by the judges. The Lord Advocate denounced him as a
demon of sedition and mischief." This case was brought before the House
of Commons, and in the course of the proceedings Mr. Fox said, " God
help the people who have such judges !" Judges are nearly always Tories.
See ' Const. His. of Eng.,' Erskine May, vol. ii, p. 293.

Thomas Muir was an advocate of Parliamentary Reform. His advocacy was held to be seditious in a time of excitement, as if reforms of that kind are attainable without excitement. Another noble Tory judge said he saw no difference between Muir's crime and high treason. The feelings of the unhappy jury were carried away by the warmth and indignation of the judges, and they found him guilty. Lord Henderland passed sentence of transportation for fourteen years ; and a third enlightened gentlemen on the bench, one Lord Swinton, said, with a ferocious aspect and diction, " If punishment adequate to the crime of sedition were to be sought for, it could not be found in our law, now that torture is happily abolished." Lord Abercromby and the Lord Justice Clerk congratulated the reformer upon having escaped with his life. Let it be observed that these judges were Tories, men of the same political persuasion as Lord Beaconsfield, the author of the Parliamentary Reform Bill of 1867, and also of Lord Salisbury and the greater part of his following, who approved in principle of the Parliamentary Reform Bill of 1884. Few of the rising generation of students who are forming their political opinions are even aware of these facts ; and we hope they will take due note of them. The circumstances attending the trial of William Skirving were equally scandalous, and reflect lasting discredit and dishonour upon the judges and lawyers engaged. These are the Tory traditions which the unthinking lawyers of to-day delight to honour by embracing the Conservative faith.

If it were necessary to bring further proof of the frequent fallibility of the judges than that which the experience of every intelligent person of our time affords, we should discover it in reference to this Law of Libel.

When the Law of Libel Bill was before the House of
Commons, the judges were unanimously opposed to it.
They contended that, under all circumstances, what had
to be decided was a question of law and not one of
fact.   However, Lord Camden, and Lord Common
Sense we might very well add, were the Court of Appeal;
and the whole Bench, with a few exceptions, suffered the
humiliation of being judged at the bar of public opinion,
and of being pronounced utterly and entirely wrong.
This may be said to have been not an instance of the
malformation of political opinion, but of judicial opinion;
and ,is, moreover, a memorable one as furnishing us
with evidence of the astonishing degree to which excep-
tionally acute and trained judicial minds can be warped
out of the straight line of truth and justice when a
point has to be considered which materially affects their
own personal prestige and power.   There is no doubt
that the institution of trial by jury, equally with the
abolition of the censorship of the press, relieved the
judges of a responsibility and of functions which
human nature is unable to exercise at all times, so as
to ensure the minimum of injustice.   Ambitious men
always wish to be supreme.   They are seldom satisfied
until they have reached the apex, whether it be of a
mountain or of the government of a State.   A sense of
dissatisfaction irritates and galls the spirit of an ambitious man until he feels that all his surroundings have
to look up to him, and acknowledge him as the mortal
Ens Entium, beyond which there is nothing and nobody
exercising a higher control.   The descendants of Adam,
one and all, have had this characteristic more or less
developed in them; and civilisation means quite as
much the curbing and reining in of the strivings after
the unattainable of hyper-ambitious men, and, for that

matter, of women too, as it does the training and education of the masses, so that they may be able to organise
themselves into a political constitution which will have
the power of using the available materials as they may
be wanted, and each unit in its place.

Statesmen, from the time of the passing of that Law of
Libel, began to discover that they were safer in the hands of
public opinion, in the now improved condition of the press,
than they were in placing any reliance, even on the Law
of Libel, now that they could be judged by their peers. ;

Concurrently with the great advance made in these
two directions, the establishment of trial by jury and the
freedom of the press, another influence, no less potent,
sprung into existence, that of public meetings. One of
the functions of the press being to report the utterances of
public men at those gatherings, journalists quickly perceived that the influence which the press might exercise
could thereby be greatly enhanced; and they did not fail
to take advantage of a new political force, which, at the
same time that it increased the power of journalism,
furnished important matter to its columns. Such
gatherings for political purposes were naturally considered by the opponents of reform to afford dangerous opportunities for able demagogues to inflame the passions
of the people, and to enlighten the ignorant upon
questions affecting their welfare. For this reason such
meetings have been only tolerated even in England
during the present century. The introduction of reforms which transferred the government of the country
from the great families to the people, would naturally
be accompanied by the development of every useful
device for making the *vox populi* easily and effectually
heard. Public meetings have on many occasions done
more to gain quickly and decisively desirable ends even

than the powerful advocacy of the press. People who are unable to judge for themselves, even when the case is explained to them in print, can be made to comprehend the salient points of an argument in favour of a certain measure by a powerful and incisive speaker. By laying emphasis here and there, by repeating the main features, and by exposing the weak points in the armour of opponents, a practised debater will exercise more influence at a public meeting than can be gained by the appearance twice or three times of the same address in the columns of a newspaper. A public meeting developes heat, which spreads and quickens the understanding of those who, when alone, remain unmoved and unenlightened as to some, if not the main points in the argument. Where numbers are collected together, and several take active part in the proceedings, valuable suggestions will often be made by comparatively incapable persons, which will be turned to account by more astute minds; and thus greater advantages are to be derived by the personal contact of thinkers of various types than can be secured for aiding the formation of political opinion by any other method. The House of Commons itself is looked up to as the *abnormis sapiens*, the almost supernatural teacher through which sophisms filter and become purified, and where fallacies and absurdities are exposed and relegated with their authors to the limbo of things whose imperfect fashioning adapts them for another sphere.

From among the lawyers who did so much to obstruct reform and keep the people out of their political rights, the name of Lord Ellenborough shines forth as a bright example. He was a man of humble origin, having risen by his talents, and by that clear perception which enabled him to see the truth and bring it to light, no less in his own profession of the law than in that of politics. His natural abilities are vouched for by the fact that on the refusal of Erskine to undertake the defence of Warren Hastings in 1785, Law served as leading counsel and gained the victory, although Fox, Burke, and Sheridan were opposed to him. From the office of Attorney General he was raised to the Lord Chief Justiceship of the King's Bench, and was made a Peer. What were his views of the political rights of the people and of the press? He laid it down that "it is competent for all the subjects of His Majesty, freely but temperately, to discuss, through the medium of the press, every question connected with public policy." He was a Liberal judge, and one, moreover, whose reliance on himself was not so feeble that he was afraid of being deprived of his office and emoluments by allowing greater freedom to the people. For that, after all, is what has and always does lie at the bottom of the fears entertained by Conservative judges, bishops, rectors, vicars, curates, landlords, &c.

Another and less enlightened gentleman, Baron Wood, belonged to the true old Tory party. His opinions were so decidedly opposed to the freedom of the press, and circumstances have proved him to be so utterly wrong as a Tory and Lord Ellenborough so completely right, that Baron Wood's words are worth reproducing here for the guidance of people who may be forming their political opinions. He remarked: "It is said that we have a right to discuss the acts of our Legislature. This would be a large permission, indeed! Is there, gentlemen, to be a power in the people to counteract the acts of the Parliament; and is the libeller to come and make the people dissatisfied with the Government under which he lives? This is not permitted to any man;

it is unconstitutional and seditious."* This unwise man's
teaching, like that of many other exalted personages of
his time, had as much effect in ultimately stopping the
progress of reform as the efforts of children to arrest
the flow of a river by casting stones into it. What a
deplorably bad system was that on which Baron Wood
proposed to constitute Parliaments, and how much
should we all rejoice that wiser and more enlightened
individuals than such as he was were born into the
world to interest themselves in the liberties of the
people, and the best mode of governing them.

While we have seen that the improvement of the
press was considerable during the early part of the reign
of George III, it is at the same time generally recognised that the last twenty-eight years of the reign of that
monarch formed a dangerous period of transition for
liberty of opinion. No man who then had leisure to
watch the course of events could fail to observe that
advantage was quickly taken by the extreme members of
the Liberal party of greater freedom of opinion being
allowed. The Government speedily realised this, and
in checking excesses repressed legitimate agitation.
But the masses of the people were beginning to open
their eyes to the fact that they had no voice in the
management of their own affairs, a circumstance which
incited them to rebel the more they reflected upon the
improvement in the wealth, power, and influence of the
middle classes. The Government, it is needless to say,
had, with the best grace they could, to give way. The
press, however, weathered the storm, and grew and
extended its influence during the reign of George IV,
furnishing ever ampler information for the guidance of
the people, which enabled them to promote legislation

* 'State Trials,' xxxi, 535.

in their own interests, and to narrow the circle in which Tory influences continued to labour for the preservation of the Constitution on the old lines. The failure of the prosecution of Cobbett in 1831 was the termination of a long sustained war between the Government and the press, since which period its complete freedom has been undisputed, while the removal of minor obstructions to the unfettered expansion of the greatest civilising agency of modern times, encouraged proprietors and editors to develop to the fullest extent their respective organs, with the marvellous results which we see to-day.

We now arrive at a stage in this branch of the task we have undertaken, which compels us to quit historical tracks and dive into the stores of our experience. The first question to be answered is : How many journals of the present day can be relied on for the expression of entirely unbiassed political opinions? The reply of every experienced reader of newspapers must be the reverse of satisfactory, and we must try and account for it being so. There are many things to consider. There is no doubt that no newspaper has reached that perfection of development which enables it to be absolutely independent until, first of all, it is financially powerful. It must be in a position to refuse, for instance, every advertisement of an objectionable nature, no matter what the price offered for its insertion. It must be in a position to use the best materials for conveying the printed matter to the eye, to secure the services of specialists of the highest public repute, to maintain educated men as its correspondents at the chief capitals of the world, and to pay well a large staff of writers who are experts in their several departments. But, to maintain a large circulation, whilst refusing absolutely to side with this or that political party, for other reasons

than that it believes the ground taken up by Liberal or
Conservative on any particular question is tenable according to the principles of justice, morality, and good
government, is the goal which all the leading journals
strive for, but which, in our time at least, few reach.
If this position, then, be unattainable except by a few,
of what real value to the public are the political views
of those journals who for existence sake must advocate
opinions which are in accordance with the traditions of
their chief supporters ? The answer is obvious.

The influence of the press is no doubt enormous ; but
it is only enormous in the present day when it tells the
truth and advocates what is just. The people are now
too enlightened and too well informed to be deceived by
any false statement but for a short time. There was a
time when journals could flourish to a certain extent
while advocating only the interests of a particular set or
party, because its readers had little or no other means
of testing its accuracy or of judging of the soundness of
its views. The set or party could afford to keep it going
because the results justified the expenditure ; but their
support to that particular paper would only be continued
so long as its influence was sufficient to visibly secure
for them the special privileges they were enjoying. It
could only pay to keep going journals of that class so
long as a considerable section of the community continued
to derive exclusive benefit from protective laws and such
like, and the sweeping away of such fallacies both as
theories and in practice means, consequently, the destruction of the journals which were chiefly supported by
those who profited by their advocacy of such doctrines.

The Conservatives of our day are wont to say that they
are overwhelmed with numbers, and that that is the reason why Conservative principles do not gain ground. It

is true that Liberal politicians and Liberals by profession who cannot exactly claim to be politicians, do greatly outnumber them. They vastly outnumbered them in 1846, and the superiority in that respect has steadily increased. It has increased moreover among the intelligent and educated classes more than among the lower and less well-informed, and the reason of this is, that Liberal principles are seen and recognised to be principles of justice, which seek to throw down all the barriers erected by the few in their own interests, in opposition to the interests of the community as a whole. The progress that has been made in this direction will be seen from the following statistics of the London and country daily press avowedly professing political opinions :

London and Country Daily Press avowedly professing Political Principles.

	Liberal.	Conservative.	Independent or Neutral.
London	6	5	7
Ashton	1	—	—
Bath	1	2	—
Birmingham	3	1	1
Bolton	2	1	—
Bowdon	—	—	1
Bradford	2	—	—
Brighton	—	1	3
Bristol	2	1	1
Burton-on-Trent	1	—	—
Bury	1	—	1
Cheltenham	—	1	—
Chester	—	—	1
Crewe	—	—	1
Darlington	1	—	1
Derby	2	—	—
Dewsbury	1	—	—
Exeter	2	1	—
Gainsborough	—	—	1
Gloucester	—	—	1

7

	Liberal.	Conservative.	Independent or Neutral.
Grimsby	—	—	1
Hanley	1	—	—
Hartlepool	—	—	1
Huddersfield	1	—	1
Hull	—	—	2
Ipswich	—	—	1
Leeds	2	2	—
Leicester.	2	—	—
Liverpool	3	2	3
Manchester	2	2	2
Middlesborough	1	1	—
Nantwich	—	—	1
Newcastle	2	1	2
Newport	1	1	—
Northampton	—	1	1
Northwich	—	—	1
Norwich	—	—	2
Nottingham	2	1	2
Oldham	1	1	1
Penzance.	—	—	1
Plymouth	1	1	1
Portsmouth	1	—	1
Runcorn	—	—	1
Scarborough	1	1	—
Sheffield	1	—	3
Shields	2	—	—
Shrewsbury	—	1	—
Sunderland	1	1	1
Wakefield	1	—	—
Warrington	—	—	1
Widnes	—	—	1
Wolverhampton	1	—	1
Worcester	1	1	—
York	2	—	—
Cardiff	1	1	—
Swansea	1	—	1
Aberdeen	2	1	1
Dundee	2	—	1
Edinburgh	2	1	2
Glasgow	2	1	3
Greenock	1	—	1
Leith	—	—	1
Paisley	1	—	—
Belfast	2	2	1

		Liberal.	Conservative.	Independent or Neutral.
Cork		1	1	1
Dublin		3	3	—
Waterford . . .		—	1	—
Jersey		1	—	—
	Total	74	41	64

Here we have 74 Liberal daily papers, 41 Conservative, and 64 Independent. The Liberal daily papers thus number very nearly twice as many as the Conservative. The English provincial newspapers numbered 680 in 1874; now the total reaches 1177 with 401 for London alone. In Wales there are now 80; in Scotland 181 as compared with 69 in 1843 and 159 in 1874, of which number 14 then belonged to Edinburgh. In 1874 16 of the Scotch papers were regarded as Conservative and 67 as Liberal. In 1884, ten years later, the Scotch papers had increased in number to 167. Of these, 84 were Liberal, 21 Conservative, 58 Neutral or Independent, and 4 Liberal Conservative. Thus in the ten years the Liberal journals had increased 17 to the Conservatives 5, while the Independent or Neutral had decreased 14. These latter therefore, it may be inferred, have in the meantime declared for Liberal principles, having during that period of ten years so reformed their political opinions as to be compelled to renounce a faith which was losing ground, and to espouse another which was daily growing in strength and numbers. Perhaps it might be more correct to say that these 14 Scotch proselyte journals had to change their creed, and only did change it after a very considerable wrench. We all know that there are few things more difficult than for people to bring themselves to confess candidly that the views which they have held for years, and are as much a part of their mind's furniture as the peculiarities of

their individual nature, are wrong. Such a change lays
the proselyte open to the insinuation that he is inconsistent, or that he formed his political opinions before
he was competent to do so, which is apt to wound the
amour propre of people, especially when they are people
of any position in life and have made that position by
the exercise of faculties which make them feel that their
judgment is about as good as anybody's else as regards
the ordinary affairs of life. But politics and the ordinary
affairs of life make very different calls upon a man's
judgment. There are politics and politics. There are
high politics and low politics. Ordinary people can
judge well enough of low politics, because this branch
of the science embraces matters of the municipal type,
in which they have had experience, and of which they
can judge very often better than, or at least quite as
well as, their nominal rulers. Liberal Governments have
always given more attention to the wants and rights of
this class, and Conservative Governments have neglected
them. Hence, while the latter have in the past lost
ground and continue now to lose ground, the former from
year to year have gained more adherents. The increase
in the number of Scotch Liberal newspapers proves this.
No one pretends to deny that it is important that all
Governments should devote a portion of their time and
energies to foreign affairs; but, in ordinary times, it is
of still more importance that they should seek to remove
all the abuses and grievances which weigh upon the
industries of the nation, and should introduce such reforms as are likely to foster the development of every
branch so as to improve the welfare and promote the
comfort of the people. Spending money in the prosecution of a spirited foreign policy, which is not the out-
come of absolute necessity, puts little or nothing in

these times into the pockets of the people, but it often takes something out. As one generation succeeds another a clearer view of these truths penetrates into all sections of the community. Even the cabman, who reads his penny newspaper in the ranks while waiting for employment, appreciates the benefits conferred upon the masses by the removal of objectionable taxes upon so many articles which minister to his enjoyment and comfort. He knows that the removal of these burdens has been due chiefly to Liberal statesmen. During the last ten years the enormous spread of cheap journalism has carried such truths as these into every cottage and hamlet in the land, and there can be little doubt that the 14 Scotch Conservative journals which have gone over to the Liberals since 1874 have done so under a pressure which threatened their existence.

The number of newspapers published in London in 1843 was 79; in 1874, 289; and in 1884, 401. The provincial papers of England numbered 212 in 1843, 680 in 1874, and 1177 in 1884.

Here again, then, we are able to show continuous progress in the spread and advocacy of Liberal principles and continuous contraction of the so-called Conservative principles, and the peculiarity of the political situation of to-day is that, notwithstanding the materially altered disposition of the Conservative party towards the larger section of the political community under the influence of fifty years' experience of the working of Liberal reforms, the Conservatives seem to have as much difficulty as ever in persuading the country to entrust them with the administration of its affairs. No one who follows the making of the history of our times can have failed to observe that since the death of Lord Beaconsfield the party has been in the position of a Cunard liner with its main shaft broken. The party ship has had just sufficient way on to be able to steer the old course marked out for her, but until that shaft is replaced there is nothing but sails to depend upon for making head-way; and the difficulty seems to be that there is no such main shaft as the broken one available. There is plenty of steam power, but the machinery by which its energy can alone be controlled continues to be out of order. There is a time in political affairs, as in seaman-ship, when it is justifiable to go full speed a-head. The attitude of the House of Lords, for instance, with refer-ence to the 1884 Franchise Bill, may be likened to a ship steaming full speed in a fog. They did not know where they were going to, and they were consequently very likely to come into violent contact with some other vessel or the rocks, just as the House of Lords did with the popular will. Another instance of the uncontrolled steam power to which we refer is to be found in Lord Randolph Churchill's speech at Leeds, on the 3rd of October, 1884, which is thus criticised by the ' Times ' : " *In that homely and elegant vernacular which he enjoys the proud distinction of having introduced into political controversy,* he avowed his ' honest opinion, that all this bobbery which the Liberals are kicking up about the action of the House of Lords is artificial, and is all humbug.' "* Both this gentleman and his half-adopted leader have never ceased to accuse the Liberal Govern-ment of blundering, and no doubt in the management of the Egyptian difficulty it is only fair to admit that they have made mistakes, as probably under the circum-stances every other Government would have done; but in all their blundering it would be difficult to find that they have committed a bigger blunder than the Conser-

* See 'Times,' Report 4th October, 1884.

vative leaders did in obstinately opposing the passing of
the Franchise Bill. Had they got this out of the way,
and thrown all their energies into attacking the Egyptian
policy of the Government, they might have aroused the
sympathies of the public in their favour. As it is,
almost everybody has been saying that they are justifying
more than ever J. S. Mill's epithet, that they are the
" stupid " party, by holding on with blind obstinacy to
a policy of uncompromising opposition when they knew
that the country was hopelessly against them.

The attitude of the press during that fight was what
it usually is in such circumstances. Conservative journals
dare not advise those whose political opinions it is their
business to help to form, to swallow the leek and wait
for a better chance. This was one of those occasions
when leading Conservative journals would have enhanced
their reputation by advising the Conservative Peers to
give way in the face of absolutely overwhelming opposition; but no, the risk was too great to run. The
journal might be deserted by the party. It might be
ejected from the Conservative political clubs; its subscribers might fall away by the hundred, and a decrease
in the circulation means a fall in the revenue. It would
expose itself to the unmerciful ridicule of the opponents
who had waged a war of words with it for the last fifty
years. It would be accused of gross inconsistency, and
of deserting the national standard in the hour of the
party's direst need. Hints would be thrown out that it
had gone over to the enemy for a consideration. All
connected with it would feel half ashamed that they
belonged to it, and would be twitted with their inconsistency by every one intimate enough with them to run
the risk of cracking a joke at their expense. In fact—
having dared to take an independent line because in

their innermost judgment they believed the adoption of
that course to be wise, sound, just, and in the interests
of the nation—would so lower them in the opinion of
their immediate supporters, that even if they only did
such a thing once, and quickly rallied to their old allegiance, they would lose so much ground that it would be
a long time before they recovered the old favour, and
would have the same chance as before of obtaining special
information when the Conservatives again came into
power.

So much for consistency.   If that is the price which
journalism has to pay for consistency, then, many will
say, virtue is not its own reward.   But consistency
of that kind is no virtue; on the contrary, it has been
abundantly proved to be a vice, and a vice of an order
which has prevented the sound formation of political
opinion to a degree which is deplorable to contemplate.
Journalists of this type have been hammering away
blindfold at the same set of opinions ever since there
were two parties to fight for office.   Generations continue to pass away and new editors come to occupy the
vacated chair, but there is no change in the political
opinions of the paper.   If there were no real Conservative editors of the unmitigated type to be had, there
would all the same be no difficulty in making arrangements for the journal to be conducted on the same lines.
Mr. Gladstone, Mr. Bright, Mr. Cobden, Mr. Mill, and
those who thought with them, and whose reforms had been
years ago accepted by a grateful country, and ungra-
ciously assented to by opponents who knew they were
wise and just, would still have to be abused in the future
as they had been in the past.   No matter how utterly
wrong and undeserved this abuse had been shown to be
over and over again, for consistency's sake the same

thing must continue to be done. If such journals were to go over to the other party, as Sir Robert Peel and Lord Derby did, its readers, most of them, would stop their subscriptions at once. Their great enjoyment for years had been to see day after day and week after week the men they hated abused, and all their actions and sayings misrepresented and explained so as to mean what the critics knew themselves they did not mean.

The great mass of the press of the country exercises its greatest influence in placing rapidly before their readers the facts of each case as they arise, and the opinions on those facts as they are delivered by the more prominent members of both political parties. When a Liberal politician turns to a Conservative journal to ascertain the opinions of the editorial columns, he may be frequently heard to remark that he could write down most of the article before looking at it. This, we do not deny, applies also to many Liberal journals, but it does not apply to the same extent. Events have proved the Liberals to be sounder in their political judgment than their opponents, and in approving of the reforms introduced by Liberal Governments they are assenting to the acts of politicians who are simply further advancing in a direction which both parties have long since agreed is one which satisfies the country, develops its resources, conduces to the happiness of the people, and extends to each member of the community the political and social rights to which he is justly entitled.

So far, then, we seem to come to the conclusion that even the press of this country, which is incomparably superior to that of any other as regards its endeavours to place the true facts before its readers and includes a greater number of journals which desire to, and do, print what they believe to be the truth, has by no means arrived

at that stage of development of which it is capable. We
hold that no journal can have reached its full development, and thereby placed itself in a position to be an
absolutely safe and impartial guide, until it has not only
placed itself in a position to be able systematically to
take up neutral ground on every question ; but until, by
the maintenance for years of an independent attitude,
it has proved that it is entirely free from partisan bias.

As we move about in the world we instinctively feel
that the opinion of ninety per cent. of. Liberals cannot
be relied on to express a strictly fair and impartial
opinion upon the acts of a Conservative Government,
and the same may be said of the Conservatives, with
the difference which we have already stated with regard
to journalism, viz. that a larger proportion of Liberal
politicians can be trusted because they have for so long
been on the winning side, and because the losers are
more permanently soured by defeat and exclusion from
power.

That the greatest journals strive for, and in some
few cases have actually realised that complete independence, through which alone they can attain to the
fullest development and the exercise of the greatest
power, is, however, known very well to close observers.

Another great struggle for this end has of late years
been going on, but there was a falling away when the
Franchise Bill of 1884 went up to the House of Lords.
That falling away seemed to show that as soon as any
party heat was developed an organ that had hitherto been
so closely associated with the fortunes of the Conservative
party, either lacked the pluck to cut itself free from the
partisan fetters by which it had been so long bound, or
feared such a decrease in the number of its supporters
that it declined the risk. If this be an accurate obser-

vation of the tactics of one of our most solidly established journals, what chance is there for the hundreds of others, occupying an inferior position, to achieve that independence without which the goal of journalistic ambition can never be reached ?

The formation of sound political opinion is only possible in the same way that a just verdict can only be returned by a jury after they have heard both sides of the case. A partisan journal, be its bias Liberal or Conservative, gives the evidence of but one side. A party journal stands up before the public, so to speak, like a counsel in a case, who has primed himself only with those facts and arguments which tell in favour of his client, be he plaintiff or defendant. If, therefore, the great majority of the journals of this country take sides like the barristers in a court of law, there can be no possibility of sound political opinion being formed at all by those whose opinions are simply a repetition of what they read in the daily leading articles. Fortunately, people are now so well educated in vast numbers of cases, and their judgment has been so ripened by its exercise in various occupations where success depends so much upon sound judgment, that the vanguard of the great army which has to weigh and pronounce upon all the great questions relating to the government of the country, use what the press supplies them with, as one of many elements which are necessary to enable them to form a sound opinion. So far, in a word, as the press as a whole is concerned, it in most cases supplies but the opinion of its editor, or, which is much the same thing, the political opinion which it has been traditional with that particular journal to hold, and which "consistency" is supposed to compel it to adhere to.

While the position of the press remains what it is,

therefore, it is evident that its greatest use to the public
is to furnish it with a truthful account of all matters
which call for notice at the time of publication.

By degrees, no doubt, the higher development of complete independence and neutrality, to which we have
referred, may be reached; but the history of the past
shows that such a transformation is a very difficult one,
for the simple reason that unless the new aspirant to
such an Olympian altitude of perfection can successfully
compete in other respects with those who have already
established themselves in that envied position, the danger
is immediately incurred of losing those adherents who
gave their support solely on the ground that their own
special views, whether Liberal or Conservative, were
consistently advocated.

There is another question—that of the impersonality
of journalism. Writers in public journals are sure more
or less to be drawn into extravagances and into committing errors of judgment if what they write is signed.
Much greater heat develops in political discussion if the
opponents can get at each other. This they do when
they sign their names or when they become the recognised guiding hand in a journal. There are many journals
of the present day which constitute the little despotism
of the editor, and in which he loves to make it felt that
his finger is in every paragraph. This is a position no
doubt personally highly gratifying, but it is almost
sure to lead to abuse. An editor, for instance, conceives
a violent dislike for a certain Prime Minister who has
perhaps criticised his paper in an uncomplimentary way.
What is the result? Hardly an issue appears without
more or less of insult being heaped upon his name, and
more or less of abuse being hurled at every act of his
cabinet. Such a course of proceeding persisted in, not

only month after month but year after year *ad nauseam*,
is wearisome and *ennuyant* in the highest degree, even
if spicely done; but it lets down the profession of
journalism from the high position of impartiality and
impersonality which ought to be the great end ever
sought to be attained.   Some few readers, whose political
principles are opposed to those of the Minister who is
the object of attack may be amused; but the majority
of those who are witnesses of this kind of performance
will sooner or later turn away from such a spectacle
with mingled feelings of pain and disgust.

CHAPTER IV.

WHAT applies to journalism in politics, as we have
endeavoured to show in the chapter dealing with the
press, applies with equal force to individual politicians.
The most perfect politician in our view is the man who
in theory takes sides, but in practice does not. A man is
perfectly right to weigh all arguments *pro* and *con*,
study the history of both parties, and then make up his
mind to throw in his lot with one or the other, on the
ground of this or that party professing what he conceives to be the best principles; but in practice he will
undoubtedly be wiser to avow it as his intention to hold
himself independent. The obvious advantage of adopting such a course in practice is, that a man escapes
placing himself in the absurd position of voting against
measures which he knows to be good for the country,
simply because they happen to be proposed by the party
whose principles in theory are not his principles.
Declared Tories have over and over again stultified
themselves by obstinately refusing to vote for Liberal
measures because Liberal Governments proposed them
in the House of Commons, notwithstanding the fact
that they knew all the while they were for the real good
of the community, and that many of their own side had
admitted this by siding with the majority. It may be

retorted, "How do you know that the Tories who voted against the repeal of the Corn Laws and the 1832 Reform Bill knew all the while they were voting against their convictions?" We should reply, that "we are justified in assuming that they did, because no sane man would allow himself to be persuaded that one portion of the nation who called themselves Tories possessed feebler judgments than those who called themselves Liberals." In those two cases referred to, events have amply proved that the free and unfettered judgment of every healthy mind could not resist the conviction coming home to it that the Liberals were sound upon that question if only the barrier of prejudice could be removed. Those who subsequently changed their faith did resist conviction at the outset, because the reform was one which the *principles* of the party did not allow them to agree to. That is the truth of it; the exercise of any judgment in the matter was, in fact, by the great majority of the Tories considered superfluous. Those who brought in the measures did not wear the Tory colours, and therefore the Tories must vote against them—which numbers in fact did, without taking the trouble to master any of the clauses of the Bill. Take warning, therefore, ye rising politicians, not to go beyond theory in taking sides; and, moreover, keep your theory to yourselves.

As regards the progress which is made by Liberalism as compared with the ground that is being steadily lost by Conservatism, we are not so much concerned with the capricious course of action adopted by either individuals or corporate bodies of Liberals, or of Conservatives under the influence of mortification at the passing of particular measures which affect their interests at the moment, as we are with the conversion

to Liberalism of individual Tories. It is highly instructive to study the changes of feeling which have
come over districts and bodies of people as the result of
a better understanding of the difference between the
political aims of Liberal Governments and those of Tory
Governments. To follow and understand the effects of
the gradual spread of education, which will inevitably
bring in its train a desire among the majority of the
coming generations to aid in the spread of Liberal principles, is more worthy of the men of our time than to
indulge the selfish inclination which prompts a man to
adopt Tory principles for fear any other shall involve
the enactment of laws which may interfere with his
special privileges. We have already remarked that the
Stock Exchange, for instance, supported Lord Beaconsfield almost to a man in his adventurous exploits.
Business with the stockbrokers was dull at the time.
They are a class of people who make money easily when
business is flourishing, and they spend it freely. Their
establishments are usually kept up nearer to the
maximum scale of their earnings than to the minimum; and people of that class are less to be depended
on for strict adherence to any principles they may have
laid down for their guidance, than is the case with those
whose profits are less fluctuating. This is no isolated
case of men's course of political action being diverted
into another channel in obedience to the dictates, at a
moment of irritation, of pure selfishness, and for no
other reason whatever. The Stock Exchange gentlemen who then " went " Tory because the prices of stocks
rose, and the public, as they very often do when prices
rise, came in to buy, never for a moment paused to
consider whether the political action of Lord Beaconsfield was sound or not. What, then, are we to think of

the future of the formation of political opinion by
corporations like that, when facts like these—and there
are and always have been many of them—are before
us? Such men, there can be no doubt, will turn round
and support a Liberal Ministry in analogous circumstances; and therefore we attach but a dubious value
to the political views held, or the principles professed,
by such bodies as the Stock Exchange, the clergy, landlords, bankers, universities, and all kinds of guilds or
corporations fattening on revenues which have been
diverted into the channel in which they luxuriate,
through their having been able to secure for their order
a privileged position. Men enjoying such special privileges are naturally irate with Sir William Harcourt and
his Government of London Bill.

The influence brought to bear by these, what we may
term, close boroughs, does not, however, materially
affect the course of events. Principles which are
founded on justice and equity are sure, as time goes on,
to gather such strength and momentum as will over-
whelm all resistance. It is always known, moreover, to
the Intelligence Department of both Liberals and Conservatives, whether the course of action taken by any
section or sections of either side is adopted in the
interests of the community, regardless of mere personal
motives, or whether it is dictated only by selfishness.
In other words, every man's and every constituency's
measure is taken. The constituency that persists in
returning members of the stamp of Dr. Kenealy, is
not treated with that serious respect which falls to
the lot of a body of voters who offer spontaneously a
seat to a man like Mr. Gladstone. The capricious
votes of either individual men or bodies of men
occupying a temporarily privileged position may do

either good or harm, more frequently harm; but they exercise little permanent effect upon the great stream of reform and the improving political condition of the community, which a sense of justice and equity working in the hearts of the people continues to force on like a mighty current obeying a law which no petty jealousies of the rival bees in the great hive can interfere with. Like the clouds whose shadows move over the landscape, they make their presence felt and seen, but they exercise no appreciable effect in the long run upon the whole surface of the earth, which yields its fruits under the influence of the sun's rays, just as the voice of truth can only be drowned for a while by obstructions which rest upon falsehood and fallacy.

The political influences we have just been referring to are, viewed from the standpoint of the history of the human race and its social and political development, ephemeral. We are concerned with something much deeper, wider, and more enduring, and that is, the spread of political light and understanding. In our day the community cannot be said to be cut up into sections, some of which are in darkness and some in light. The light in these times penetrates everywhere in civilised countries. Where the true science of governing a nation is best understood and practised, there the light by means of newspapers — even newspapers whose political principles are wrong—and through various forms of teaching penetrates everywhere. Wherever despotism, in however mild a form, still prevails, there the voice of justice and equity will be smothered. What, however, we are now concerned with is the formation of political opinion in the leading countries like our own. On this subject Sir G. C. Lewis remarks:* " In the free

* 'Influence of Authority,' &c., p. 175.

states of recent times, the direct action of the mass of the people under the Government has been moderated by the representative system, which has established an intermediate stage between the popular suffrage and the legislative measure. This circumstance, combined with the invention of printing, and the consequent diffusion of knowledge, has caused the democratic action to be regarded with less alarm. Nevertheless, a certain amount of intelligence and education has almost always been pointed out as a qualification for the exercise of the powers of Government, and the existence of a fran-chise founded on property has been defended, in part, on the ground of its securing a requisite amount of education." Then he goes on to say, which is more to our immediate point : " This feeling in modern societies has likewise been sharpened by the fact, *that the entire community* consists of freemen, and that the working classes, forming the bulk of the poor population, *are not slaves* as in the ancient republics. The alleged defect of capacity for government, and of a respect for order and the rights of property, in the multitude, has repeatedly been urged as a reason for excluding them from political power."

The new additions to those bodies of men, who live and work in clusters or large organisations, get to form their political opinions and their estimate of prominent men very much like a baby forms its opinion of its mother's milk, with its eyes shut. Opinions formed simply by the light of self interest, grows into a tradition, for instance, as we have said in large banks, Govern-ment offices, universities, &c., and from the moment a young man joins such an organisation it is no disrespect to him to say that his ideas expand under the influence of the partisan heat which prevails there. In the for-

mation of political opinion the danger of this kind of
political education is, that the other side of the question
gets no chance of being weighed in the balance until the
individual's political bias has become so confirmed, that
he is probably immoveably prejudiced.   None but the
newspapers which favour that party come under his
notice.   He hears the more prominent members among
the opponents of that party habitually abused.   He
wishes to gain the favour of his superiors, and smilingly
acquiesces in their views when appealed to.   He hears,
on the other hand, their political idols extolled, and he is
proud to know some of the circumstances which have
contributed to their greatness.   Thus, by degrees, he is
brought to admire what in his youthful ignorance he
believes to be the virtues of the one set, and to despise
the other for what he is told are their vices.   His
worldly wisdom does not yet enable him to read between
the lines of people's opinions, or he would know that but
a very small percentage of those who can express intel-
ligently their political views, work them out on any
broader lines than those of mere self interest.   Thus it
becomes evident that the formation of political opinion
depends very much upon the special influences under
which young men may come in their early life.

To go into detail, let us take the City of London
proper as an instance.   At the election of members of
Parliament in 1880, the City of London returned three
Conservative members and one Liberal.   This means
practically that the voters of the City of London profess
Conservative principles.   Well, how is this, that the one
central spot in England at which is gathered during the
day the representatives of a larger class of wealthy,
cultivated, and refined people than anywhere else, should
with a few exceptions all profess the same political prin-

ciples ? The main reason of it is, that in some way, directly or indirectly, the merchant princes and great traders, the chairmen of shipping companies, of dock companies, of this, that, or the other corporation, guild or institution, are lending their material and moral support for the maintenance of privileged positions through whose aid the few gain at the expense of the many. Who, for instance, could expect private bankers to support a bill for the incorporation of joint-stock companies on the limited liability principle ?

On the other hand, it is quite right for Governments to concede certain privileges to corporations of merchants *for a period*, just as the patent law protects the patentee for a number of years ; but, as soon as it becomes apparent that the continuance of those privileges enables those to whom they are extended to use them exclusively in their own interests and at the same time to the detriment of others, who have a right after a certain time to share in the benefits, it is the duty of the Government to step in and say, as they virtually do to the patentee—you have enjoyed an exclusive right to the benefits accruing from your invention or from your special privilege to trade, to enable you to acquire a substantial profit, and now you must share it with the public. The equity of that method of dealing with those who have been granted certain privileges has been acknowledged in the past, and it must be acknowledged in the future. There is, for instance, among others, the case of the Hanse merchants. This league, founded in 1241, acquired such strength that they went to war in 1348 against the King of Denmark, and again in 1428 with forty ships and 12,000 regular troops, besides seamen. They enjoyed many privileges in England by treaty which were abolished in 1578 by Elizabeth. The

members of such a league would naturally be Tories.
What right, say they, has any one else to derive any
benefit from a trade which they have created and fostered?   The answer is, that their privileged position
could not have been acquired without the aid of the
Government with which they made the treaty, and
which secured to them that privileged position.   Such
privileged positions are, and always have been abused,
and that alone is sufficient reason for withdrawing the
privilege, when the circumstances under which it was
granted have entirely changed.   But, apart from the
abuse, as in the case of the patentee, there must be a
reasonable limit beyond which the protection should not
be afforded.   Without the public demand for the mer-
chandise in which they traded, neither the one nor the
other could make any use of his privilege, and therefore,
as in the further parallel of the annuity, it must fall in,
some time or other.

In the same way as the Hanse merchants would have
kept their special privileges for ever if they could, all
other corporations struggle to retain the benefits attaching to their order, and band themselves together for
mutual protection to resist the action of the Liberal
reformer.   In his celebrated phrase, Lord Beaconsfield
would have called it " plundering " for Queen Elizabeth
to abolish the treaty by which the English merchants of
the Hanse League enjoyed so many privileges, and
ultimately at the expense of her other subjects.   Lord
Salisbury endorses that view.   We read in his article in
the 'National Review' for October, 1884, the following: speaking of a Conservative opposition, he says,
" They have to prevent 'plundering' as well as
'blundering;' and the performance of this duty interests
their followers throughout the country quite as much as

the leaders in the House. When a Radical Government now-a-days comes into power with a strong
majority at its back, a feeling spreads itself abroad
among all sorts of people who belong to any class
electorally weak, similar, at least in kind, to that which
is felt in a Turkish province on the announcement that
a new Pasha has been appointed. They know that the
process of ' conveyance ' is about to begin. Whether
they be landowners or shipowners, or belong to an old
corporation, or are members of an endowed church,
they look forward to the future with misgiving, for they
know that reform, *of the predatory species,* is in the
air." Lord Salisbury believes in strong minorities. He
further remarks in the article referred to : " A certain—
though small—portion of every majority is accessible to
argument, especially on this subject ; and a strong Conservative opposition can usually prevent any serious
wrong from being done. The calm and moderate legislation of the Liberal Parliaments of 1837, 1847, and
1859 show the enormous advantage which a strong
opposition may confer on the Conservative interests of
the country." It is no doubt highly important that the
Conservatives should obtain the largest minority they
can, when a Liberal Government is in power. The
more they can get to think with them the less there will
be to think with the other side. But no matter how
large the Conservative minorities were at the dates mentioned, they never stopped the great reforms which
were carried at those epochs. They never, for example,
stopped the Protectionist landlords from plundering the
consumer by imposing a duty on the corn imported into
the country. That was " plundering " with a vengeance. It was not the plundering of a corporation or
guild of the privileges which were being, and had been,

supported for, perhaps, a couple of hundred years on the dues of the Port of London, which belong to the municipality, which is the corporate servant of the people. The Conservative opposition to the repeal of the Corn Laws meant the " plundering " of the poor by the rich. It was the " Society for the *Protection* of Agriculture," of which the Duke of Richmond was Chairman, and which was established as a corporation of landlords to counteract the efforts of Messrs. Villiers, Cobden, Bright, &c., who had formed an association to procure the repeal of the Corn Laws, which might much more appropriately be accused of " plundering and blundering," than any Liberal administration. Lord George Bentinck distinguished himself by being the head of that party from 1846 till his death, September 21st, 1848. That is, perhaps, the most notorious case of " plundering " on record, and also the most renowned instance of "blundering," which is proved by the fact that the landlords were entirely overthrown and routed in their attempt to continue to plunder the people by protecting their own interests at the expense of the community, when a Conservative Government came into office in 1852. The Derby administration, it is well known, dare not propose the restoration of the Corn Laws ; and the Protectionist Society was therefore abolished.

In the face of such evidence as the above, the insinuation of Lord Salisbury, " for they know that reform of the *predatory* species is in the air," is singularly inappropriate. It is proposed now to reform the government of London, a Bill with that object having been introduced last session. That is, of course, according to Conservative ideas, " a reform of the predatory species." The members of the Corporation of the City of London are probably actuated by much the same motives as those who constitute the corpus of similar large organisations, and they have much the same interests. What the leading members of the organisation do to protect the society in which their own interests are bound up, the other members are likely to do also. As their acts will be alike, so their opinions will not be likely materially to differ.

It is worth while further to analyse the process of the formation of political opinion by men who belong to such societies, which we have also touched on elsewhere, because we shall then see clearly how it is that the City of London practically returns Conservative members to the House of Commons. Let us hear what Sir George Cornewall Lewis has to say about a man's opinion being influenced by personal interest. * " The qualities which render a man a trustworthy authority in matters of opinion are much rarer than those which render a man a credible witness in matters of fact. Accordingly, the honesty which induces a man to speak the truth is more common than that which induces him to form sound opinions. There are many men who, under other circumstances, would never be seduced by interest to report a fact falsely or to express an insincere opinion, whose judgment might nevertheless be perverted by interest. It is commonly said that the belief is independent of the will—that is, of the desires or inclinations; and everyone must be conscious that he cannot change the state of his belief on matters either of fact or opinion by merely wishing it to be otherwise. But the operation of a personal interest, bearing closely and directly on the question, generally causes a man, unless he be remarkably honest or perspicacious, *insensibly*

* ' Influence of Authority,' &c., p. 25.

to adopt prejudices, or *partial and unexamined opinions.*
The dislike of listening to unpalatable truths induces him
to shut his ears against evidence and arguments opposed
to the views which he considers favorable to his own
interest; while, on the other hand, the desire of hearing
evidence of a different character leads him to read only
the books and to frequent only the company of persons
where opinions in accordance with his interest are likely
to be expressed."

Again, on p. 26, we read : " Men utterly incapable of
telling a deliberate untruth or deliberately expressing
an insincere opinion, are nevertheless liable to be warped
by personal interest in the deliberate formation of
opinions.   When a strong bias of this sort exists, their
minds, *ready to receive every tittle of evidence on one side
of a question, are utterly impervious to arguments on the
other.*   Hence we see opinions, founded on a belief (*and
often a radically erroneous belief*) *of self-interest, pervade
whole classes of persons.*   Frequently the great majority
of a profession, or trade, or other body, adopt some
opinion in which they have, or think they have, a common
interest, and urge it with *almost unanimous vehemence
against the public advantage.*"

No man possessing a sound judgment can read the
foregoing remarks—be he Liberal, Tory, or anything
else—without feeling that they are true.

The members of the constituencies which return the
Conservative Members of Parliament for the City of
London are really Protectionists in disguise.   As men
of business they have learned by experience that Protection, as opposed to the principles of Free Trade, is
a fallacy; because the fortunes so many of them have
acquired under a system of free-trading are the proof
beyond which no trader desires any clearer demonstra-

tion. But in spite of their having been entirely won over from error to see the truth as regards the protection of trade, they are as much in the dark, or pretend to be, as regards another set of interests. They, in other words, still band together to protect special privileges which they now enjoy in the City of London, as the Protectionists endeavoured to resist the repeal of the Corn Laws. The formation of their opinion regarding the Corn Laws was not due to any consideration of principle, but solely to that of self interest. But they were then defeated, and their own interests were ultimately advanced in spite of their own wilful opposition. The reformation of the Corporation of the City of London is not an analogous case, because the operation of the proposed reform can only be in a limited area, and therefore only affects a limited number of people, whereas Free Trade affects more or less the whole world. The result of the existing management of the revenues of the Corporation of the City of London is, that all but a section of the City of London community are systematically shut out from participating in the benefits which a select few now enjoy through being relatives, friends, or acquaintances of those gentlemen who have managed to place themselves in a position in which they can dispense the hospitality of the Corporation. The system or organisation as it exists has been allowed to grow up, and no doubt in some respects it is worthy of admiration as representing the united efforts of generations of men who, one set after another, have been able to vie with each other in their endeavours to still further expand and embellish the luxuriance of those great gilded shows and civic banquets for which lord mayors and aldermen are famous. But the questions always remain : How has this been done ? who has found the

money ? and whose money was it by which select coteries
of individuals feasted and enjoyed themselves year after
year ?   Does, for instance, the man and the woman who
are units in those two walls of human beings lining the
roadway from Guildhall to Westminster on Lord Mayor's
Day contribute out of their earnings to furnish the
luxuries under which the banqueting table groans in the
evening ?   If so, the satisfaction is hardly enough that
that man and that woman should be allowed to see the
lord mayor's and the alderman's daughters driven along
the road in gilded coaches to partake of those costly
viands and sip those cabinet wines.   These banquets
resemble the bright electric light which shows the
guests the road to the Guildhall ; but there are the dark
shadows, the darker in proportion as the light is bright.
The time has come to see whether or not the money
which has for so long made the light of the banqueting
hall bright and cheerful shall not be diverted with a
view of dispersing those dark shadows.   The age in
which we live is not a feudal age, when the surrounding
splendour of ephemeral potentates is supported at the
expense of the lower orders.   A monarch in our day,
in the most civilised countries, lives in his exalted position on the sufferance of his people for a purpose which
is designedly in the interests of the nation, which brings
with it its cares and its burdens, which are often, indeed,
heavier to endure than those of the meanest of his loyal
subjects.

Outside those interests, which are bound up with the
municipal functions of the members of the Corporation
of the City of London, we come to the ramifications
from each member composing that Corporation.   With
very few exceptions, those members have always held
the same political views, because it was in their interest

to do so. In fact, their entry into that body as a member depended absolutely upon their holding the same political creed as those already composing the Corporation. We may take it for granted that a man openly professing Radical principles would expose himself to the same opposition and the same ill-favour as a Radical curate, if there is such a person, taking holy orders. In other words, the traditions of both fraternities are and always have been bound up with Tory principles. We see occasionally Tory bishops siding with the Liberals in the House of Lords. Is it because they have no further preferment to look for, and they can, therefore, allow free play to convictions which had previously been held in check, and had remained unexpressed through fear of damaging their prospects by incurring the displeasure of their superiors? All the dependents of those seeking admission to a society, like the Corporation of the City of London, would be induced to think like their principal. The members of his family would agree with his political views, and repeat his political maxims; and so his influence radiates. And as one generation follows another, the politics, it may be called, of the Corporation would take deeper root, and spread their branches wider, until an entire district votes practically one colour.

To probe further into the cause of the City of London returning practically all Tories, we find that the Corporation of the City of London is a large Conservative fortress, surrounded and supported by a number of small fortresses, all of which, with perhaps one or two exceptions, are prepared to concentrate their political fire in the same direction. Taken as a whole, the banks in the City, both joint-stock and private, vote for Conservative members. Nearly all the members composing the larger City Livery Companies are Conservatives. The members of the Stock Exchange, as we have said, are at present Conservative, and so are the leading traders and merchants. In other parts of the country there is at least a mixture of creeds; but here, in the City of London, the voters are professedly so much one way of thinking, that the conclusion seems to be irresistible, that the individual voters do not or will not, take the trouble to think for themselves, or to reason out the why or the wherefore ; but that they do, even in our day of enlightenment, what those before them were accustomed to do. " My father," says one, " was a Tory, and of course I am also a Tory," and the creed of the majority seems to be simply that and nothing more ; because the father was a Tory the son is, and there is an end of the matter. Well, and why was the grandfather of this man's father a Tory ? If we look back into history a little we shall see why it was. The common councilmen, sheriffs, aldermen, and some other of the superior officers of the City of London, are elected by the liverymen of London; and down to the passing of the Reform Bill in 1832 they had *the exclusive privilege* of voting at the election of the Members of Parliament for the City. Those who do not know, or who do not remember that they enjoyed that *exclusive privilege*, will understand why the Tories fought so hard to prevent the Reform Bill of 1832 from passing.

The passing of the Reform Bill of 1832 was, the liverymen think, an invasion of their rights ; and the whole generation of them, and probably their sons too, must have passed away before they would allow that they had not an exclusive right to that privilege. In fact, the circumstance that the City of London returns all Conservatives but the member who represents the minority, seems to show that the liverymen are still of opinion that the reforms introduced by the Bill of 1832 were a gross injustice to them, and they do not even forgive the Whigs yet. In other words, the ready-made political opinions continue to be passed on, on the old Tory lines ; and we seem to be justified in asserting that from a political point of view, Tories of the City of London are as far behind the times as regards political enlightenment in 1884 as they were in 1832.

It being the custom in these times for large numbers of voters in the City to live out of London, it is obvious that where they cluster outside the town, there will the political principles of the City prevail to a large extent. In the majority of the districts of London, such as Lambeth, Chelsea, Marylebone, Finsbury, Hackney, and Southwark, Liberal or Radical principles prevail ; but outside the radius of London proper it will be found that the political principles are Conservative ; and this, it will be seen, is due largely to the cause we have mentioned. Berkshire, for instance, returned two Conservatives in 1880, Buckinghamshire two, Chatham one, Essex four, Greenwich two, Hants four, Harwich one, Hastings one, Hertfordshire two, Kent six, Lewes two, City of London three, Maidstone two, Middlesex two, Norfolk four, Shoreham two, Suffolk four, Surrey four, Sussex four, and Westminster two. Here are fifty-four Conservative members all clustering round London. They own land, most of them, of course, and whatever a man's unavowed political tendencies were before he became a landowner— it being the fashion to be a Conservative if you own land—he will probably declare himself for that political creed. A country place is generally too hot for a

Liberal of masculine character if he buys an estate and
settles there. He naturally wishes to be received into
his neighbours' houses, and to receive them in return in
his ; but a Liberal in most rural districts is looked upon
by Conservatives, even in this age of enlightenment, as
a sort of abandoned political heretic, to be avoided by
all respectable people. If he is an educated Liberal
he can, however, generally give a very good account of
himself, and can explain his reasons for being a member
of the larger and more enlightened body, which are as a
rule found very awkward to reply to. The historical
facts in connection with the rise of the Liberal party,
which are at the same time the historical facts in connection with the simultaneous decline of the Tory party,
are not at all palatable to a Conservative who finds
himself inside four walls, where he must stay for a time
and defend himself, if the conversation happens to drift
in the direction of politics ; and his method of defence,
therefore, is generally to stay away and dub the Liberal,
" one of those Radicals who are upsetting the Constitution, and destroying the British Empire." In country
districts, where the " land, the Church, and the hereditary principle " are represented by three corporate
bodies holding the same political views, and standing
shoulder to shoulder, like the swarthy Aborigines do for
mutual protection against the advance of a white
civilised race, a single Liberal invader has anything but
a comfortable time of it. In such a case the progress
made must of necessity be very slow. It *has* been very
slow. The proof of this is that, even at the present day,
forty years after the repeal of the Corn Laws, the City of
London, which has profited so enormously by free trade,
and the abolition by the Liberal party of a vast number
of vexatious imposts which hampered and restricted

trade in all its branches, is as much Conservative as ever. A city which may be said, from a political point of view, to have been the dwelling place of such men as Cobden, Bright, Stuart Mill, Ricardo, and Gladstone, with a small host of minor teachers such as Bagehot, Jevons, Tooke, and Newmarch, &c., still closes its ears to the truth, and sticks obstinately to the old exploded errors, as if the voters in the City proper were deaf, and bereft of understanding. They have seen men like Sir Robert Peel forsake them and their cause, and with a rare courage turn his back upon opinions which he had discovered, too late, to be unsound. They know that Pitt was twice foiled in his attempt to reform Parliament on the lines afterwards adopted by the Liberals; and they even now try to claim him as one of themselves, when they know only too well, as Macaulay has told them, that Pitt was in his heart a Free Trader and a Liberal, and would have been one of the brightest ornaments among the great Parliamentary reformers of this century if he had been free from those engrossing troubles with foreign powers, which allowed him no leisure to devote to domestic politics.

It is idle to look for sound political opinions from the members of corporate bodies, such as we have referred to, until they can cut themselves free from the political traditions which have for so long warped their judgment. Some day, no doubt, the heads of these institutions will be men who can afford to disregard the effect upon their own personal interests, as some of the bishops do, of taking a new departure by assuming an independent attitude. The men who take action of that kind with such surroundings are very rare. They shrink from rendering themselves conspicuous in a branch of thought which is outside the scope of their immediate

9

duties, and so the formation of political opinion is allowed to drift until some great man shall arrive who will have the courage to set an example, by which the corporate body of the University he honours with his presence may be able to distinguish itself by changing a creed overgrown and decaying with error and fallacy, for one that knows only the never ending spring time of justice and truth.

That the political principles of the seats of learning known as Universities should be Conservative, is intelligible enough to those who know the origin of these institutions. Universities are believed to have originated about the twelfth or thirteenth century, and to have been either offshoots of, or to have grown out of, the cathedrals or monasteries. The heads of the Church have, during all time, fought against the spread of education, because the enlightenment of the people has, as experience amply shows, so emancipated the ignorant from the tyranny which the priest has always exercised over him as long as he dare, that he very naturally, like his co-Tories the Protectionists, feared his privileges would be invaded by too much of the truth being known. Every freshman who enters a University naturally desires to stand well with his superiors, as they themselves did when they first entered the college. Celebrated Liberal statesmen, who have enjoyed the privileges of a college career, have in nearly if not all cases, developed into Liberals after leaving the University. This shows clearly enough that their first political opinions were formed under circumstances in which the evidence by which their judgment was guided was *ex parte*. At Universities, as in Rectories, and in peers and squires' houses, the journals taken in will of course support Conservative principles. The whole atmosphere is redolent of but the political odour of one party, and the students, as in the case of the banks in the City of London, and the members of other institutions similarly influenced, in consequence come naturally to imbibe Tory ideas and views, and, influenced by the traditions of the place, look in their ignorance upon those outside the colleges who hold opposite opinions to theirs, as "destroyers of the Constitution, of which their college forms an important part." It is thus evident that whether we investigate into the origin of the political views held by landlords or clergymen, peers or bankers, we find that the Tory is actuated by but one motive, and that is the preservation of the ring fence which prevents any laws from being passed which shall interfere with his special privileges. If we are asked " Is this not, after all, but human ?" we must without hesitation reply, Certainly ! But we must add, that if all the Liberal as well as the Tory members of humanity had continued up to this period of time to act upon those selfish lines, we should in this country be no further forward on the path of civilisation than the Boers in South Africa, whose idea of meting out justice in politics to all the members of the community is not through the instrumentality of bills passed by a Parliament which as nearly as it can be made is a reflex of the will of the people, but by the short and more summary process of shooting those who object.

CHAPTER V.

Miss Toulmin Smith says, " The essential principle of
the guild is the banding together for mutual help,
mutual enjoyment, and mutual encouragement in good
endeavour." We make the following extracts from the
article in the 'Quarterly Review,' No. 317, on the
London Livery Companies :

" To promote each other's advantage in business was
one of the objects of their union."

" Adulteration, bad work, the use of worthless materials, and cheating in every form were discountenanced
and punished ; but, except in this general way, it would
be a mistake to suppose that the public good was the
animating impulse of this system of co-operation."

The guild statutes ordained that " no one was to
work longer than from the beginning of the day until
evening, nor at night by candlelight." Dr. Brentano
remarks on this ordinance : " The real ground doubtless
was rather regard for the well-being of the guild
masters." They did all they could, in other words, to
keep up prices in their own interests. It is amusing to
note how the writer in the 'Quarterly Review,' on the
London Livery Companies, apparently without meaning
to, discloses the devices of these corporations for
hedging themselves in in the true old Tory fashion.
Their method of procedure was first to band together
and form themselves into a powerful trades union, and
then to consolidate their position by obtaining a charter

from the State. In other words, their object was to secure a legal monopoly. This was not possible until they accumulated sufficient funds to be in a position to tempt the needy Plantagenet kings into granting them those privileges in return for a sum of money. Most of these charters were obtained in Edward III's reign, and by them the Companies acquired large powers; they established trade rules by which they could prevent anyone from practising a craft unless he joined its guild, and these powers were subject to confirmation by the City Corporation. The importance of their monopolies being secured by law was that they could take offenders before the Mayor and Aldermen, and that they could invest their property in land. These Companies were in fact established ostensibly with a view to the public benefit, but in reality only for the benefit of those immediately concerned. It is the same old story as the baronial rights conferred by the feudal conquerors. The 'Quarterly' Reviewer, to whom we have referred, says, " We are far from saying that the Crown in granting these important privileges to the City Companies was conscious or unmindful of the advantages which the State derived from having the trade of the Capital supervised without trouble or expense to itself; *yet that was not the main object in view.* The charters were granted to the Companies for valuable consideration, not only in money, but also in the shape of well-grounded confidence that, so long as the King befriended the City, the City would always be ready to help the King with men and means in the hour of need. The charters were intended therefore by the King, and they were received by the Companies, as benefits and gifts to be used for the advantage of the recipients." It is only fair, however, to state that these Companies exposed and punished fraud, and thus did much to prevent articles, which were not of the quality they appeared to be, from being sold to the public. What would the adulterating wine merchants of the present day say to having to stand in the pillóry, and " drink a draught of their own stuff, while the remainder was poured over their heads?" While the Companies, who derived great benefits from their charters, exercised such a salutary influence as that, there would naturally be less objection to their continuing to enjoy the privileges upon which they have so long fattened; but wealth seems as usual to have brought with it demoralisation, and is the Government of our day not right in saying, "You have long neglected to act up to your original motto of *do ut des ;* now your privileges must be withdrawn?" There can be no objection in principle to privileges being granted by Government to corporations of a similar character, provided it can be proved that the community does not suffer by their abuse. But everyone knows that the community nearly always does suffer, or the members of these guilds would not need to stand so firmly on the defensive. Nearly all the members of the City of London Livery Companies are Conservatives for the same reasons as the old Tories stuck together to try and conserve privileges exclusively for themselves, which have had to be wrung from them at the point of threatened revolution. About the middle of the fourteenth century these craft-guilds reached their full development, owing to a twofold change that then occurred. Labour commenced its competition with capital by the villeins flocking from the country into the towns for the sake of the higher wages there paid. The 'Quarterly' Reviewer tells us that the Companies " allowed jealousy rather than prudence to guide their policy,"

just as the old burghers had done long before, and with
the same result. " They placed all sorts of impediments
in the way of the workmen who wished to join the craft-
guilds, and they succeeded in excluding them. But their
success undermined the inherent authority of the guilds
themselves, which henceforth ceased really to represent
the crafts." The Tory reviewer opens his article in the
' Quarterly' by calling attention to the fact of the proposed Royal Commission for investigation and inquiry
being composed of nine members of the " dominant
political party" out of twelve. No one surely can make
himself believe that if the Conservatives had had to form
such a Commission that they would have constituted it
entirely of Liberals, or that the results of the investigation could be expected to be thorough and searching if
the Conservative element had preponderated in the Commission. Nor does it further the reviewer's cause to
say that two of the members, if such was really the case,
were avowed enemies of the Companies. The reviewer
has himself furnished us with the material to enable us to
prove that as long ago as the middle of the fourteenth
century these guilds commenced to abuse their privileges, and have done so ever since; and yet he inveighs
against a Liberal Government for proposing to examine
their title to continue to enjoy exclusive privileges, of
which, by implication, the reviewer himself disapproves,
and which have not been interfered with for upwards of
four hundred years. This, to say the least, is not logical.
The article we quote from states that there are altogether
7319 Liverymen, and the total number of individuals
with vested rights in the Companies is put down at
17,300, while a rough estimate of the total value of the
property makes it out to be not less than fifteen millions
sterling. Here then we have, say, at an estimate that

is probably within the mark, 90 per cent. of these 17,300 voters whose political opinions are in fact no opinions at all, but are what may be more appropriately termed a foregone conclusion. We shall of course be met with the retort that the opinions of most Liberals are also a foregone conclusion. Our rejoinder is, that Liberal opinions are the opinions of the vast majority, and that the principles which guide Liberal action have been in all their main features not only approved of by all Liberals, but by most of the intelligent Conservatives; and that they not only approve of them, but for years have worked on the lines marked out by the great Liberal reforms which have been carried since 1832. These 17,300 Liverymen will of course admit that they are Conservatives, first, because they wish to conserve their vested interests in these fifteen millions sterling, which they would stand a good chance of losing if they espoused the Liberal creed for other reasons.

The 'Daily News' in its remarks upon the City Companies Commission gives certain details, which are of course left out in the 'Quarterly Review' article, but which are essential to enable a right judgment to be formed as to the cause of the action taken by the Liberal Government. We there read that of the £750,000 or £800,000 a year, " a considerably larger capital and income than is possessed by Oxford and Cambridge put together," £400,000 may be said to be spent on entertainments, "as it is all spent in or upon the halls where the entertainments take place." The impartiality with which their hospitality is dispensed is shown in the fact that "the Courts meet at the halls and decide what Conservative statesmen are to be asked to dinner." The question of technical education was raised on one occasion, when the Livery are related to have exclaimed as one man, " We don't want technical education, we want more wine. We don't want technical education, we want a song." The quotations which Mr. Hare makes from the wills of the benefactors show that " they never intended to leave the present diners anything whatever." " They desired to relieve poverty and support education." The course proposed to be pursued, and against which the Conservatives so stoutly protest, has many precedents. " In Paris, Belgium, the Netherlands, and Portugal the guilds have been suppressed, and their property has been applied to the relief of poverty; while in Germany, Austria, Italy, and Spain the guilds have been reorganised by the Legislatures." In fact, Switzerland and England are the only countries in which the necessary reform remains to be carried out. The 'Daily News' concluded its article upon this subject by giving the following particulars, of which we find no trace in the 'Quarterly Review' article, and without which it is quite impossible to form a right judgment as to whether or not the Liberal Government were justified in appointing the Commission which will no doubt result sooner or later in the proposed reform being carried out:—

" The tables are of three kinds—(1), tables showing the growth of the so-called private income of the Companies during the ten years over which the inquiry has extended; the rateable value of the halls, almshouses, schools, and other buildings in the possession of the Companies; the value of their plate, pictures, wine, and furniture, and that of their livings; (2), tables showing the application of their trust income, and the extent to which the objects are promoted out of the so-called private income; (3), tables showing precisely how the so-called private income has been spent for the ten years, the amount eaten and drunk, or disposed of in 'Court Fees,' salaries, and the embellishment of the halls which the municipal reformers have, with their natural profanity, termed 'shrines of gluttony.' 4. Tables showing exactly what the present 20,000 members of these fossil institutions pay annually in the way of entrance money and fees for their privileges, and the precise amount of public money which they spend upon themselves in feasting, 'Court Fees,' and the relief of poor members. These figures appear likely to rivet the attention of the workmen to whom Mr. James Beal lectures at the Eleusis Club and other centres of political education. Mr. Alderman Cotton speaks in his 'protest' of 'thrift.' The Saddlers' Company, to which he belongs, spent in 1879 upwards of £3000 out of an income of £11,000 in 'Court Fees,' which means that the 'Court' which is or calls itself the 'governing body,' declared in that year a dividend of about 27 per cent. The Mercers' Company, of which the Lord Chancellor is a hereditary member, and which consists of an interesting group of scions of about eight or nine families, distribute among its Court, or rather its Court distribute among itself, stipends of about £300 a year. This is the body with which he says that the State has no right to interfere. The Commissioners find that the amount paid annually by members of the Mercers' Company to the common purse, the sum which nowadays represents the 'pence' paid to the 'ale' and the pilgrimages in the Middle Ages, is £40, and that the members actually receive in 'Court Fees,' dinners, and relief in poverty or old age, £19,000 a year. The Grocers contribute £150 annually, and spend on themselves £9,025. The Drapers contribute £270 annually, and spend on themselves £14,000. The Goldsmiths contribute £550 annually, and spend on themselves £15,700. The Salters contribute £200 annually, and spend on themselves £8000. Altogether, whereas in the reign of Edward VI all the funds which the Companies had inherited were devoted to public purposes as opposed to dining, at the present day the actual and constructive expenses of their entertainments involve probably an expenditure of £200,000, taken from funds which belong to the poor of London.

"However, University College and King's College have become a prey to the 'research of endowment;' Lord Reay's scheme .for an Educational University of London is well supported; technical education is a prosperous cause, thanks to the 'deathbed repentance' of the Companies; and finally Lord Derby and his colleagues have drafted a Bill for Sir William Harcourt. which will, it is hoped, become law this session."

The immediate question in dispute between the two political parties is, does the corporate property of these Companies belong to the public, or do the individuals composing them possess an indefeasible right to it? It will be interesting to clear this point up if possible, because if it can be shown to be public property, by proving that it is and that the individuals must relax their hold, we should *pro tanto* prepare the ground for converting to Liberal principles 90 per cent. of these 17,300 Liverymen.

The first question is, have these corporate properties ever existed in the form of a constitution founded on distinct shares transferable with a legal title and which the individuals composing the Companies could dispose of, like the holder of shares in a modern joint-stock company in the market? The answer is No! they have always been trust properties. (2) Do they consist in the aggregate of the distinct and separate accumulations of

individual traders which each possessed the right to
bequeath to whomsoever he chose ?   The answer is No !
They acquired their wealth to a great extent through
advantages derived at the expense of the community.
The ' Quarterly. Review ' article tells us that they kept
up prices in their own interests ; that they acquired a
legal monopoly ; that they established rules for preventing others practising a craft unless they joined the
guild, and that subsequently, when it suited their purpose, the same order of craftsmen were excluded ; that
they invested the funds, thus acquired at the expense of
the community, and under cover of the protection of
needy Plantaganet kings, in land, which has many times
doubled in value.

If Henry VIII seized and perpetually vested in the
Crown the property and revenues of these guilds, the
proposal to apply the large amount of funds that has
been accumulated, for the benefit of the community
upon a more extended scale than was the original
intention of the founders of the societies would seem to
be justifiable.   What a King in the old Tory days did,
no doubt in the interests of those for whose benefits
special privileges had been granted, to enable the guilds
to amass their wealth, a Liberal Government could do
on the plea of more widely extending the charitable
relief which from the first it was the intention should be
dispensed upon eleemosynary principles.

The foregoing extracts from the history of these
guilds furnishes us with further evidence of the way in
which political opinion has been formed in the past.
Here we find small political fortresses manned by
Conservatives for centuries, wholly inaccessible to the
influence of Liberal opinion.   No one with even the
faintest trace of a reforming spirit about him would

have been allowed within gunshot of the place. There was one password, and one only, " Tory." If the new-comer was not furnished with that and prepared to swear that he would act up to and support the Tory traditions of the sect through thick and thin, he could not only not be admitted as a member of the brother-hood, but he would be hunted from the little territory upon which they maintained their feudal tyranny. Again, however, the hour has struck; and another triumph is about to be added to the long list of Liberal reforms.

CHAPTER VI.

IT is not often that the last paragraph of a great book
enunciates one of the wisest maxims of its author; but
this is the case with John Stuart Mill's ' Principles of
Political Economy.' On the last page of the second
volume we read, " Even in the best state which society
has yet reached, it is lamentable to think how great a
proportion of all the efforts and talents in the world are
employed in merely neutralizing one another. It is the
proper end of government to reduce this wretched
waste to the smallest possible amount, by taking such
measures as shall cause the energies now spent by
mankind in injuring one another, or in protecting them·
selves against injury, to be turned to the legitimate
employment of the human faculties, that of compelling
the powers of nature to be more and more subservient to
physical and moral good."

The student of the history of the political wars which
have been waged between the rival parties who have
contended for ascendancy in the management of the
affairs of the State during the last hundred years, must
be struck, on reading the above quotation, with its
applicability to the contests between Tories and Whigs,
and between Conservatives and Liberals. Much as
there is to be said against the opposition of the Tories

as a body to reform in almost any shape since the government of the country divided itself into the Executive Government and the Opposition, all impartial critics must allow that that opposition has been greatly intensified and embittered by the action of the Liberals when out of office.   In fact one of the great blots upon our system of government is the sustained obstruction practised by those out of office against legislative or other measures proposed by those in office.   However much we may agree with the principles of the one party and differ with those of the other, we are bound in fairness to admit that the opposition and obstruction, of which Mr. Gladstone has often so loudly complained, is largely due to the course he has thought proper to pursue himself when out of office.   The relentless animosity which characterised the attitude of both Mr. Gladstone and Mr. Disraeli towards each other, practically throughout their career, and which waxed fiercer as the latter rose higher in the political scale, is a spectacle not calculated to set a good example to men in humbler walks of life.   The degree of heat which had been generated by years of rancorous contests in which, as leaders of their respective parties, they engaged, showed evidently no signs of abatement when the elder statesman, after having passed his threescore years and ten, could sit down deliberately and compose such a bitter *coup de bec* as that which described Mr. Gladstone's volubility of speech-making as due to his being "inebriated by the exuberance of his own verbosity, &c."   No one can pretend to say that the formation of political opinion, by people, either inside or outside the House of Commons, was aided by the utterances of rival statesmen whose main object seemed, as a rule, to be to discredit and overthrow each other at

whatever cost. In this case instead, as Mr. Mill says,
" of compelling the powers of nature to be more and
more subservient to physical and moral good," we seem
to be well inside the truth when we say that " physical
and moral good" were on nearly all occasions made subservient to the desire to show each other's actions and
motives up in the worst light possible. To what an
extent not only these two eminent statesmen, but many
others previous to their time who were rivals, have
neutralized the efforts of each other it is impossible to
say, but one thing is certain, and that is, that a vast
amount of time has been wasted and much good that
might have been accomplished has had to wait while the
two combatants stepped into the arena to settle their
personal differences.

As far as the existing constitution is concerned, the
question which at present presses for a solution is, how
long is the political business of the nation to continue to
be obstructed by the defects which for years past have
hindered and encumbered the working of the machinery
of the Legislature ? Two forces stand opposed to each
other, the one, the House of Lords, constituted of
elements which in some respects carry within them the
seeds of certain and rapidly progressing decay, no
efforts being made by themselves to arrest it ; while the
other, the Members of the House of Commons, continue to do their best to include among their number
representatives of all classes of the people, and to alter
as necessity dictates their system of procedure with a
view to obtaining the maximum results, throwing at the
same time an amount of energy and zeal into the work
which makes the self-imposed burden sustained by all
other political senates, both ancient and modern, to pale
by comparison.

The kind of rabid statement which comes from writers and supporters of the Tory party may be seen for instance in the October number of the 'Quarterly Review,' for 1884, where we read, "A strong Second Chamber is the dread and abhorrence of the demagogue, who trades on popular ignorance and passion, on party organisation manipulated for the ends of faction."

Nothing could be more the reverse of the truth than this statement. The "dread" has been all on the other side, ever since the House of Commons became the real ruling power in the country. The readers of the following pages, if they did not know it before, will see how the House of Lords gave way time after time, in respect of proposed reforms, through "dread" of having what remained of their privileges taken from them if they persisted in opposing the will of the nation. As to "abhorrence," the word is altogether out of place. The country, on the contrary, has been proud of the Upper Chamber on account of its containing so many honoured names of its most distinguished citizens who had been elevated to the Peerage for more substantial merits than simply because their fathers had been Peers before them. Then as to the demagogue trading on "popular ignorance and passion" we have always understood that the Tories and the stock from which they spring, especially the clergy, have done all in their power, more it is true in other countries than in this, to keep the people ignorant, since clerical influence and opulence depended so much upon the classes beneath them not being allowed to understand how they were being kept out of the privileges they ought to enjoy. This is no mere matter of opinion; the pages of history bristle with facts in support of it. Then, which of the two parties has done the most to educate the "demagogues" with a

10

view of enabling them to join the ranks of the Liberals, to aid in furthering their own interests by legislation such as the repeal of the Corn Laws, the Reform of Parliamentary representation and a hundred other measures? As far as the "trading" goes, both figurative and literal, the upper classes have fattened all through this century at the expense of the classes below them. They are beginning now to find it out. The middle and lower classes are now having their innings. The telegraph now tells the consumer the real price of the prime articles of necessity. The merchant can no longer "make" the price of colonial produce to suit his own purpose, and the vast army of middlemen has been reduced to a skeleton battalion. No, the Tories make a great mistake if they fancy the people dread the House of Lords. People generally dread what they cannot control and feel is too strong for them. In fact the refutation of this statement is to be found in the pages of the very number from which our extract is taken. On p. 591 we read, "Already our Second Chamber is one of the weakest known to history, weaker than any but those recent imitations which some foreign states have attempted to construct upon the same lines without the strength derived from tradition, wealth, hereditary rank, and social influence. It is incomparably weaker than the American or Roman Senate, weaker even than the present Senate of France or the Council of Victoria." Well, if that description of themselves by themselves is accurate there is not much to "dread." What *they* have chiefly to dread is destruction at their own hands. The one condition of their existence as a branch of the Legislature is their recognition of the will of the people as being supreme.

There is no doubt that at the time at which we write

the long struggle between the House of Lords and the House of Commons is arriving at a point at which either the Upper Chamber must join the cabinet of curiosities towards which the Sovereign may be said already to have crossed the threshold, or so reform itself as to become not an obstruction to legislation, but an aid. There are, as most people admit, elements in the Upper House, like those which once constituted an active part of the Sovereign's duties, which are not exercised for the benefit of the community and which must, like those obsolete sovereign functions, be incorporated into the figure-head of the State. Every serious struggle between the two Houses has left the one weaker and the other stronger. Hitherto it has been but the bumping of the earthen pipkin against the iron one in their passage down the stream of time; but the violence of the collision evidently increases, and the question is how long the weaker vessel can resist the blows, which can have but one end if continued. As regards the effects of these contests upon the formation of public opinion, it is patent to everyone who studies political affairs that the maturity of sound opinion upon all subjects has been materially retarded by the animus which is a motive largely actuating both sides in the prosecution of their contests. The primary desire is to get into office—to enjoy power, with its attendant prestige and benefits. Human nature being what it is, no opportunity is lost of the " Outs " discrediting the measures brought forward by the " Ins." However good a Bill may be in itself, and however loud may be the call of the people for its being passed into law, it always has to run the gauntlet of the rival jealousies of the two parties. This, on the surface, may seem to be a very good thing, and in one sense it is; but could not more than the ultimate results

achieved be secured if a body of legislators were so
constituted as to ensure the elimination of those elements which give rise to such continuous personal conflicts and to such bitter party hatred which at times,
and in no time worse than our own, brings the whole
system of government into that sort of contempt which
is now and again felt for the deliberations of a local
vestry ?   How are people outside the walls of Parliament
to form their opinions of particular measures brought
forward, if the men in Parliament do their utmost in
many cases to misrepresent the intentions of the framers
of the Bill, with the object of discrediting the party in
power and getting them turned out ?   This is literally
the chief business which the party out of power devotes
its energies to.   We do not require to fortify the position here taken up by citing instances, because it is well
known that, if it were not for the two middle strata of
politicians, the moderate men of both parties, which may
be said to constitute the warm lining of both houses,
there would be a continuous deadlock.   It is, in fact,
this element of sober and undemonstrative sound and
deliberate judgment that " licks into shape " the proposed measures of even the greatest masters.   No one
man's judgment can be as good as the judgment of all
other men.   What we want to arrive at, therefore, is a
constitution of the legislative machine that shall get rid
of the defects which for so long have obstructed the
business of Parliament.   In other words we require to
increase the number and power of the "warm lining" of
Parliament, the men who like General Moltke, are
satisfied to do a minimum of talking and a maximum
made up of thinking and action.   The brilliant demonstrative Members are all very well when restrained
within proper bounds ; but when they are to follow each

other day after day with three or four columns apiece, of much the same arguments differently attired, we feel very much inclined to echo the wise remarks of the men of business who in their criticisms of the commercial columns of our journals say, " Gentlemen, as many facts as you like and as little fancy."

In the Parliamentary utterances there is a great deal too much fancy, and particularly of fancy having reference to persons. It is no doubt highly gratifying for the House of Commons to witness Mr. Gladstone in a white heat " smashing and pulverising " the arguments of Lord Randolph Churchill, or Mr. Chamberlain raising a Liberal laugh at the same gentleman's expense, over the Birmingham riots in October, 1884; but the nation says, "This is not business, gentlemen." You do not draw your thousands a year to keep back the business of the nation, waste its time, and the money which the people subscribe to defray the expenses of keeping the Parliamentary machinery going, for the purpose of meeting to amuse yourselves by bitter personal conflicts. The sober strata in the House should assert themselves, and establish a Speaker's bell to ring down all such exhibitions as these. Immediately any anger is developed, authority should step in and quell the disturbance, no matter by whom raised.

CHAPTER VII.

THE FORMATION OF POLITICAL OPINION IN TIMES OF
DEPRESSION OF TRADE.

MANY instances could be cited of the way in which
Governments have from time to time been accused of
directly causing depression in trade, when neither the
general policy they had been adopting nor particular acts
had anything whatever to do with it. The influence of
authority in such matters, it is well known, is at all
times considerable. If a Member of Parliament can be
referred to as having given this or that opinion, ordinary persons, with less means of acquiring correct
information, are naturally satisfied to rest their case
upon evidence furnished from such a source without
questioning it. And yet this is one of the fertile sources
from which so much error is imported into political
opinion. If business in any department becomes depressed there are never wanting persons who upon the
slenderest unconfirmed evidence, will accuse the Government for the time being of having been the cause of
the mischief. In this way it is evident that a Government lasting out the full term of seven years must
depend to a large extent upon luck for gaining or losing
supporters. If trade happens to be depressed they will
lose credit and *vice versâ*. People are to be met with,
in one's walks abroad, by the score, who declaim against
the Government or approve of their general policy very
much in accordance with the state of the particular

industry or trade from which they draw their revenue. This may to some extent be excusable in the case of irresponsible persons, but cannot on any showing be allowed to be a venial offence when committed by an individual who is a Member of the House of Commons. Mere empty declamation unsupported by any attempt to give carefully tested chapter and verse for the statements is of course accepted for what it is worth, which is nothing at all; but we propose to deal with a case for the purpose of illustrating our argument, which is founded on facts, to which all who are interested can turn and verify for themselves.

On the 31st October, 1884, in the House of Commons, the adjourned debate on the Address was resumed by Mr. MacIver, in whose name the following amendment stood on the paper:—"'But humbly to direct Her Majesty's attention to the depressed condition of commerce and agriculture, and regret that Her Majesty's gracious Speech contains no reference to a subject of such paramount importance.' He said that he did not wish by this amendment to anticipate the bringing forward of the question of a general inquiry into the condition of this country in due time by those who had more right to speak on the subject than he had himself. It seemed to him, however, that, representing as he did a large and important trading constituency, he had some right to be heard upon such a question as this (hear, hear), and since no one else had stood forward to undertake it, he felt it his duty under the circumstances to do so. In his opinion the consideration of this question was of greater importance than that of a Franchise Bill, and he regretted that the Government had been so blind to the condition of matters around them in every centre of industry as to suppose that they could satisfy

starving men with a Franchise Bill. He wished to
approach the consideration of this question from a non-
political point of view, as he thought they were too
apt to treat in a party spirit even important problems
such as this. He wished to say that he had the
greatest sympathy with the question which had been
addressed to the First Lord of the Treasury by the Hon.
Member for Sunderland with reference to shipbuilding in
the Royal Navy, and knowing as he did the present
condition of our navy, and that ships could be now
cheaply and advantageously built at those ports where
there was so much distress, he thought that the Hon.
Member had been justified in asking that the Government should take some such steps. The position was
now far too grave to be treated as a party question.
Manufacturers and those engaged in agriculture were
bound up in each other, and neither could prosper without the other, a truth that was too often forgotten. He
had no sympathy with those politicians whose political
existence depended upon setting class against class,
the manufacturing artisans against the agricultural
labourers, and who saw in a state of affairs such as this
a field for sowing dissensions. Then, speaking in
another place, Lord Kimberley had argued that there
was distress all over the world, and that the condition
of other countries was worse than our own. That was
partly true; no doubt trade was not good in the United
States or on the Continent; but it was impossible for
any member of the Government or the House of Commons to make any accurate comparison as to the state
of trade here and elsewhere. Those who were opposed
to him pointed triumphantly to the statistics of the
Board of Trade; but for his own part he was inclined
rather to doubt the Board of Trade statistics; he

had less faith in statistics and in newspaper information than was the case with many Hon. Members opposite."

Mr. MacIver doubted the Board of Trade statistics
and also what he read in the newspapers, possibly, we
may add, because he could gain nothing from either
source which favoured his theory. As an instance of
the way this gentleman got up his case, and also of the
way opinions were given in consequence, upon the basis
of which numbers of others believing in him went about
abusing the Liberal Government as an incompetent and
blundering one, we will take his statement regarding
French shipping passing through the Suez Canal. He
said it had doubled while British shipping had only
increased 7 per cent. What was Mr. Mundella's reply
to this? He is reported as follows :—" Then the Hon.
Gentleman had said that the amount of French shipping
passing through the Suez Canal had nearly doubled,
whereas the amount of English shipping had only increased by about 7 per cent. But in considering that it
must be remembered that the increase in French shipping was mainly due to purchases made in this market
(hear, hear), and that the increase of 7 per cent. in
English shipping was a vastly different thing, and
represented a much larger increase than was represented
by the doubling of the French shipping, for at least 80
per cent. of the shipping passing through the Canal was
British. From a statement of the shipping which he
had in his hand it appeared that the total tonnage of
British ships clearing in cargo or ballast in British ports
in the years 1878-79 and 1882-83, that was to say, the
two last years of the late Government and the two
first years of the present Government, was in 1878,
35,291,000 tons, and in 1879 37,434,000 tons, and in

1882 43,607,000 tons, and in 1883 47,039,000 tons. (Hear, hear.) The foreign shipping, on the other hand, was in 1878 only 16,304,000 tons, and in 1883 18,000,000 tons, so that there had been a much smaller proportionate increase in foreign shipping."

That statement regarding French shipping had, there can be little doubt, furnished numbers of people with an argument, used by them on the authority of a Member of Paliament, against the Liberal Government. Their opinions had been influenced by what he had told them he was going to use in Parliament in support of his motion on the depression of trade, and yet those who will take the trouble to investigate the other side of the case will find that Mr. MacIver had shut his eyes to facts which when brought forward cut the ground entirely from under him. This is one of the innumerable instances of how political opinion is formed on false evidence—and the mischief that is done does not stop there. Numbers of people will not take the trouble to read what Mr. Mundella said in reply at all. They will take Mr. MacIver's statement as accurate, because it suits their political proclivities, just as he took the doubling of the French shipping as compared with the increase of 7 per cent. in the British without thinking of the relative proportions to which those increases referred, and without either caring to find out whether or not the increase in the number of French ships was due to an increase in the quantity of British goods to be carried by them.

Mr. MacIver did not wish to say anything personal against the President of the Board of Trade, but he thought the department over which he presided " was useless and mischievous," which could hardly be considered a compliment, although it measured with tolerable

accuracy the value of the speaker's opinions upon things
in general.

Mr. MacIver subsequently stated that "many Free
Traders would agree with him that what was called Free
Trade had disappointed everyone;" but no Free Traders'
names were given, neither was there any evidence as to
everyone having been disappointed.

Then it was attempted to be argued that the depression
of trade here was due to English manufacturers taking
their capital abroad, setting up rival manufacturing
establishments and thus injuring this country. Mr.
MacIver said:—"An idea prevailed very widely that
certain members of Her Majesty's Government were now,
or had been, concerned in manufacturing enterprises in
foreign countries. It was only due to the Right Hon.
Gentleman, the Vice-President of the Council, to give
him an opportunity of explaining to the House whether
there was any foundation for that idea as regarded
himself or the firm which used his name, and which, it
was said, were interested in manufactures at Chemnitz
in Saxony, in opposition to the manufactures of this
country." The sort of basis which this allegation rested
on is shown by Mr. Mundella's reply as follows :

" The Hon. Gentleman mentioned, in addition, that the
Hon. Member for the North-West Riding carried a great
deal of British capital abroad. He thought, on the
contrary, that his Hon. Friend had brought a great deal
of foreign capital to England. As far as he personally
was concerned, he was almost ashamed to make a statement to the House. The facts were these, and he
would show the House what use was made of them
up and down the country. Hon. Members opposite had
denounced him by name, in the most unmeasured terms,
as an employer who carried his machinery and capital

abroad. Indeed, he believed it had been alleged that his object in advocating the Factory Acts was to limit the hours of labour at home, so that advantage might be taken of the long hours of labour abroad. This was the revival of an old story, circulated at the time of his original election for Sheffield, nearly a quarter of a century ago. In 1853 he was a partner in an old-established concern in the town of Nottingham. Having thrown all his energies into the business his health broke down, and he was ordered to go abroad. During his absence the concern was converted into a joint-stock company, and when he came back he took his share in the undertaking, and continued his active connection with it till a short time after he became a Member of the House of Commons. It happened that in 1860, or 1861, when the American war broke out, there was an old-established business in Nottingham, which had a branch in Germany, where the old handlooms were very widely utilized for German and American business. But the German and American business came to a standstill, and his firm bought the whole of the plant and machinery of the concern. He went over to see the business in Germany, and he thought it would be a very good thing to continue it, because it gave an opportunity of insight into the whole system of German manufactures and education. He wished more manufacturers would make themselves acquainted with the method of their foreign rivals. (Hear.) He had already told the House that his active connection with the business ceased soon after he became a Member of Parliament. He had since been a small shareholder, but his *maximum* interest in this foreign enterprise never at any time reached the sum of £3,000. As he did not know to what extent the large business at Nottingham had gone on increasing its capital

and machinery he sent a telegram to-day for information
on that point, and he had just received a reply that the
capital applied to English work had trebled, and that
the buildings and plant had increased nearly fourfold.
He had now shown how far he was a manufacturer
abroad, and how far he had injured English workmen
by his connection with foreign affairs. But why was it
wrong to import anything from abroad ? " (Hear.)

Mr. MacIver was followed in the debate by Mr.
Ekroyd, who supported the motion, and among other
things referred to the depression in agriculture as
follows :

" In fact, agricultural depression was making itself
felt by the occupier of land as severely as at any time
during the last seven or eight years. Reduction of
rents was no remedy for the existing state of things.
It was a partial remedy locally, but viewed from a
national standpoint it was no remedy whatever, for the
reduction was equivalent to a loss of circulating wealth.
This matter could not, in a national sense, be met by a
reduction of rents. A reduction of rents or of the
letting value of the lands and buildings in any country
had always been regarded as an indication of decay."
(Hear hear.)

We are informed that a reduction of rents is no
remedy whatever as the reduction was equivalent to a
loss of circulating wealth. The insinuation here again
is that the suffering of those engaged in agriculture was
due to the Liberal Government, both the Members
referred to being Conservatives. It was a curious circumstance that the introduction of the Franchise Bill
was deprecated by the Member for Birkenhead while
trade was so depressed. By the passing of the Franchise Bill the position of those coming next to the

landlords in the agricultural districts will to a certainty
be improved.   The two millions of voters who are to be
admitted to their electoral rights by means of that Bill
know why it is that there is so much suffering among
the country-people and labourers.   As more land comes
into cultivation all over the world and the supply of food
increases the value of land that has for many years
been high in price relatively to its productive powers,
it must of necessity come down, just as silver has come
down owing to the production of more than is wanted
for current requirements.   It is a common thing in
passing through country districts to be told that the
only people who are making a living are the parsons and
the auctioneers.   The fact is, the land will have to be
re-valued.   In other words, the price must be lowered
by existing owners being compelled either to lower their
rents or to sell their holdings.   This is the true remedy
for the depression and by which alone the tenants and
their labourers can make a living.   The land in England
is above its value, when estimated by the quantity of
produce it affords as compared with that of the same
description of land in other countries.   To pretend, as
the Fair Traders do, that food shall be taxed in order
to raise the market value of a commodity which is finding its true level on the same principle as everything
else, is like a speculator asking other people to pay losses
which are the result of his own bad judgment.   Every
landowner in England, as elsewhere, is at perfect liberty
to buy or sell land as and when he chooses.   Enormous
tracts of land have of late years been purchased by
English capitalists in the United States, the British
colonies, the River Plate, and in many other parts of
the world, where it is to be had cheap and offers a good
prospect of a high return on the investment in the

future. Owners of land in England who did not realize when they could obtain higher prices than those now ruling, have themselves to blame. They doubtless had their own reasons then for the course they took, and it is the height of absurdity to expect the Legislature to step in and impose taxes which shall be a burden on an innocent community for their personal benefit.

Mr. Ekroyd compared the prices of 1884 with those of 1871, 1872, and 1873, which he said were prosperous, because wheat was then 57s. 5d. a quarter; but his argument was shattered to pieces by Mr. Mundella's reply, that those prices were inflation prices caused by the Franco-German war. This is another and the last example we shall take from that debate on the depression of trade. It shows how little care is taken to look up the facts from which deductions are made. The importance attached to that debate is shown by the amendment being supported by only 67 Members, while 86 were against it, showing a majority of 19.

CHAPTER VIII.

"ONE-MAN POWER."

WE have heard a good deal of late years of what is called "one-man power," a phrase which is intended to mean that the Prime Minister for the time being is virtually a dictator, and can do exactly what he likes. The complaints against this "one-man power" have come chiefly from the Conservatives, one occasion upon which it was made being Lord Salisbury's speech at Dumfries on October 21st, 1884. He then said:

"In this country of Scotland you have had some people who have even improved upon Mr. Chamberlain's lessons. Sir George Campbell, who in his time was charged with the government of 64,000,000 of people, and would have disposed of anybody who had incited to disorder with extreme rapidity (laughter), is reported to have said: 'I entreat you now to be content with lawful proceedings' (hear, hear)—these were his words—'but if the House of Lords does not pass the Franchise Bill, why then we will take stronger measures.' (Laughter.) That is to say stronger measures than lawful proceedings. That is the kind of result which Liberal doctrine, as preached by Mr. Chamberlain, is producing in this country. (Laughter and cheers.) Now, there are other indications of the same tendency— a tendency against which I think all good citizens should watch (cheers); and there are indications which show at once what danger attends this one-man power."

The "one-man power" Lord Salisbury says is the result which Liberal doctrine is producing in this country. Is it any more the result of Liberal doctrine than that which is due to the "one-man power" of Lord Salisbury himself when he incites the House of Lords to obstruct legislation which there is the clearest evidence to show the great majority of the people are anxious for? What about Lord Beaconsfield's "one-man power" in Afghanistan and the Transvaal? Was that the result of the preaching of Liberal doctrine?

But to take a wider view, there must surely be some radical mistake here. Lord Salisbury has put the saddle on the wrong horse. The whole course of Parliamentary Reform, which William Pitt himself endeavoured to initiate, is synonymous with the destruction of the "one-man power," which in the persons of generations of military and civil despots had ridden roughshod over the people for centuries. We need go but a very few years back, comparatively speaking, to find an example, of which history affords hundreds. For instance, Pitt himself was frustrated in his efforts to reform Parliament by George III, who personally opposed the proposals of the Minister for reforming the House. As the Tories were of course opposed, and a large portion of the Whigs were indifferent, the matter was decided virtually by the "one-man power" of the King himself. Again, in 1696 a measure was proposed to establish a qualification in land for Members of Parliament. Both Houses were in favour of it, but the King, who "leant rather to commercial interests, withheld his assent." Again, when William IV dismissed Lord Melbourne's Government there was an arbitrary exercise of "one-

11

man power." There is, however, no more any possibility of such a " one-man power " as that being
exercised, and it is a curious circumstance that a
Tory leader should refer to a kind of government which
is chiefly remarkable for disgracing the annals when Tory
principles prevailed and the country was governed first
by a " one-man power " and then by an oligarchy, both
of which have been swept away for ever.

It is very much the fashion nowadays to look upon the
nation and its affairs as handed over helplessly to the
man who is at the political helm—in other words, to the
Prime Minister. But this allegation will not stand the
test of close inquiry. Not long ago Mr. Gladstone proposed to lend the Suez Canal Company eight millions
sterling, and to make certain concessions which were
considered too liberal. The whole fabric of that scheme
was shattered to pieces in a day. It did not even survive
the evening of the day the details were made known.
What became of the " one-man power " in that case ?
There never has been a more conclusive proof that no
man, be he ever so eminent, and no Ministry, be they
ever so powerful, can do what the nation does not
approve of if they only know the facts. No Ministry, be
they ever so skilled, both individually and collectively,
can at all times exercise such a sound judgment as can be
secured by submitting for the approval of the nation particular proposals of the Government ; and this undoubted
fact emphasises the contention that Parliament should
insist upon reviewing all the acts and promises of the
Cabinet, while foreign Powers should come to understand, once for all, that bargains made with them were
liable to repudiation by the nation if not approved of.
This view is supported by Mr. J. S. Mill :—" It must be
remembered, besides, that even if a Government were

superior in intelligence and knowledge to any single individual in the nation it must be inferior to all the individuals of the nation taken together. It can neither
possess in itself nor enlist in its service more than a
portion of the acquirements and capacities which the
country contains applicable to any given purpose. There
must be many persons equally qualified for the work
with those whom the Government employs, even if it
selects its instruments with no reference to any consideration but their fitness."* The fault, if fault it can
be called, is that they do not always know, and the
reason is that they cannot always know. It is so perfectly well known that the details of delicate international
negotiations cannot be made public at the time the negotiation is being carried on, that to insist upon their
being conducted openly would for most practical purposes put an end to diplomatic intercourse between
nations. Nor is it necessary that such negotiations
should be made public while they are being carried on.
The time has gone by for the Cabinets of a nation
governed as England is, irrevocably to conclude compacts
of a serious nature with foreign Powers without the
authority of Parliament. They ought on all serious
occasions to be absolutely subject to the approval of
Parliament, unless they are of such a nature that the
dozen men forming the Cabinet are so completely unanimous and satisfied in their own minds that what is being
done is the best that could be done for the country, that
they do not hesitate morally to bind the nation by the
promise given. The case of the Suez Canal loan is the
exception that proves the rule. There evidently was
doubt in the minds of Ministers whether the nation
would agree to that proposal, and they did wisely to

* 'Prin. Pol. Econ.,' vol. ii, p. 553, J. S. Mill

have it published at once.   Government is, it is true, the
most important organisation for the management of
public affairs which we have; but there are hundreds of
institutions of various kinds in the country which in a
sense exercise a "one-man power" in the same way *ad
referendum*, and the acts of all managers are supervised
and kept within well-defined lines by boards of directors,
and their acts again by the whole body of shareholders.
A Prime Minister is the manager of the Executive
Government, supervised and controlled by the other
members of the Cabinet, and they again by the people.

CHAPTER IX.

It is no matter for surprise that Tory writers should ransack all that historical record has to tell them of Pitt's opinions, acts, and principles, with the object of endeavouring to establish in their own minds a belief that he was in his heart a Tory. But, although he governed this country for seventeen long years without a break, at a time when Tory principles had not yet been passed through the crucible which was subsequently to purge them of their many fallacies, there is the clearest evidence, to our mind, that William Pitt was a true Liberal at heart; and it is as morally certain as anything can be that had he lived he would, if not avowedly by his vigorous efforts in the interests of Reform and the abolition of abuses, have left no less clear and conclusive evidence of his being a Liberal than that which is so overwhelming in the case of Sir Robert Peel.

Another attempt to prove that William Pitt was a true Tory appeared in the 'National Review' for October, 1884, from the pen of Mr. T. E. Kebbel. We there read "that the navy was the true defence of England, and that in the extension of our colonies and our commerce lay the true interest of England were old Tory doctrines to which Pitt most heartily subscribed." It is something new, at all events, to learn that the maintenance of the navy and the extension of our colonial possessions were more articles of the Tory than the

Liberal creed. Indeed, everybody knows that while the Tories did, in their own exclusive interests, all they could do for years to hamper the trade of this country with her colonies by advocating protective tariffs and imposing harassing duties on imports as well as exports, the Liberals, on the other hand, did all in their power to set the trade of the country free, and thus allow all traders to buy in the cheapest and sell in the dearest market. Does Mr. Kebbel pretend that the Tories as a party have voluntarily furthered Reform either in Parliament or out of it? Does not he blush to think that they have constantly obstructed the path of Parliamentary reform from the moment the first attempt was made to carry a Reform Bill down to the present day? Can he claim that William Pitt was one of those Tory obstructors, when history and well-authenticated fact tell us that on the 7th of May, 1782, he made a motion in Parliament to reform the representation of the people, and so well did he expound his views on that subject, and so persuasive were his arguments, that that motion was only lost by a majority of twenty votes in a House of 300 Members? So staunch a Liberal was Pitt at heart, and so satisfied did he feel after losing his motion by that comparatively small majority that he would succeed if he tried again, that the very next year he renewed the attempt, when he was again defeated by 293 votes to 149. Unhappily for him, and also for the country, the fears inspired by the French Revolution checked the tendency towards Liberal principles, and he was compelled to relinquish efforts which there is little doubt would otherwise have given the country a Reform Bill much earlier than 1832, and would in addition have enrolled Pitt, by the realisation of his own scheme for the reform of the representation of the people, among the avowedly great Liberal statesmen of this century. Pitt further showed what were his true political principles by carrying through a commercial treaty with France in 1786 on Liberal principles; and again he tried to forestall the celebrated Roman Catholic Relief Bill, which Mr. Peel succeeded in passing in 1829, by including in his scheme of Reform—when he effected the union with Ireland in 1799—the relief of the Roman Catholic laity from civil disabilities. The King frustrated his design, and he resigned in disgust. This is the man whom Mr. Kebbel claims as a Tory. A more flimsy pretence it would be difficult to match.

We observe no reference in Mr. Kebbel's article to Pitt having urged upon the King the necessity of a coalition with Lord Grenville and Mr. Fox, with the object of forming a strong Ministry. Thoroughgoing Tories do not as a rule propose to ally themselves with members of the Opposition, one of whom was an extreme Liberal—so extreme, indeed, that George III said he would not admit him to his councils, even at the hazard of a civil war. How little Pitt was a Tory at heart is as clearly proved by this genuinely Liberal proposal of his, that one wonders how he could, with his temperament, have got on with the King and the Court for so long as he did. The explanation, of course, lies in the fact that such power as that enjoyed by a Prime Minister is too much temptation for human nature. Although, however, Pitt swallowed his principles at the start, they peeped out through his actions and utterances, and when he had had his fill of power he virtually declared himself to have been a Liberal from the beginning.

It is instructive, in following the political history of this country at the opening of the present century, to observe the strong undergrowth of Liberal opinion traceable in

the minds of the statesmen in power, notwithstanding the
many impediments to its development which then existed.
What we have already had to say regarding the views
and actions of William Pitt, especially in the latter part
of his career, establish, we should think, to the satisfaction of all reasonable men, that that statesman was in
the bottom of his heart a Liberal, and had been so from
the beginning.   Knowing, as we all do, how weak human
nature is, and how often it has suited others to profess
principles which they did not really believe in, to gain
power and wealth, we can hardly affect to be surprised
that Pitt yielded to a pressure which has made many
other eminent men nominally Tories ; but his career,
nevertheless, affords a valuable study, and supplies ample
material for an essay on the formation of political opinion.
There is no question in our mind that had Pitt started in
his life untrammelled by the political opinions and traditions of those around him he would have begun and
ended his career as an avowedly Liberal politician.

While the King and the Court exercised so much
political power and the people so little, no more than a
stunted growth of Liberal principles could be looked
for.   While the King, likewise, could dismiss his Ministers because they proposed, as they did, concessions to
the Catholics, for instance, it could hardly be expected
that reforms in a Liberal sense could make much
progress.   And yet all the time very solid progress was
being made.   No building can stand for very long that
has not good foundations.   Good and solid foundations
were being laid upon which to build up the Liberal
principles, which to so large an extent preponderate in
our day, while William Pitt was Prime Minister.   The
degree in which all efforts to introduce just and reasonable reforms were frustrated even as long ago as that

period, which is what we may call the dark ages of the formation of political opinion, has shown the public how eager those who ruled over them and their satellites struggled to preserve for themselves the loaves and the fishes. There was no attempt to conceal the objects of the Tory politicians of that day, and the consequence was, that when those professing Liberal principles once gained the upper hand they did not then, and have not since, relaxed their efforts until the series of abuses, which are well known to have been swept away, including the one-man King power, were all finally got rid of. Pitt himself, as we have said, tried to deal with some of them himself, but he was too weak in supporters of the type who could make his efforts successful to . afford any chance of gaining his end in the circumstances in which he lived.

Pitt's Liberal tendencies may be described as a light struggling to illuminate the surrounding darkness of Toryism. Mr. Addington, who was a weak tool employed by the King to frustrate the efforts of reformers, particularly those who advocated the Catholic cause, we cannot say *enjoyed* a brief reign as First Lord of the Treasury after Pitt's seventeen years of power, because he was much too timid and limp in character to derive any pleasure from holding a position which carries with it such a burden of responsibility. The King in fact must have felt like a schoolboy freed from the control of the master, when he changed the autocratic Minister who had compelled him from 1783 to 1801 to play second fiddle in all affairs of State, for the subservient and docile statesman who resigned after a vain struggle with embarrassments with which nature had not fitted him to contend. As far, therefore, as Mr. Addington is concerned we are bound to confess that

during his brief reign the cause of the Liberals made
little or no progress. Mr. Addington's one idea of
political action seemed to be to follow the shadow of
the King, and through thick and thin support the principles of him and his Court. His mind had not been
formed in the large mould which enabled his predecessor
to look beyond the small circle of his immediate surroundings and grasp the principles and truth of a higher
and nobler faith.

In February, 1806, Lord Grenville acceded to power in
the company of Mr. Fox, a Minister for whom the King
felt the strongest aversion. As is usual, however, in
lower grades of society, he liked Fox more as he knew
him better. Pitt was virtually a Liberal convert, as we
have already several times affirmed, and Lord Grenville
was an avowed convert to Liberal principles, although it
must be admitted that he was a convert of less robust
faith than some others, for he deserted Liberal principles
and the Whigs in 1817 ; so that with the brief interval
of Mr. Addington's Premiership, Liberal principles, if
not openly, were secretly being nurtured on the very
steps of the throne and in defiance of the Court and its
supporters, who, prohibited by the law from using
physical force to prevent their privileges from being
encroached upon, were no less impotent intellectually to
withstand their being assailed. Lord Grenville joined
with Pitt in making favorable intimations to the
Catholics, but their efforts to bring about Catholic
emancipation being frustrated they resigned, and Lord
Grenville went over to the Opposition, with which party
he acted till Pitt's death in 1806. In the Cabinet which
followed he filled the office of First Lord of the Treasury for one year and sixty-four days, and on the dissolution of the Ministry he continued his efforts in the

interests of the Catholics, having been a constant advocate for their emancipation. It was evident that a man holding the wider and more Liberal views which alone harmonised with his nature, as they did with Pitt's, could not get on for long in immediate contact with such a narrow and selfish mind as that of George III, whose long reign of sixty years was marked by an amount of royal obstruction to the development of Liberal principles which sadly mars the interest with which the now predominant party in politics review the events of that otherwise momentous period in the history of this country. Lord Grenville, like other Liberal converts, was a man of considerable intellectual attainments. Had it not been for these, he would probably, like Addington, have remained in the ranks of a party which is less renowned for the brilliancy of their intellectual gifts than for the stubbornness with which they have endeavoured to preserve institutions for times for which they were entirely unsuited. He held the office of Chancellor of the University of Oxford, in which he was succeeded at his death, in 1834, by the Duke of Wellington. Lord Grenville's Liberal tendencies were manifested in another direction, which did not increase the favour with which the King regarded him. Like all true Liberal politicians he could not understand the doctrine of the administration of the army being under the exclusive control of the sovereign. In a country like ours, having a representative Parliament and a chosen number of that body constituting a Cabinet to advise the King on all important matters affecting the welfare of the nation, it seems almost incredible in our day that the sovereign should have so far presumed as to take it for granted that the management of the army rested with the King alone; yet such was the case. And when we know it, we cease to wonder that Liberal

Administrations, unsupported by .the power of public
opinion, as it happily makes itself felt in these days,
endured but for a brief period. No Liberal statesman in
fact with any independence of character would submit
to serve under such circumstances. Lord Grenville we
are told was much astonished at such a doctrine, which
he thought quite unconstitutional. The difficulty,
however, was overcome by an arrangement by which
any proposed changes should be submitted for the
approval of the King. The occurrence of these little
differences showed that the Government of the country
continued in reality to be under Tory control although
the Administration was a Liberal one, and it is no wonder
under such circumstances that the Grenville Ministry
only lasted a couple of months beyond the year. Pitt
after a long struggle had succumbed, and Grenville after
a very short one, in both cases for much the same reasons,
which brings us to the Government of the Duke of
Portland, who took office as Prime Minister on March
31st, 1807. In conjunction with Mr. Perceval, he
restored strength to the Tory party by supporting the
King in his resistance to the emancipation of the
Catholics. The Administrations of these two statesmen
were in fact nothing more than Governments carried on
by the King and his friends. Alarm seems to have been
taken by the Tories at the dangerous tendencies in a
Liberal direction manifested under the Pitt and Grenville rule, and now that these statesmen were out of the
way, coercion and repression were to be more than ever
resorted to, with a view to obstruct as much as possible
all Liberal reforms. Mr. Perceval died, and with him
disappeared for the time all hope of Whig ascendancy,
Tory rule having regained that which had been imperilled
by the proposals of Reform to which we have referred.

Although there was now to be a Tory reign for nearly fifteen years under the Premiership of Lord Liverpool, that Administration did not even commence its work without showing the effects upon political opinion of what had been done by the advocates of Catholic emancipation. This circumstance shows, indeed, the value of agitation in a cause by men of position and authority. The fact of Pitt, who was and is claimed by the Tories as one of themselves, whatever impartial and Liberal politicians may think, having advocated a reform which the King and his supporters strenuously fought against, was calculated to impress the public mind much more than if he had been án avowed Liberal. The consequence was, that after the question had been reopened by the Grenville Government it had evidently taken such a hold upon the public mind, that even Lord Liverpool himself, with his prospect of a long lease of power, did not think it wise to pronounce decidedly against the removal of Catholic disabilities. He showed himself, in fact, the sensible statesman which there is no doubt he was, by deciding to leave it an open question.

The fact, however, of the members of his Cabinet being allowed freely to express their individual views on a question which had, comparatively speaking, so recently been considered almost a breach of Court etiquette even to refer to approvingly, showed the tendency of the times. Indeed, whether Lord Liverpool and his friends foresaw it or not, it is certain that the license thus permitted to Ministers on such an important subject led, as might very well be expected, to such differences and divisions that the dissolution of the Tory party was the result. The formation of sound political opinion could not have been more successfully promoted than by countenancing the expression of unreserved individual opinion by Ministers in whatever society they found themselves.

Lord Liverpool retained his hold upon power, but the party of which he was the chief was being gradually undermined. The ancient fabric which Tory government may be said to have resembled was composed of elements which were gradually becoming anachronisms, and was beginning to assume to the mind's eye the hue which characterises the deserted feudal castle. The elements in themselves would continue for the most part to retain some of their old vigour and freshness, but it was in their combined form as the ruling power of the nation that dissolution might be observed. The King was there, and would be succeeded by other kings and queens; the Lords were there, but their power and prestige were at no distant date, as we know too well, to be rudely shaken with the introduction of each successive measure of Parliamentary reform, apart from the self-inflicted damage which a number of minor reforms were the occasion. The House of Commons was there, to a large extent recruited from their own nominees and through their own influence. The Church was theirs, for reasons too well known. The land was theirs, as well as most of the institutions which had their origin in royal foundations like the great colleges. But the time had come when the one-sided political influence exercised by all these combined forces was to be brought to a standstill by an opposing stream of democratic sentiment; and not only to a standstill, but was to give way and be rolled back by a mightier flood than had even up to that period of history borne the fortunes of England to such an unprecedented pitch of prosperity.

Liberal converts were henceforth not to be limited to individual statesmen of eminence. There were to be converts by the score and by the hundred, independently of the new recruits who would approach the consideration of the question of the formation of political opinion with an unbiassed mind and by the help of historical records, which showed the unrepresented classes that their manual labour and skill was being used mainly in the interests and for the benefit of those who ruled them. The clearer the perception of this fact the stronger flowed the flood which was to shake the Tory foundations.

Not only were there Liberal converts among the increasing populations of the large towns, but the position and influence of the old country squires was gradually being also undermined by wealthy capitalists who were in a position to buy up the estates with money gained by the war, by manufactures and by the expanding commerce of the country. At the same time the new generation was less disposed to be trammelled by the narrow political views which their fathers had entertained under different circumstances, and as the growing manufacturing industries formed the centres of new towns and attracted the surplus population of the counties, it is evident that with easier access to information and instruction on the passing political events of the day, a far larger body of recruits would be gathered to the Liberal standard than the Tories could hope to secure. In a word, while the increase in the number of those professing Liberal principles was large and continuous in the towns, the counties were either stationary or retrograde.

The descendants of the old country gentlemen, many of them, have been heard to lament the departure of the good old times, and to curse a fate which has destined younger sons to turn out fortuneless into the world and compete for a livelihood with others no better off than themselves; but every man of sense and reason must be able to understand that the higher civilisation which mankind is obviously destined to reach could never be attained while one section of the community permanently rolled in riches and luxury, while the other as permanently shivered at the great men's gates, or toiled in the fields for a pittance, downtrodden by forced exclusion from the political rights which they have now at last secured. In the first quarter of the present century society may be likened, by a stretch of the imagination, to one of the greatest discoveries of our day, the electric light. The Tory party and their satellites, in their several strata, resembled the bright light, and the struggling Liberals the dark shadow without which the light would lose half its brilliance. But for the downtrodden peasantry and lower orders of that time the splendour of the Court could find nothing to support it; but for the brawny arms of the docile rustic the noble domains of the squirearchy must have tumbled into ruins; but for the indomitable pluck and matchless sinew of our hardy seafaring population the empire that was in great part won, we admit, during the period of " the one-man power,"—in other words a Government of which the King was Prime Minister—could never have been won at all. Is it just and right that electoral rights should be denied to the more enlightened descendants of the one part of the nation, while it is wholly monopolized by the other ? Many Conservatives will no doubt say, "We never contemplated anything of the kind." Those who would thus exclaim, and there are many of them, are in reality Liberal converts. Their minds have been undergoing a process of reformation under the influence of teaching, which has not been voluntarily imparted, by members of their own creed, but which has been administered to them day after day for fifty years, by the organs of the press, by Tories converted into Whig statesmen, by Whig statesmen further converted into Liberal and Radical statesmen, and among others by Liberal preachers who have seceded from the Established Church. The process of reformation by which a large body of moderate men of both parties has been created into national political ballast, has, besides, been urged forward at an ever-accelerating speed, which has at last, at the moment we are writing, nearly crushed the House of Lords itself, by the gradual but sure education of the great bulk of the nation into the belief that Liberal principles have been sound and just principles from the beginning, and that Tory principles are unjust and have been visibly decaying from the birth of the present century up to this very hour.

The momentous change that was taking place in the feelings of the people at the time of Lord Liverpool's advent to power justifies our dwelling upon details which otherwise are not exactly germane to the question of Liberal converts, which is the subject of this chapter. The events of various kinds which had occurred in the domain of politics up to this period of history had had the effect of making the people entertain a higher respect for themselves and less for their rulers. This being the case we are justified in remarking that during Lord Liverpool's Premiership the borderland between the narrowest of Tory rule and the rapidly widening principles of Liberal rule had been crossed, never to be re-crossed. Lord Liverpool's reign was distinguished by many legislative measures of a wise and liberal character, which historians are agreed marked a new departure. In domestic reforms the names of Huskisson and Peel

stand out in prominent relief, while George Canning,
who was destined to succeed Lord Liverpool, was pre-
paring the way for a more liberal system of international
diplomatic intercourse, by which the old filibustering
method of kings and potentates, grabbing whatever they
could lay their hands on, and initiating wars to afford
them the required opportunities, would be followed by a
due recognition of the just rights and claims of other
nations and peoples.   Greater forces than those ope-
rating within the limits of these islands were slowly but
surely exercising an influence over the minds of the
people in a Liberal sense.   They had before them the
spectacle of a great Republic, which had burst the bonds
that tied North America to the mother country, and they
had themselves set out, untrammelled by the effete diplomacy of a monarchy which was itself struggling in vain
to support an oligarchy and maintain privileges for the
few at the expense of the many, upon a political crusade
which was only to experience a check from the opponents
of the movement which would afford them breathing
time while they recovered their strength for renewed
efforts.

The motto of that time, and which was henceforth to
be inscribed over the halls, wherever they might be,
where political meetings were held, was *Non sibi sed
patriæ*.   The ruler, in other words, must spring from
the people, and be justified by his ability and his acts
from the commencement of his career.   No more rulers
by hereditary right.   The system was an exploded one.
It had been proved to be unsound and fruitful of evil
results in a variety of forms, and the nation would have
no more of it.   The Duke of Wellington's Premiership
is in itself a proof of the wisdom of that view, which
. may be said, indeed, to have given the *coup de grace* to

the idea that eminent soldiers must necessarily be eminent politicians. It may be just as well taken for granted that he will be an eminent sailor, and therefore appoint him to command the Channel fleet. That such a man, indeed, should have been allowed to tarnish his magnificent military fame by political blundering of the kind the great Duke perpetrated, is sufficient evidence alone that politics are a business which require a training of half a lifetime before the man is fit to command, and, moreover, his training must be gone through in the open, before the nation's eyes, so that he may be tried and tested at all points, even before he is allowed to have one voice among the ten or a dozen who sit in the Cabinet Council.

The nation, as we have said, had been at this period educated into a higher estimate of themselves, and, as is nearly always the case, they had found out that their rulers, the kings and queens and emperors, were not fit for the work which circumstances had allotted to them to perform. Wherever we look over the face of the earth we see not only the conversion of individuals to Liberal principles progressing, but we see the conversion having arrived at that stage which enables the country to substitute the one form of rule for the other. Russia is heaving like a highly-charged volcano labouring on the eve of a violent eruption. The government of the " one-man power" in force in Germany is tolerated only out of respect to the man who has forged the links which bind as yet only loosely together the new empire. Even now, thirteen years after the Franco-German war, the fabric has not by any means settled down. It vibrates with discontent and irritation from within, and from dread of a combination of foes from without. The " one-man power " there, although justified in that case, it must be allowed, on the ground of commanding ability, if on no other, is as doomed as it is everywhere else, and the nation knows it, and suffers for that reason the system to remain in force, because they know that with him it must and shall end. The chronic rumbling of the Socialist agitation is only the same kind of rebellion in Germany, on a smaller and less dangerous scale, than the Nihilism which threatens any day to fill the streets of the Russian cities with blood. In France the process of conversion is so far complete that, for the time at least, the " one-man power " is dead. The account with the emperors was ruled off at Sedan, and a pretty account it was.

The period embraced by Lord Liverpool's Premiership is that in the political history of this country during which the last great effort of the Tory party was made to obtain ascendancy over the rising power of Liberal principles. . The complete and permanent change of colour then took place which is synonymous with the substitution of the designation of Conservative for Tory. It was, in fact, more than a tacit admission that the party had undergone conversion under the pressure of influences it was useless to attempt further to oppose. Although Lord Liverpool was himself ·to preside over the Government which was in office during that period of the conversion of the party from their extreme Tory views, and was consequently the whole of the time an avowed Tory, he, like many other Tories, showed by his acts and views, although in a less pronounced form than Sir Robert Peel or the present Lord Derby, that the truth had taken a permanent root in his mind, and that in reality he was a Liberal convert. That this view is supported by facts we shall now proceed briefly to show, the reforms to which we shall refer being evidence like-

wise in a general way of the continued conversion of
the Conservatives to principles more or less Liberal.
This changed attitude of the Conservative party in fact
marked the boundary of a new departure in the annals
of legislation.

In the concluding chapter of Sir Erskine May's ' Constitutional History of England '* we read, "Responsibility
and *popular control* gradually forced upon them larger
views of the public interests, and more consideration
for the claims of all classes to participate in the benefits
of enlightened government. With freedom there grew
a stronger sense of duty in rulers—more enlightenment
and humanity among the people; wiser laws, and a
milder policy. The asperities of power were tempered,
and the State was governed in the spirit which society
approved." The good old times to which the Tory
descendants are so fond of referring were a period in
our political history when the revenues of the nation
were freely used by the governing aristocratic families
to patch up the broken fortunes of their own relations
and supporters. " No example more aptly illustrates
the altered relations of rulers to the people than the
revision of official emoluments. Ministers once grew
rich upon the gains of office, and provided for their
relatives by monstrous sinecures and appointments
egregiously overpaid. To grasp a great estate out of
the public service was too often their first thought.
Families were founded, titles endowed, and broken
fortunes repaired at the public expense. It was asked
what an office was worth, not what services were to be
rendered." A good deal of the system of abuses which
had thus grown up was demolished by Joseph Hume,
who had to fight his way to the attainment of his object

* Chap. xviii, p. 385, vol. iii.

amidst every possible obstruction and against even
a sustained fire of ridicule. No wonder the admirers
and supporters of the sovereign employed their ingenuity
in the composition of a national hymn containing such
lines as

> "Confound their politics,
> Frustrate their knavish tricks."

To continue in our times to sing such ridiculous words
is to heap ridicule upon the authors of them and the
order in whose interests they were written, because
events have proved that if the politics of either party
has been confounded, in the sense of subverted, it is
certainly those of the Conservatives.

The conversion of Tories to Liberal principles and
the enlistment into the Liberal political ranks of people
of previously no political colour, has been largely due to
such men as Joseph Hume. He consistently worked
for the purification of a stream which had for very long
been polluted by almost every form of irregularity in
the keeping and auditing of the public accounts and in
the dispensing of the public revenue. The financial
abuses which he laid bare must have seriously impressed
many minds at the time, which had no other means of
expression than is conveyed through the vote at the
polling booth, and there is no doubt that Hume is one of
the many Liberal politicians whose preaching in the
House of Commons, and out of it, brought many converts and political proselytes into the Liberal fold. The
biographers of Hume say of him, "No sooner had he
entered the House of Commons than he commenced
his crusade against financial abuses. He commenced it
almost single-handed, and for a long time he could
number few supporters in the House of Commons.
But he was neither to be dismayed nor put down.

Nature had not made him an orator, and the glib
speakers of the House and turners of sparkling para-
graphs in the press attempted to laugh him into silence.
But in spite of sneers and frowns he persisted in his
course; his minorities at last became majorities; and
the great triumph of his long Parliamentary career will
be, that he taught the House of Commons to exercise in
reality its functions as auditor of the national accounts."
—" Religious toleration, Parliamentary reform, universal
education, free trade, and every scheme of popular
improvement, found in him an uncompromising champion
and advocate. Long before the close of his career he
had the gratification to hear his disinterested services
eulogized by the greatest statesman of his age." In
that lay his principal reward. While kings have been
crowned, dukes, marquises, and earls have been robed in
ermine, and bishops in their lawn, one and all, with
some few exceptions, for advocating and supporting
political principles which are being rapidly swept from
the sullied pages of the statute-book, an apostle—one
Joseph Hume—who preached consistently from his birth
to his death the true doctrine of Liberal principles, died
in 1855 at the bottom of the political ladder. But his
was a crown more lasting than the glittering tinsel of
royalty or the faded trappings of the peer or the bishop.
His biographers may well say with shame, " It is not a
little curious that among the strange party combinations
that have of late been witnessed in England, no exalted
office should have been found for a man whose personal
character was unimpeachable, whose talents were
acknowledged, and most of whose views, political,
economical, and financial, maintained with undeviating
constancy for a long series of years, *were finally sanctioned
by the Legislature.*"

Among other improvements introduced into the legislation as practised at that period our investigation causes
us to stop at once when we light on the work of Lord
Brougham. Nature had been more liberal to him than
to Joseph Hume, and besides he chose a calling which
in itself raises a man to a higher position in the estima-
tion of the public than is attainable by a financier or
political economist unless he be a phenomenon. To the
aspirant to Parliamentary honours, above everything a
ready tongue and a good delivery are essential to great
success. In this respect Brougham was incomparably
Hume's superior. But both men have earned a lasting
fame, and both were Liberals, which is what we are
chiefly concerned with. They are men who were
engaged heart and soul in uprooting errors and abuses,
and they cleared, both of them, a vast deal of ground
which before their appearance on the stage of life had
grown thick with the weeds of Tory neglect and mismanagement. Let us give our chapter and verse also
for the reforms introduced by Lord Brougham, and we
can turn again to no better authority than Sir Erskine
May.* "The abuses in the administration of justice,
which had been suffered to grow and flourish without a
check, illustrate the inert and stagnant spirit of the
eighteenth century. The noble principles of English law
had been expounded by eminent judges, and applied to
the varying circumstances of society, until they had expanded into a comprehensive system of jurisprudence,
entitled to respect and veneration. But however ad-
mirable its principles, its practice had departed from the
simplicity of former times, and by manifold defects went
far to defeat the ends of justice. Lawyers, ever following precedents, were blind to principles. Legal fictions,

* 'Const. Hist. Eng.,' vol. iii, p. 387.

technicalities, obsolete forms, intricate rules of procedure accumulated. Fine intellects were wasted on the
narrow subtilties of special pleading; and clients won or
lost causes—like a game of chess—not by the force of
truth and right, but by the skill and cunning of the
players. Heartbreaking delays and ruinous costs were
the lot of suitors. Justice was dilatory, expensive,
uncertain, and remote. To the rich it was a costly
lottery; to the poor a denial of right, or certain ruin.
The class who profited most by its dark mysteries were
the lawyers themselves. A suitor might be reduced to
beggary or madness; but his advisers revelled in the
chicane and artifices of a lifelong suit and grew rich.
Out of a multiplicity of forms and processes arose num-
berless fees and well-paid offices. Many subordinate
functionaries, holding sinecure or superfluous appointments, enjoyed greater emoluments than the judges of
the court; and upon the luckless suitors again fell the
charge of these egregious establishments. If complaints
were made they were repelled as the promptings of
ignorance; if amendments of the law were proposed
they were resisted as innovations. To question the
perfection of English jurisprudence was to doubt the
wisdom of our ancestors, *a political heresy, which could
expect no toleration.*" So matters went on in the time
of Lord Eldon; but as in other departments, where the
Liberals have entered with the pruning knife and the
reforming spirit, that of the law was at length to be
taken in hand by one Henry Brougham in 1828, whose
work was eventually rewarded by his elevation to the
Woolsack. The character and energy of this great
Liberal reformer and converter may be seen from the
various directions in which he continued with unabated
vigour to exercise his untiring abilities. His biogra-

phers describe him as advocate, politician, author, law
reformer, educational reformer, man of science, and Lord
Chancellor. His speech on law reform in the session of
1828 took six hours to deliver. In 1830 he prominently
advocated Parliamentary reform and prepared a Bill;
and took part with Earl Grey in carrying through the
great measure known as the Reform Bill of 1832. He
made another great speech on law reform in 1845.

Curiously enough, the energy and spirit with which
Brougham entered upon his task of reforming the law
exercised very much the same effect upon the minds of
the lawyers of that period, who thought the dormant
condition of mind upon the subject which had characterised their predecessors for several generations was all
that was required of them, as was produced upon the
minds of politicians generally by the Liberal crusade
against Tory selfishness and neglect by the preaching, in
Parliament and out of it, of the great reformers, whose
work forms the great and lasting monument, felt though
not seen, which will for ever rear its topless pinnacle to
mark an era in the annals of our country when Justice
and Freedom were unbound, that they might henceforth
exercise an impartial control over the affairs of the Parliament and the people. When this great law reformer
was able to give real effect to the schemes he had at
heart he carried the profession with him, and then
there came what we may call a wholesale conversion.
Following in his footsteps came Sir Richard Bethell,
Lord Denman, and Lord Campbell, besides others of
eminence. *" The procedure of the Court of Chancery
was simplified; its judicial establishment enlarged and
remodelled; its offices regulated. Its delays were in
great measure averted and its costs diminished. The

* ' Const. Hist. Eng.,' May, vol. iii, p. 390.

courts of Common Law underwent a like revision. The effete Welsh judicature was abolished, the bench of English judges enlarged from twelve to fifteen, the equitable jurisdiction of the Court of Exchequer superseded, the procedure of the courts freed from fiction and artifice, the false system of pleading swept away, the law of evidence amended, [and justice restored to its natural simplicity. The law of bankruptcy and insolvency was reviewed, and a court established for its administration, with wide general and local jurisdiction. Justice was brought home to every man's door by the constitution of County Courts. Divorce, which the law had reserved as the peculiar privilege of the rich, was made the equal right of all. The Ecclesiastical Courts were reconstituted, and their procedure and jurisdiction reviewed. A new Court of Appeal, of eminent and learned authority, was found in a Judicial Committee of the Privy Council, which as the court of the last resort from India and the colonies, from the Ecclesiastical Courts and the Court of Admiralty, is second only to the House of Lords in the amplitude of its jurisdiction. The antiquated law of real property was recast, and provision made for simplifying titles and facilitating the transfer of land. Much was done and more attempted for the consolidation of the statutes. Nor have' these remarkable amendments of the law been confined to England. Scotland and Ireland, and especially the latter, have shared largely in the work of reformation. Of all the law reforms of this period, indeed, none was so signal as the constitution of the Irish Encumbered Estates Court."

Such were the more conspicuous improvements of the law during the thirty years preceding 1860. Before they had yet been commenced Lord Brougham eloquently foreshadowed the boast of that sovereign who should

have it to say " that he found law dear, and left it cheap;
found it a sealed book, and left it a living letter; found
it the patrimony of the rich, and left it the inheritance
of the poor; found it the two-edged sword of craft and
oppression, and left it the staff of honesty and the shield
of innocence."

If the Liberal ranks had had but this one great
triumph to boast of they would be rich in the possession
of the boundless gratitude of the community. What
have the lawyers to say to the political principles
espoused by a man who could thus carry his reforming
spirit into the department of the law, root up the abuses,
inconsistencies, and entanglements of our effete, cumber-
some, and obstructive system of practice, and substitute
order for chaos, and justice and expedition for injustice
and harassing delay? Moreover, in his own department
of the law this great reformer converted everybody.
All acquiesced in the changes he introduced, and pronounced them good. Yet, by themselves advocating
Conservative principles in politics they sided with a party
whose motto is *Semper eadem*. Where should we be now
if the whole country had remained Conservative, and in
so remaining had left undone the work of the Liberal
Reformers to which we have referred?

It was the light of the truth born in the mind of
Brougham that in the first place made him a Liberal
politician, and, being a Liberal politician, his was far too
big an intellect to allow itself to creep in the narrow
channel from which so many embracing the legal profession have not the courage to emancipate themselves.
They let go their anchor, we know well enough, into the
sea-bottom of expected preferment, and there it remains.
If they feel they have been converted, as no doubt scores
of them have, like those expecting preferment in the

Church and in the army, they have to keep their new-born faith to themselves. Presently the test comes, and they either sink their new convictions altogether and go in avowedly for Conservative principles, or they shrug their shoulders and announce themselves as neutral, which everybody knows is equivalent to striking the Conservative flag.

It seems almost superfluous to say that the Lord Chancellors and judges were, with scarcely an exception, Tories up to the period of the ascendancy of Liberal principles. Some of them, although they were eminent judges and learned in the law, were as shortsighted and narrowminded outside their special province, at all events as regards politics, as the most ignorant suitors who listened with breathless awe to their sentences. If there is one science more than another in our day that is a flourishing one, and which most intelligent people have from the beginning foreseen would increase in power and usefulness, it is the press, and yet the learned Lord Mansfield we are told incurred much odium in his time for the doctrines he laid down regarding the liberty of the press. The Earl of Rosslyn (Loughborough) entered upon his career with his mind imbued with Liberal principles. As plain Alexander Wedderburne he obtained glimpses of the truth, no doubt partly owing to his having been educated at Edinburgh, where his young political views would be formed on the Liberal model. But the atmosphere of the Bar interfered with the right development of his political views. As showing, however, how personal interest affects the attraction which the truth naturally has for a man's mind, on getting into Parliament he joined Lord Grenville in opposition to the Administration. He even adhered to the party of which Fox was an associate when Pitt came into power; but he was, or pretended to be, frightened out of his faith by the French Revolution. We will not be so uncharitable as to say that, like many others in different walks in life, he saw his way to the Woolsack, which he eventually reached, sharing the office with Lord Thurlow during Pitt's seventeen years of office from 1783, *but* on the condition that he turned his political coat. The French Revolution, no doubt, furnished a large number of weak-kneed Liberals with a pretext for trying their fortune with the other party, and that portentous event, as we know only too well, threw the civilisation of politically 'more advanced countries back to a degree which is incalculable. But for that great revolutionary upheaval England might by this time have been well through the political training which the last section of the unenfranchised must go through before the country may be said to have been perfectly ballasted. Politicians hitherto unclassed are coming into the Liberal fold by thousands. They are naturally elated at the prospect of at last obtaining a voice in the government of themselves, and there will be more or less very rough action and expressions of opinion, as was the case at the Aston riots, until their spirits have settled down. This lower class of politicians are, happily for the great cause of the truth, far away from any such temptations as have caused many a Tory convert to desert to the enemy.

Lord Eldon was a friend of Pitt and owed his advancement to him, and moreover would have stood no chance whatever, in the time of George III, of reaching the highest dignity known to the law if he showed any sympathy with the principles of such men as Fox. What the principles of the son of a coal-fitter, one William Scott, of Newcastle-upon-Tyne, would have been, had he not come within the influence of the governing powers of that period, we need not inquire, because we know that all things in nature have but one way of growing unless they are warped out of the straight. One of his biographers very properly remarks, " His Tory politics will be viewed through the various lights and shades of party feeling, but no one will attribute to Lord Eldon a want of integrity." Edward Law, Lord Ellenborough, was born the son of a bishop, and lived and died under the influence of the traditions with which ninety-nine out of every hundred of that order have felt bound to associate themselves. Lord Erskine harboured a more independent and daring spirit, fostered no doubt by a wider range of experience, acquired through a somewhat chequered early career. First a sailor, then a soldier, he was eventually called to the Bar, but the naturally Liberal tendency of his mind caused him to incur the displeasure of the Prince of Wales, and the loss of his appointment of Attorney-General to him, by defending one Thomas Paine. This man had written a book called ' The Rights of Man,' which rights neither the Prince of Wales of that period nor the governing powers were at all disposed to recognise. Young Erskine, however, thought otherwise and was no doubt a Liberal politician in his heart. In fact the proof of this lies in the fact that he was raised to the Peerage by a Liberal Administration in 1806, and refused to serve under any other, for he retired on the dissolution of the Grenville Ministry in the following year. This case of the son of a Peer becoming a true Liberal convert was rare in those days. Lord Lyndhurst, at first intended for an artist, his father being the painter Copley, was drawn away from his natural inclination for Liberal

principles in politics by breathing the atmosphere of
the Bar. Some surprise, we are told, was excited by the
great speech of Sir John Copley against Catholic emancipation, delivered in March, 1827, " which could not
have been anticipated from his earlier Liberal opinions."
Is that conversion to Tory principles to be accounted
for by the circumstance that in the April following he
was appointed to succeed Lord Eldon as Lord Chancellor, and was raised to the Peerage as Baron Lyndhurst, of Lyndhurst? Contact with the great Duke,
among other influences, whose close ally he became,
seems to have allured him still further from the political
path he was disposed to follow in his early life, for it is
recorded that he was a formidable opponent of the
Reform Bill. This was perhaps only a natural sequel of
his having become a "trusted councillor of the King."
From that time his divergence from the tendencies of
Peel became more and more marked, and the only con-
solation the Liberals can gather from this circumstance
is, that by far the greater statesman was being rapidly
drawn out of the Tory political orbit towards the truth,
while the great lawyer's views were being narrowed and
falsified by influences which were born of the very
heresy which they imputed to their opponents.

Every man, we are all willing to admit, is entitled to
his own opinion. But when we are upon such a theme
as the formation of political opinion, the inquiry must of
necessity lead us to some extent into the probing of
motive, and in the case of public characters, whose
actions and course of procedure in life are matter of
historical interest such an investigation may, we think,
within limits be held to be justifiable. The political
views of Lord Truro afford another instance among the
comparatively few that are to be found of a man being

able to rise superior to the Tory influences around him
and adhere, as he did for the most part, to Liberal principles. This may in part be due to his having come
under the influence for some time of Mr. Brougham, in
whose company as a junior he defended the cause of
Queen Caroline. He shared the Whig vicissitudes, and
was happily rewarded for his persistence in the right
cause by the Great Seal being at the disposal of a
Liberal Government under Lord John Russell, at a time
when he was eligible for the office. From a political
point of view the career of Lord St. Leonards was a
remarkable one, and suggests curious reflections as to
the influences under which his political opinions were
formed. He begun life far outside the sphere of Tory
traditions, his father being a hairdresser. But he is
one of the many remarkable instances of men rising to
the highest positions equipped with but little besides
their own abilities. He perceived, as many others have
done, that to publish a good treatise on some branch of
the science which he had determined to take up is a
good advertisement. He was evidently a man of no half
measures, for he took up at once the position of a
thoroughgoing Tory. How little trouble he had taken
to mature his opinions; however, is shown by his introducing a Bill for amending the law regulating the proceedings of the Court of Chancery, a few weeks only
after he had in his maiden speech in the House of Commons violently protested against any inquiry at all into
the abuses which prevailed. The very principles of
Toryism being opposed to all reform, his first trumpet-
blast in the Legislature must, he thought, be strictly
consistent with the attitude he had assumed. The
better judgment which afterwards assumed the mastery
over him showed him the error of principle he had

13

fallen into, but he continued to fight against that better judgment, the Tories being in power, and he obtained the prize he was no doubt aiming at. The highest distinction of all he received at the hands of Lord Derby in 1852. Curiously enough, however, some people might be inclined to say, his Toryism abated some of its vehemence after he had gained the highest prize, and he then assumed the character of a cautious law reformer. Lord Cranworth was the son of a clergyman and was no doubt imbued with Tory ideas at an early age, which in the course of things would be confirmed as he passed from his home to Cambridge and from there to the Bar. Yet for all this he entered Parliament representing the Liberal party, and being eligible while a Liberal Government was in office, he held the Great Seal throughout the Administrations of Lord Aberdeen and Lord Palmerston, and again in 1865 when Earl Russell was Prime Minister. This was no doubt a case of conversion to Liberal principles, since it may very fairly be taken for granted that until he thoroughly comprehended the divergent aims of the two parties he followed in the footsteps of his father and was under the same influence through a part, at all events, of his college career.

While conversion upon a Liberal scale was going on among those whose function it was to administer one branch of the law, no less progress was being made in reforming the criminal code. Up to this period, it may be said with truth, that the criminal code was administered upon a system which was little better than that which prevails in a backward despotic nation, and that society revolted against such barbarities. Honorably associated with the reforms introduced at the beginning of the century is the name of Sir Samuel Romilly, whose Bills mark the limit of transition from a policy of

hasty and ill-considered judgments whereby trifling
offences were punished with wholly unjustifiable severity,
to one characterised by judicious clemency and the adoption of safeguards against despotic rigour, as those of
Lord Brougham did in the department which he reformed.
Starting on the right course from the beginning, so far
as we know, Sir Samuel Romilly was one of those
whose political backbone was proof against the influences
under which young lawyers are brought at the commencement of their career. His general politics agreed
with those of the Whigs, and it is highly honorable to
the cause of Liberal politics for adherents to be able to
number among their great men, who substituted so much
that was good for so much that was bad, the name of
one of whom history records that he was "the highest
legal authority of his time." Although the Liberal
Peers supported him, a lifelong struggle with the Tory
section of the House of Lords left this enlightened
reformer with results achieved which constituted a
solid foundation for those to work on who followed him,
rather than the reconstructed edifice which it had been
his great object to raise. In fact it may justly be said
that it was Romilly who paved the way for what was
subsequently done first by Sir James Mackintosh and
more effectively by Sir Robert Peel. After showing himself to be an able man, although to some extent inconsistent in the views he expressed, he set to work in 1818
to continue the labours for the reform of the criminal
laws which had practically ceased with the retirement
of Romilly. Sir James seems to have been to some
extent prevented from prosecuting the reforming task
he had set himself through being called to the assistance
of the Government during the short Canning Administration—and again when Lord Grey took office in 1830.

The expression of public opinion against the continuance of such a system of law as that which punished
with death forty kinds of forgery, was beginning to
undermine the resistance to any change of the upper
classes, even the bankers themselves petitioning Parliament against the continuance in force of such an
extreme penalty.   The Lords, true to the traditions
which have so weakened their position as a part of the
Legislature of the country that their influence is but a
mere shadow of what it otherwise might have been,
restored the clause petitioned against, which the Commons had removed. from the Bill.   The Commission
appointed in 1833 to revise the criminal law found in
Lord John Russell the man, and in 1837 came the hour.
During those periods the obstruction of the House of
Lords was successfully overridden, the Master of the
Mint being successful in abolishing capital punishment
as the penalty of false coining.   The voice of public
opinion was increasing in volume, to the evident dismay
of Tory opposition, which continued to give way first
before the determination of reformers in one direction
and then in another, until the one crime of murder alone
was punishable by death.   The names of Denman,
Leonard, and Ewart are honorably mentioned among
the Liberal politicians who left their mark upon the
reforms of the period.   Improvements involving a more
humane treatment of criminals of all types were introduced.   The prison and transportation systems which
had hitherto, under a lax Legislature, been the means of
hardening and rendering irreclaimable the criminals,
were reformed so as to afford the unhappy prisoners
some chance of becoming decent members of society
when their period of punishment expired.   The light
thrown upon the generally fearful state of the prisons of

that time was due to the efforts of the great philanthropist John Howard, whose account of what he had seen so impressed the House of Commons that it drew from Burke one of his most splendid eulogies. Great respect for his humane efforts was shown by the Russian authorities when his body was laid to rest at the Russian settlement of Cherson on the borders of the Black Sea, and a statue was erected to his memory in St. Paul's Cathedral. No great warrior could die more happily than did Howard, who, on one of his benevolent missions to a suffering member of the little community who was prostrated with a malignant fever, himself caught the infection and was gathered to his fathers, a noble example of a man who almost from first to last sacrificed himself for the benefit of his fellow-creatures.

Roused by the efforts of individual reformers, the State at length took the matter of the prisons in hand and erected spacious buildings suitable for the purpose. Although the improvements erred perhaps in the direction of leniency, the change was a wise one, for it has been proved in all ages that undue severity only hardens the criminal. Although little was done at that epoch compared with the scholastic reforms which distinguish the era of Queen Victoria, an effort also was made to teach the lower orders that the path of virtue was better than one of vice. The year 1829 also saw the introduction of measures for providing for a more efficient police force, which up to that period had been very inefficient and had furnished the wits of the age with many opportunities for exercising their powers of satire and ridicule.

Efforts in other directions were made to improve the social and moral condition of the people, reforms being introduced into the system of dispensing alms. Hitherto money had been distributed without due discrimination to all who begged for it, the result being that all who could relied upon charitable relief in preference to working for their living. Commissioners were appointed to supervise those in charge of lunatics, and adequate provision was made in new buildings for those suffering from this awful disease. The Factory Acts were passed, together with other measures designed to improve the condition of the working classes. In 1816 Mr. Brougham lent his powerful aid in calling the attention of Parliament to the necessity of educating the poor. Endowments were restored to the objects for which they were originally granted, and one is ashamed to write that such an all-important question as the education and elevation of the ignorant classes was sought to be kept in the background, and the efforts to bring it into the front obstructed, by the very party whose unfounded fears for their own welfare and the safety of the State had done all they could to keep the government of the country in their own hands, not so much for the good of the country as a whole, but for the good of themselves.

Then, as regards the commercial policy, it is too well known how the system of monopolies and protections, bounties and drawbacks, was destroyed by the development of political science and liberty to need any further detailed mention here. The declamations of the Fair Traders and the reciprocity-mongers, although repeated year after year, fail to disturb the convictions of the sound thinkers in the country, whose faith in Free Trade principles cannot be shaken by the recurrence of normal periods of depression, or the cries of those who are incapable of changing their modes of conducting business in accordance with the altering circumstances of the times in which they live. Although all but a very few

Conservative politicians are now satisfied that Free
Trade is the sound theory, the Conservatives can count
none among their ranks of any importance who have
lent a helping hand in establishing a system which has
done so much for the country which gave it birth, while
on the other side are arrayed the names of Cobden,
Bright, Huskisson, Villiers, Hume, and last, but not
least, Peel and Gladstone. But it must always be remembered that the men could have done nothing but for
the growing enlightenment of the nation, whose will
nothing could withstand. The Tories wisely, though
reluctantly, recognised that, and have gradually yielded,
year by year, what otherwise must have been forcibly
taken from them. Progressive reform in the Customs
tariff, which in 1842 embraced over 1100 articles, had
in 1860 removed all but about fifty.

We have now given an outline of the enormous benefits
conferred upon the nation by the strong movement in
the direction of "more consideration for the claims of all
classes to participate in the benefits of enlightened
government," and also in the direction of enacting new
and better laws in all branches of domestic legislation,
as well as of purifying all the channels through which
the laws were administered, and of rooting up what was
bad and unsuited to the times. What has been effected
during the period we have traversed is of itself the best
proof that the statesmen who then and have since been
entrusted with the government of this country have administered its affairs in a more liberal spirit than they
were ever administered before, and that that fact alone
shows what a marvellous conversion to Liberal views
there has been under a true conviction on the part of
professed Liberals that such a policy was the best for
the country, and on the part of Conservatives under the

pressure of a more enlightened public opinion, which they have found it more in their own interests to submit to than to continue to oppose.

Lord Liverpool may have belonged to the class of statesmen which comes under the category of mediocrities, as some of his critics assert, but it should be remembered that he enjoyed the co-operation of one of the ablest Foreign Secretaries that ever filled that high and important office, George Canning. About the time when Lord Liverpool took office the period of Napoleon's triumphs was drawing to a close. The bully of Europe was at last being driven into a corner where, some three years after Lord Liverpool became Prime Minister, more than Bonaparte's match was to beard him in his own den. The brilliant stroke of Canning in forestalling Napoleon's design to capture the Danish Fleet in 1807 and use it against this country, was one of the feats which was of itself sufficient to lift that man into the front rank of statesmen, and was no doubt one of those moves on the political chessboard without which there is no saying for certain that this country might not have sustained an irreparable disaster. The era which furnishes statesmen in power with opportunities for gaining a reputation for being brilliant was, as we have said, drawing to a close. After Waterloo this country enjoyed profound peace for many years, and Lord Liverpool would show his wisdom by doing all he could to preserve that peace and allow the country breathing time for the development of the Liberal reforms which were so much needed.

The differences of opinion on the Catholic question, which had been a bone of contention between the two parties all through Lord Liverpool's Premiership, were at length to be the rock upon which the Tory party

was to split. Tory critics are no doubt sore with Lord
Liverpool for not using his opportunities to frustrate
the efforts of those who were in favour of that measure.
They could not offer stronger testimony as to their
real opinion that the leaning of the man was in the
direction of Liberal principles. Without openly pro-
claiming himself a Liberal convert, his conduct showed
plainly enough to which side he really belonged and
in whose interests he may be said to have passively
worked.

Rather more than one year before Lord Liverpool
died, the most able member of his Cabinet, George
Canning, obtained the reward he so richly deserved and
was appointed Prime Minister. As far as principles are
concerned Canning's character will not stand too close a
scrutiny. His biographers say of him that " as a statesman his aim was to uphold the honour of the country
and to pursue a Liberal line of policy at home and
abroad." Early in life Canning was tempted to leave
the path which the natural inclination of his mind had
caused him to follow, by Mr. Pitt, who in return for his
support in Parliament rewarded him with an Under-
Secretaryship of State. Ministers in Parliament above
all things require the aid of able young men who can
talk. Ambitious young men may perhaps be excused
for hovering ön the confines of the two parties with a
view of seeing which offers them the best chance of
office, but, as in the case of Mr. Canning, they must not
complain of criticism if in accepting office they violate
the principles which their action and utterances in early
life shows them clearly to have espoused. Mr. Canning
was sent for by Pitt. The haughty statesman, in his
precise way, said that " he had heard of Mr. Canning's
reputation as a scholar and a speaker and that if he con-

curred in the policy which the Government was then pursuing, arrangements would be made to bring him into Parliament."

*"It has been said that the temptations held out by this offer were too strong to be resisted by the young man, and that Canning deliberately changed his political principles to advance his personal interests. At first sight there appear to be some grounds for this statement. Canning had been the favourite nephew of a conspicuous Whig; he had lived much in Whig society; he had held strong views with regard to the French Revolution, and all that he had written and spoken had led his friends to believe that he was far more an adherent of Fox than of Pitt. Again, when a man by the change of his political creed obtains advantages that he would not otherwise have possessed, he naturally lays himself open to misconstruction. To an ambitious genius like Canning, the scion of no great house, and heir to no great fortune, adherence to the Whigs signified political extinction. The Whigs were an exclusive party; among their body were men of the highest distinction. In taking his seat among them Canning would therefore find himself surrounded by celebrities who had claims far beyond his own, and thus might have to wait for years till the Whigs, who always rewarded sparingly outside their immediate coterie, thought him worthy of notice. On the other hand, in accepting the proposal of Pitt an assured career opened out before him. Pitt was Prime Minister and had almost everything in his gift; his tenure of power seemed secure; it was acknowledged that he stood staunchly by his friends; above all, the Tory party, though daily increasing in strength, was deficient in rising talent. Every advantage was thus on

* 'Representative Statesmen,' Ewald, vol. ii, p. 75.

the side of Pitt; every disadvantage on the side of Fox. Canning accepted the offer of Pitt, and through the influence of the Prime Minister was returned, in 1793, as Member for the Borough of Newport." Mr. Ewald says, " Yet there was no apostasy." His friends apparently thought otherwise, and quizzed him as follows:

" The turning of coats so common is grown,
   That no one would think to attack it;
But no case until now was so flagrantly known,
   Of a schoolboy turning his jacket."

Many other politicians who had previously been true Liberals turned tail and rushed into the camp of their opponents when they were scared by the consequences of the French Revolution, and no doubt Canning thought that event furnished him with a very good excuse for "turning his jacket." At all events, we are told that whilst at Oxford and during the first years he was reading for the Bar he was in favour of the French Revolution. *"As long as France was struggling for freedom he, in common with many in England, cordially sympathised with her, but when she became the tool, first of the demagogue who massacred her people, and then of a despot who used her for his own ends, his sympathy was turned into disgust." That is no doubt a plausible excuse to urge on his behalf; but because another nation, after having freed itself from Tory bondage, rushes for a time to extremes, that is no valid reason or excuse for an Englishman changing a creed which he had deliberately formed during a series of years. However, the weakness which induced him to throw his principles overboard when he came within the dazzling enchantment of a Prime Minister, notwithstanding the possession of naturally brilliant gifts, caused him to

* Ewald, vol. ii, p. 77.

revert without scruple to a creed which had its root still in him, though its growth had been dwarfed by its removal into the frigid zone of Toryism. He probably saw that the Tory light would be for a long time extinguished after the death of Lord Liverpool; and he was right. He, therefore, associated himself with no less a Free Trader than Mr. Huskisson. The two, as Canning's biographer says, "now advocated a course of both home and foreign policy strikingly at variance with that of which he had for years been the wittiest defender. His new policy was as popular as his old had been obnoxious." In spite of that, he achieved his main object, and in April, 1827, he became Prime Minister. He now shared what Liberals call the "honours," which Tories heaped upon Sir Robert Peel when he deserted them. In the case of Canning we have a man whose political career does not entitle us to call him exactly a Liberal convert. He was more than that. He began a Liberal; he turned Tory, owing to Pitt having turned his head by offering to get him into Parliament, and after having been nominally a Tory until just before the death of Lord Liverpool, he throws those principles to the winds and declares for his old faith, which no doubt all the while had been struggling to burst the bonds with which he had bound it, to gratify a young and hot ambition, his real Liberal feelings all the time eating the heart out of him. How little Canning really sympathised with Tory principles is shown by his having forfeited his fondest hopes of representing in Parliament the University where he was educated, when the question arose of having to choose between that and advocating the removal of Roman Catholic disabilities. It is said of him, that he desired to represent his University *" be-

* ' George Canning and his Times,' p. 250.

yond all the blandishments of power, beyond all the
rewards or favours of the Crown," and yet he chose the
nobler part, holding that the discontent would disappear
if the Legislature passed a measure in favour of Catholic
Emancipation. Although, like many others before and
since, he was wrong in that opinion, he was right in
supporting the enactment of a law which, if it failed to
appease those for whose benefit it was designed, was an
act of justice which freed the governing power from the
reproach to which they would otherwise have exposed
themselves. To have represented all the universities in
the world would not have conferred upon him the same
distinction, as to have it recorded of him in the political
history of his country that he was the man through
whose generous efforts the Roman Catholics were in the
main and finally indebted for emancipation from their
disabilities.

Canning was a brilliant statesman in the sense that
Lord Beaconsfield was, but he was of the two probably
less farseeing, unless we may persuade ourselves that
had Canning lived to see the reforms carried out that
Mr. Disraeli did he too would have seen farther and held
broader views on the subject of Parliamentary reform.*
"The House of Commons," Canning declared, "was
not to be the organ of the people, but of an educated
minority. Institute universal suffrage, and a military
Cæsarism would have to be created to control it." We
are now as close as we can be to universal suffrage, and
there is no danger of the throne being swept away.
Mr. Ewald did not himself perhaps imagine when he
was writing his book, to which we have referred, that
the House of Lords needed the support of the moderate
men of both parties to save it from being exposed to a

* 'Representative Statesmen,' Ewald, p. 126.

severe crisis over the Franchise Bill of 1884. How far the Tories looked upon Canning as one of themselves is proved by the fact that when the King was .at last obliged to commission him to form a Cabinet all the leading Tory followers retired, Lord Palmerston, Mr. Huskisson, and Mr. Wynn alone remaining faithful to him.

Our task of examining in outline the political· bias of the heads of Administrations during the first quarter of the present century, with a view to ascertain which of them, although nominally Tory, were really Liberals, and which of them were converted to Liberal principles, brings us to a point at which the growing power of Liberal principles was destined to be checked rather sharply by the advent to power of one whose natural aristocratic tendencies, no less than the constitutional temperament of the man, formed the political bias of his mind very much in the absolutist mould. Everybody knows that Wellington was a great soldier, perhaps the greatest general there ever was; but nobody can say this of him as a politician. In the category of Prime Ministers he is not probably entitled to be ranked higher than third-rate. This is not so much his fault as that of the circumstances in which he had been placed. Politics is one science and war another. That of war rather teaches a man whose whole business is to command that the Government should be the master and the governed the servant; whereas the enlightened politician, both Liberal and Conservative, has developed so far as to admit that the proper and lasting principle prescribes that the Government shall be the servant and the governed the master. A general instinctively feels that all the power of his forces goes down from the top of the organisation to the bottom, and that if his skill, strategy, and tactical combinations fail, disaster almost inevitably follows. The difference between the organisation of an army and of a body politic differs in respect of the units in the former case being nothing better than muscular machines, while in the latter, when civilised and educated to the point at which the foremost communities have arrived in our time, there exists the power of forming and expressing opinions upon the questions arising to be dealt with by Government, and, what is of more importance than either, of having them carried out, which is superior, on the whole and in the long run, to that which any single individual can lay claim to. This obvious truism signally exemplifies the importance of education, even to minds of the highest order. On the subject of politics the great Duke had been in the dark, or, as one politician said of another, " up in a balloon," while he was fighting his great campaigns. That the Iron Duke was therefore of the order of Tory who refused to budge was perfectly natural. If he once took up a position in the field of politics he was much less likely to budge than any other politician.

After the feeble stopgap reign of Viscount Goderich Liberal principles received a check in 1828 and the Duke of Wellington took the helm. A military Premiership could hardly mean anything else than a revival of Tory principles of the narrowest school. However, like retrogression in other branches, the onward movement of Liberal principles would be only further stimulated by the public having another opportunity of being governed on a system which was already in process of decay. A few Liberal Members assisted the Duke for a few months, but it was certain that such an arrangement could not last and in a short time they receded. Invincible in the field, Wellington had to retreat

before the first political assault of Lord John Russell on
the question of the repeal of the Corporation and Test
Acts.   To the disgust of himself and his supporters
the Bill was carried through both Houses of Parliament,
and he was no more fortunate in dealing with Ireland.
In fact, whether from conviction or with a view to saving
his Government, the Duke, in companionship with Mr.
Peel, became Liberal converts.   Both virtually renounced
their Tory faith and agreed also to the removal of the
civil disabilities which had for so long exasperated the
Catholics.   Their followers were of course furious.   The
importance, however, of the Duke having taken office is
obvious for the purpose we have in view.   If he had
remained in opposition he would have as steadily declined
to agree to that measure being passed as he had previously opposed reform in general.   The responsibilities
of office compelled him to recognise the justice of the
demand, and consequently, notwithstanding his professions, we have the proof in his acts that, like many
others, he perceived the truth when he had time and
opportunity adequately to study the question and
understand its merits.

It is somewhat difficult to make oneself believe that
in so persistently opposing Parliamentary reform Wellington really understood all the bearings of that great
question.   If his mind was filled with apprehension as to
the consequences of the government of the country
being handed over to the people, it is no matter for
surprise, since many other great men who may be said
to have been brought up in the same political nursery
entertained fears of a like kind.   He afterwards found
them to be quite unfounded, and the great Duke would
no doubt have made the same discovery had he lived.
He never realised that the successive Reform Bills were

for the public good, or it is tolerably certain he would
have entertained quite different opinions on the subject.
*"Like all men whose standard of duty is unusually
high, Wellington never allowed an interested ambition
to militate against the public good. 'I have never
had much value,' he writes to the Hon. H. Wellesley,
'for the public spirit of any man who does not sacrifice
private views and convenience when it is necessary.'"
This biographer thus speaks of our great general when
touching on his qualifications for a politician. "Unfortunately for political history 'the Duke, though splen-
didly qualified as a soldier, was but slenderly endowed
with the gifts of a statesman; his prejudices narrowed
his sense of judgment; he was too hasty in arriving at
his conclusions; he was too unsympathetic and exclusive
to interpret aright the feelings and wishes of the
country, and whilst in the belief that he was in the
right path he was often led astray. Duty is after all a
relative phrase; what one man considers as meet and
right another regards as mischievous and unwise. It is
therefore most important that he who makes the performance of duty his great aim in life should be sure
that he is being guided by a polestar and not by a
will-o'-the wisp. Born in the purple, surrounded by all
that was great and noble, and with strong aristocratic
sympathies, the Duke was a Tory in his loyalty to the
throne and to all that appertained to his order, but a
Whig in his pride of birth and social exclusiveness."
To expect, in these circumstances, that the Duke would
proclaim himself a Liberal convert is not reasonable. It
was indeed a thousand pities that he ever consented to
take any part in politics at all. He was a renowned
warrior, and with the great reputation he had earned in

* Ewald, 'Representative Statesmen,' vol. ii, p. 147.

a field in which he was master he should have remained content. He would then have escaped the ever-to-be deplored incidents which occurred in June, 1832, when he was hooted and personally attacked owing to the part he took with the Opposition in Parliament during the Reform debates.

Earl Grey's assumption of the office of Prime Minister in November, 1830, was accompanied with the announcement that it was the intention of his Government to resume the Reform operations which had been broken in upon and interfered with by the Tory rule of the past three years. That it was the intention to carry out that programme may be gathered from the fact that Lord Brougham was to be his Lord Chancellor. Earl Grey rendered signal services to the Liberal party, and so pronounced were his Liberal views, which were entirely impervious to the influence of his surroundings at Cambridge, that he actually belonged to a political confederation from which Fox thought it prudent to hold aloof. He commenced in the right path and adhered to it consistently until he could achieve two objects for which he had striven—the furtherance of Parliamentary reform and the abolition of slavery. The excitement which is caused by a general election was accompanied by a startling incident which followed the dissolution of the Ministry on July 24th, 1830. Charles X of France attempted a *coup d'état*, and was rewarded by losing his crown and having to fly to England. That was one of those high-handed one-man power attempts to establish absolutism which, instead of achieving the object aimed at, signally advanced the interests of the Liberal cause and stimulated the efforts of reformers. At a period when the press in England had gained so substantially free and powerful a footing, the attempt to violate its liberty and overturn the representative institutions of a neighbouring country was sure to give rise to indignant protest, which it did. Nothing could have happened more calculated to bring in converts to Liberal principles and strengthen the faith of proselytes.

Lord Melbourne also kept steadily on in one path, adhering to the Whigs from the opening of his career. The principles which this Minister upheld were apparently more congenial to the tastes of the Sovereign during the early years of her reign than was the case when her experience had been enlarged and her knowledge of political affairs more extended. Whether this was actually so or not, the Queen apparently had no objection to a Liberal member of the aristocracy acting as her private tutor in all that related to the duties of her high office.

It is a remarkable circumstance, which, perhaps, Conservatives may be able to account for to their own satisfaction, that among the eminent politicians who have lived, a far larger number of Conservatives have gone over to the Liberal ranks than *vice versâ*. Indeed, so far as we are aware, the professed Liberals who have changed their creed have been quite among the minor lights of their generation. The conversion of a great man under the influence of irresistible conviction, and his open avowal that he had through ignorance espoused the wrong cause, is a noble example which smaller men need not be afraid to follow; yet how few there are among amateur or even professional politicians who possess courage like that of Sir Robert Peel, the most remarkable statesman of his time. The truth is that really great men possess minds far above that standard of narrowmindedness which is characteristic of little men. Little men see only far enough into a subject to be able to embrace with their understanding just those elements of the question which harmonise with the views they happen to have formed in the special circumstances in which their lot in life has been cast. A great man, on the other hand, possesses a large and broad mind, which enables him to rise above entertaining those petty jealousies and that narrowminded conceit which cause the great majority of people who are in error wilfully to shut out the true light from their minds.

In our view the only way to satisfy oneself that a man is competent to give an intelligent exposition of the reasons for the opinions he holds, is to put him through his paces as they say of a horse. The mere dogmatic assertion that this or that policy of a Government is wrong counts for nothing, although it is in very many cases the alpha and the omega of what the average politician has to say on the subject. In the case both of Sir Robert Peel and Mr. Gladstone it became evident early in their career that they would go over very soon to the opposite camp. It was quite clear to all sound thinkers who closely observed those men, that both of them would ultimately go over to the Liberals, because they possessed far too much intelligence for there to be the least fear that the minds of men of such extraordinary powers could continue for any length of time to be impervious to the truth, or that they could resist its forcing them from the wrong into the right path.

Another circumstance should arrest the attention of the political student, and that is, that notwithstanding the violent opposition of all Tories to the abandonment of the principle of Protection in favour of Free Trade, there is no statesman of any standing in our time who has any regard for his own reputation who dare venture in any public place to avow his belief that the principles

of Protection are calculated to benefit a country more
than those of Free Trade. On this particular point there
has been uncompromising conversion on the part of the
whole Tory party. This is a matter which admits of no
dispute. That the advocacy of the principle of Protection was an error is as clearly demonstrated as that the
sun does not go round the earth. Any Conservative in
these days who still maintains that the principle of Protection is better than that of Free Trade, is looked upon
even by the leading lights of his own party as a person
whose opinions are unworthy of serious attention.

No more remarkable incident could be introduced into
a history of creeds than that of the conversion of Sir
Robert Peel, which began to declare itself in 1829, notwithstanding the fact that while this change in his
views was visibly maturing he headed an attack of the
Tories against the Whig Administration of which Lord
Melbourne was the chief. Curiously enough, he was at
the very climax of his political power, as the leader of
the Tories, when his mind had ripened for a plunge,
which landed him among the Liberals, prepared to
sweep away burdensome imposts, which only finds a
parallel in the drastic measures in the same direction
proposed and carried by Mr. Gladstone when he was
Chancellor of the Exchequer. Biographers of Sir
Robert Peel tell us that "in 1842 he proposed one of
the most extensive alterations in the tariff of the country
that had ever been effected. Hundreds of imposts—
many of them insignificant, but all of them vexatious—
were swept away." But this change in his views fell
among the party which he led like a thunderbolt, and we
are told that " the confidence of the Protectionists in
their leader was grievously shaken, and their complaints
of being duped by him were loud and clamorous. But,"

we are further told, that " in losing their confidence he gained that of the opposite party, who began to look upon him as the man destined to realise their hopes." This action was followed, as is too well known by all Conservatives, by what we may call a political eruption commencing with a split in the Peel Cabinet, followed by an attempt of Lord John Russell to form a Government, which, however, he soon abandoned, and Sir Robert Peel was reinstated. Then at the opening of the session of 1846, he formally announced, to the surprise, rage, and dismay of his old friends and the immense delight of all Liberal politicians and political economists, that he intended not to modify, but entirely to repeal the Corn Laws. From this moment, the army of Tory Protectionists, seeing that their friend had led an assault on their strongholds, which had been for so long maintained for their own personal benefit at the expense of the people, hurled at him unsparing invective, and from that moment he became the object of the most bitter reproach. Although openly accused of having betrayed and deceived them, he bore it all with firmness and equanimity, comforted no doubt by the thought that he had passed from the depressingly cold atmosphere of error into the light and warmth of the truth.

If we did not write another sentence for the edification and enlightenment of young politicians, who may with open minds be seeking that same light, which a great man walked fearlessly into before a gazing nation and an admiring world, this episode is sufficient of itself to demonstrate how erroneous have been the principles which on the whole Tories have advocated from the point of view of national interests.

No one knowing anything of the subject will be so bigoted as to maintain that Conservative politicians have done no good for their country. Such an assertion is nonsense. The earlier history of this country shines in all its pages with the glorious achievements of those who had a large share in building up the wonderful fabric of the British empire. What they did in the days of Elizabeth, for instance, will always be remembered by Britons as among the most brilliant achievements in the history of the world. No one grudges them the fullest credit to which they are entitled for the statesmanlike qualities and the memorable pluck which so enhanced the prestige of the nation in those days. That is not the point with which we are dealing. Our object is to show, and we can show it conclusively, that having achieved that magnificent position for themselves and their friends, like the barons in their strongholds on the Rhine and other places, they tried to keep all the spoils for themselves. They endeavoured to fence round what they had won for their own personal benefit, to the exclusion of the descendants of those by whose strong arms and bulldog pluck and endurance, all their successes were mostly due.

Why, may we ask, did not some confirmed Tory, who at the same time that he proposed to relieve the people of their burdens, suggest the abolition of those hundreds of burdensome and vexatious imposts which Sir Robert Peel swept away?

If the Earl of Derby, who was Prime Minister in 1852, '58, and '66, had the comfort and wellbeing of his countrymen at heart, why did not he propose to sweep away the burdensome and vexatious taxes which Mr. Gladstone abolished when Chancellor of the Exchequer? How is it, may we ask of young political students, as well as of the old, whose Tory principles have over and over again been proved to be unsound, that the great reforms proposed by Cobden, Bright, and others, and carried by the Liberals and acknowledged by all the world to have been acts of justice and an example for all other nations to follow, were not only not suggested by the Tory party, but were always opposed tooth and nail? And why, because they feared that such measures would curtail their special privileges and deprive them of benefits which enabled them to fatten at the expense of those less well placed in life.

There is no escape for Conservatives from the position in which they find themselves.   No arguments will avail to relieve them from the stigma which rests upon their order of having opposed, with all the might of artifice and money, the passage through the House of Commons of measures like the following:

LIST OF BILLS

REJECTED BY THE HOUSE OF LORDS,

WITH PARTICULARS FROM ORIGINAL SOURCES.

List of Bills Rejected by the

Year	Bill	Date	Con.	
1812	For abolishing and regulating sinecures and offices executed by deputy. Negatived.	3rd July.	Con.	35
1813	Ditto.	...	...	
1819	Roman Catholic Disability Removal Bill.	10th June.	,,	82
1821	Ditto, as connected with Legislative Rights.	17th April.	,,	120
1822	Roman Catholic Peers—to enable to sit and vote.	21st June.	...	
1823	English Catholic Elective Franchise.	9th July.	,,	73
,,	Dissenters' Marriages Relief. Second reading.	13th June.	...	
1824	English Catholic Relief. Rejected.	24th May.	...	
,,	Unitarian Marriages Bill. Passed the second reading. Thrown out on committal.	2nd April. 4th May.	... ...	
1825	Ditto. Second reading.	3rd June.	,,	52
,,	Roman Catholic Disability Removal.	17th May.	,,	130
1829	...	...	...	
1833	Jewish Disabilities. Second reading.	1st August.	,,	54
1834	Ditto, ditto.	23rd June.	,,	38
1836	Ditto.	19th August.	...	
1848	Ditto.	25th May.	,,	125
1850	Ditto.	17th July.	,,	108
1851	Ditto.	17th ,,	...	
1853	Ditto.	29th April.	,,	115
1857	Ditto Oaths Bills.	10th June.	,,	139
1834	Tithes (Ireland). . Rejected on second reading.	11th August.	...	
,,	Bribery at Elections.	7th ,,	...	
,,	Admission of Dissenters to the Universities. Second reading lost.	1st ,,		
1835	Roman Catholic Marriages. Rejected.	11th ,,	...	
,,	Constabulary (Ireland). Second reading rejected.	26th ,,		

House of Lords, with Particulars.

Not Con.		Majority		
Not Con.	8	Majority	27	The Lord Chancellor's amendment to be read a second time that day three months carried.
...		...		...
„	141	„	59	...
„	159	„	39	...
		...		This Bill passed the House of Commons May 17th. The Lords rejected it on second reading by 171 to 129.
„	80	„	7	...
...		...		Rejected by 27 to 21.
...		„	38	...
...		„	4	...
...		„	39	...
...	56	„	4	...
...	178	„	48	This Bill passed the second reading in the House of Commons April 21st by a majority of 27, and the third reading May 10th by a majority of 21, 248 to 227. Twenty-seven bishops voted not content. Only two, the Bishops of Norwich and Rochester, supported the Bill. The Bill brought in by the Duke of Wellington passed the second reading April 4th by a majority of 105, and the third reading April 10th by 104.
...		...		...
„	104	„	50	...
„	130	„	92	Bill put off for six months.
...		...		Withdrawn.
„	163	„	35	...
„	144	„	36	...
...		...		...
„	164	„	49	...
„	171	„	32	...
...		„	67	...
...		...		Lords' Amendments not agreed to by the Commons.
...		„	102	This Bill passed the third reading in the House of Commons July 28th by a majority of 89.
...		„	26	To repeal an Act of 19 King George II, as makes void all marriages celebrated by any Popish Priest between Protestant and Papist.
...		„	12	To provide for General Inspector for all Ireland, and to transfer the appointment of, from the Magistrates to the Crown.

List of Bills Rejected by the

1835	Tithes (Ireland). In committee, clause 61,which provided that upon next vacancy in a parish with not more than 50 members, English Catholics, such church may be sequestrated during pleasure of Lord Lieutenant, and the rents, profits, &c., to be received by the Ecclesiastical Commissioners, was struck out by a majority of 97 August 24th. The Bill was therefore abandoned.			
1836	Roman Catholic Marriages. Rejected.	4th August.	Con.	19
,,	Civil Offices' Declaration. Rejected.	16th ,,	,,	27
,,	Post-Office Commissioners. Second reading negatived.	12th ,,		
1837	Municipal Corporations. Rejected in committee.	9th June.		
,,	Reform of Parliament. Rejected on second reading.		...	
,,	Parliamentary Electors.	...	...	
,,	Final Registration of Electors. Second reading postponed for three months.	7th July.	...	
1838	Ditto.	...		
,,	Parliamentary Electors. Negatived on second reading.	8th March.	...	
,,	Municipal Corporation (Ireland).	...		
1839	Electors Removal.	18th July.	,,	80
,,	Copyhold Enfranchisement. Rejected on committal.	29th ,,	by	39
	Slave Trade (Portugal). Second reading.	1st August.	Con.	32
1840	Affirmation. Second reading.	4th ,,	...	
1841	Jews Declaration. Second reading.	3rd June.	...	
,,	Ditto. Third reading.	11th ,,	,,	64

House of Lords, with Particulars.—Continued.

Not Con. 39	Majority 20	...
„ 43	„ 16	For the relief of persons elected to municipal offices, and entertaining conscientious objections to subscribe the Declaration.
...	„ 35	To appoint for executing the duties of Postmaster-General.
...	„ 86	...
	„ 38	...
...	...	To enable electors to vote if the rates had been paid to within six months.
	„ 33	...
...		House of Commons reinstate the Boundary Clause by a majority of 18, and refuse to consider the Lords' Amendments.
...	„ 65	To extend the time for the payment of rates, &c., due April 5th, from July 20th to October 11th. The Lords insist on their amendments by majority of 30. House of Commons postpone going on with the Bill August 15th. The Lords reject the Franchise Clause. House of Commons reject the Lords' Amendments by a majority of 15, and reinstate the Franchise Clause, which the Lords again rejected August 7th by a majority of 17.
„ 39	„ 41	Lord Redesdale moved that the Bill be read that day three months, on which amendment the House divided.
to 28		...
Not Con. 38	...	...
...	...	Put off for six months.
...	...	Carried by 48 to 47.
„ 98	„ 34	Against the Bill. Amendment to be read that day three months.

List of Bills Rejected by the

1846	Corn Importation Bill.*	15th May.	...
1848	Ditto. Second reading. Bribery at Elections.	28th ,, 24th August.	Con. 211 ...
1849	Second reading put off. Affirmation. Second reading.	22nd June.	,, 34
,,	Tenants at Rack Rent Reliefs. Postponed for six months.	...	...
1850	Ditto, ditto.	7th May.	...
1851	Inhabited House Duty—Bill to repeal the Window Tax, and to impose other duties in lieu thereof, passed under pro- test, signed by a small number of the Lords.	...	...
1857	Oaths Bill. After long debate negatived.	15th June.	,, 139
1858	Church Rates.	2nd July.	,, 36

*   *Analysis.*

The Majority—Ayes 329.

	Conservatives.	Liberals.	Total.
English Counties	12	13	25
English Boroughs	68	142	210
English Universities	2	—	2
Welsh Counties	4	—	4
Welsh Boroughs	3	6	9
Irish Counties	4	16	20
Irish Boroughs	7	19	26
Scotch Counties	5	9	14
Scotch Boroughs	1	18	19
	106	223	329

Majority (Tellers Included)
Conservatives .   .   106
Liberals .   .   .   223
              329

House of Lords, with Particulars.—Continued.

...	...	Third reading in House of Commons—Ayes 327, Noes 229, Majority 98.
Not Con. 164	Majority 47	...
...	...	...
„ 10	„ 24	Against the Bill. List of non-contents—Bishops of London and Chichester; Earls Carlisle, Minto, St. Germans; Lords Campbell, Denman, Kingston, Sage and Sele, Wrottesley.
...	...	The Earl of Harrowby "could have no hope of carrying it against the opinion of the Landlord Class in that House" June 22nd, 1849.
...	...	Bill dropped.
...	...	...
„ 171	„ 32	...
„ 187	„ 151	...

* *Analysis.*

The Minority—Noes 231.

	Conservatives.	Liberals.	Total.
English Counties	103	4	107
English Boroughs	78	4	82
English Universities	2	—	2
Welsh Counties	8	—	8
Welsh Boroughs	2	—	2
Irish Counties	13	1	14
Irish Boroughs	2	—	2
Irish Universities	2	—	2
Scotch Counties	10	—	10
Scotch Boroughs	1	—	1
Isle of Wight	1	—	1
	222	9	231

Minority (Tellers Included)
Conservatives . . 222
Liberals . . . 9
231

List of Bills Rejected by the

1860	Church Rates.	19th July.	Con. 31

of the Reform Bill of 1832, it was impossible to excite public interest from East Retford to Birmingham. The Government of Lord Melbourne shillings on corn, and in 1846 the Corn Laws were swept away from Jews to seats in the Legislature was even more analogous to the present duced and thrown out. In 1845 it was carried by Lord Chancellor the Jews to Parliament was carried in the House of Commons by a of 25. It was reintroduced in 1853, and in 1858 the Bill was again their Lordships, by which the Jews were allowed to gain admission during the last half century, it was painful to think how little had entered Parliament, the claims of Roman Catholics had just been granted from the fear of English commotion. The Corn Laws were

1860	Paper Duty Repeal Bill.		8th May.	...
	Ditto.	Second reading.	21st „	„ 104
1861	Customs and Inland Revenue.		11th June.	...
		Third reading.		
1867	Admission of Dissenters to the Universities.	Second reading.	25th July.	„ 46
1868	Irish Church.	Second reading.	29th June.	„ 97
1868-9	Admission of Dissenters to the Universities.	Second reading.	19th July.	„ 54
1870	Ditto.		...	„ 83
1871	Ballot.	Second reading.	10th August.	„ 48
1872	Municipal Elections (Wards).	Second reading.	18th July.	„ 56
1873	Register for Parliamentary Elections.	Second reading.	...	
„	Public Worship Facilities.		...	
„	Rating (Liability and Value).		...	
1876	Law of Burial.		15th May.	„ 92
1880	Compensation for Disturbance (Ireland). Second reading rejected by 282 to 51.		...	

House of Lords, with Particulars.—Continued.

Not Con. 128	Majority 99	Lord Lyvedon, in introducing the Bill, said : "A few years before the passing in the subject of Reform, and Parliament refused to transfer the Franchise were expelled from office in 1841 for proposing a fixed duty of eight the Statute Book. The conduct of Parliament upon the admission of case. In 1841 the Jewish Civil Disabilities Removal Bill was intro- Lyndhurst. In 1848 the second reading of the Bill for admitting majority of 70. In 1851 the Bill was read a second time by a majority brought up to their Lordships' House. The door was then left ajar by into the other House. Looking back to the course of Legislation been yielded to reason and how much to fear. In 1829, when he first yielded to the fear of Irish insurrection. The Reform Bill was next repealed from the fear of a famine in Ireland."
... ...	... ...	Third reading in the House of Commons— Ayes 219; Noes 210.
„ 193 ...	„ 89 ...	Paper Duty repealed by this Bill. Many of the Lords objected to this being dealt with in a "Supply Bill," and recorded their protest in the journals of the House.
„ 74	„ 28	...
„ 192	„ 95	In the House of Commons the second reading was carried by 312 to 258.
„ 91	„ 37	...
„ 97	„ 14	...
„ 97	„ 49	...
„ 77	„ 21	To facilitate the division of Boroughs into Wards. Second reading put off for three months— 62 to 26. Second reading put off for three months— 68 to 52. Second reading put off for three months— 59 to 43.
...	...	
...	...	
„ 148	„ 56	Lord Granville's Resolution : "That it is desirable that the Law relating to the

Burial of the Dead in England should be amended."
(1) By giving facilities for the interment of deceased persons without the use of the Burial Service of the Church of England in churchyards in which they have a right of interment, if the relatives or friends having the charge of their funerals shall so desire.
(2) By enabling the relatives or friends having the charge of the funeral to conduct such funeral in any churchyard in which the deceased had a right of interment, with such Christian and orderly religious observances as to them may seem fit.

| ... | ... | In the House of Commons the second reading was carried by a majority of 78, and the third by a majority of 56. |

15

Sufficient time has now elapsed to render it as certain as anything can be that the foregoing reforms have been for the good of the nation at large, and that they have been acts of justice which no Government could withhold when demanded by the popular voice without laying themselves open to the charge of legislating for party purposes and not for the national good. The legislation of the Tories, when not undertaken under compulsion of being unable otherwise to retain their places, as was the case with Mr. Disraeli's 1867 Reform Bill, has invariably been in the interests of a class. Either it has been of that type or they have not legislated at all.

Great care seems to have been taken by those who were responsible for the political education of Lord John Russell that he should not come under Tory influences when his mind was in the plastic condition peculiar to youth. He was actually sent to Edinburgh to avoid those strongholds of Toryism, the English universities. How clearly this one circumstance shows how handicapped the Whigs were at an early stage of the development of Liberal principles! All who went in for the land, the law, the Church, or the universities were schooled into looking upon Whigs as persons of whom they were taught to sing—

"Confound their politics,
Frustrate their knavish tricks."

Lord John was one of those politicians who was kept in the right path from the commencement, and has done as much if not more than anybody for the Liberal cause. Many were the conversions to Liberal principles as the direct result of his teaching and example. Suffice it to say here that in the part he took in the drafting, introduction, and explanation of the first Reform Bill to the House of Commons, he rose to be the first statesman of

his time, and he steadily adhered to the principles which
he had espoused from the commencement. His achievements, like the tombs erected to the memory of famous
Roman emperors on either side of the Appian Way, stand
out as landmarks to guide future generations along the
path to the liberties and power which their predecessors
have enjoyed, and which, but for such men as he was,
they might still be sighing for in the galling toils of
political bondage.

The political career of the Earl of Derby, the father
of the present Earl, is one well deserving the careful
study of the student who is searching for the true light
in the domain of politics. The course pursued by this
gifted man is still one more signal example of how the
formation of political opinion depends upon self-interest.
There are cases, as we have said before, like those of
Cobden, Bright, &c., where the truth had obtained such
a strong hold upon the mind from the beginning, that no
amount of self-interest could turn the man aside, or
induce him to forsake the principles which had become
the dominating influence of his nature. But such cases
are rare. A very large majority of even the greatest
politicians have not been proof against the allurements
of high office and the love of power. Lord Derby's
career suggests unmistakably that his political principles
in early life had developed only a weak backbone to
their system, which gave way under the strain which
bent the backbone of the political principles of so many
others ; and there was no possibility after the elevation
aspired to had been reached, to straighten it out and
leave no trace upon which the political historian could
fix his criticism. If ever a Tory was to the manner
born it was Lord Derby. Haughty, proud, arrogant,
impatient of opposition, he might have been George III

himself, who looked upon society as his camel whose one
object and destiny had been to develop the hump for him
to sit upon.   The feebleness of Lord Derby's foresight
in matters regarding the industrial and social development of the country is seen in his strenuous opposition
in 1826 to the Liverpool and Manchester Railway Bill,
which he characterised as "a mad and extravagant
speculation." Being a young man of intellectual promise, he overcame the scruples which Eton and Oxford
had imbued him with, and joined the Canning Administration in 1827, and again in 1831 became Chief Secretary
for Ireland in a Liberal Government. While sitting for
the Borough of Windsor he energetically promoted the
cause of Parliamentary reform, and having grown in
wisdom since he tried to stop the construction of the
first bit of railway projected in the kingdom, which was
the beginning of what has done more for the country
than all other reforms put together, he took part in the
establishment of the Shannon Navigation scheme.   His
elevation to the dignity of Lord Stanley in 1834 raised
him into an atmosphere where at that time the profession of Liberal principles was not the fashion, and so his
politics had to be changed, no matter apparently what
his real convictions might previously have been.   The
question of the reduction of the Irish Church Establishment furnished a pretext for differing with the policy of
Earl Grey, and Lord Stanley walked across to the Opposition bench, never to return.   This is the way political
opinion was formed in 1834.   The accession of his father
to the earldom in the same year was an event which, it
was apparently thought, ill accorded with the circumstance of his son being a Liberal reformer.   In 1841
Sir Robert Peel had not yet changed colour sufficiently
to justify Lord Stanley in refusing again to take office

under him, so he returned to the post of Colonial Secretary in 1841, which afforded him the opportunity of adopting principles which landed him in the camp of the Protectionists. In less than twenty years he had been able, therefore, in obedience to the dictates which caused him to espouse Liberal principles at the start, to traverse the distance between one political pole and the other. In 1844 he was made a Peer. His measure, however, had been taken, and although opportunities on three different occasions opened to him the highest place in the State, he was rewarded as so unsound and vacillating a politician deserved to be. In 1858 he followed Lord Palmerston as Prime Minister, and being defeated on a question of Parliamentary reform, he dissolved, but a vote of want of confidence showed him that he was not the man for the times, and although afforded yet another chance in 1866, his health then failed him and his star set. In many ways he was a kind and liberal man, but he was spoilt as an exemplary political character by the existence of a House of Lords. If there had been no such institution for either his father or him to be raised to by hereditary right, he might and probably would have fulfilled his early promise and have left his name on the great roll of Liberal statesmen and reformers. Although, therefore, we cannot claim the father of the present Lord Derby as a Liberal convert, the son has made up for the parent's shortcomings by deliberately throwing overboard all the principles and traditions which were unbroken through a succession of no less than fourteen Earls of Derby. The rising politicians of our day are so familiar with the circumstances of the conversion of the present Earl that we need occupy no space in recounting them. No stronger case, however, than his could be cited as showing the unsoundness of the principles of Toryism, for no impartial and healthy mind can resist the conviction that the cause which has been so deliberately forsaken by a statesman of such eminence, who is above all renowned for his common sense, is one that is lost.

No Peer of the realm who voted for the repeal of the Test and Corporation Acts, for Catholic Emancipation, and for the repeal of the Corn Laws, could be classed otherwise than as a politician of Liberal principles, although so far back as 1802 he succeeded to the earldom. This was the case with Lord Aberdeen, who was Prime Minister for two years from December, 1852. His biographers in some cases claim him as a Tory, as Mr. Kebbel does Pitt; but in neither case can the claim be allowed. Politicians must be judged by their acts. A man very often talks on politics in a way which affords no real clue to his creed, but when it comes to voting and taking sides he attaches himself to one side or the other before the public eye, and cannot explain away his act or escape from the position he has taken up. The early surroundings of George Hamilton-Gordon were no doubt of the Tory type, and he was nominally a Tory himself, and sided with them both at Harrow and Cambridge; but his mind, like that of many other nominal Tories, was open to conviction, and when he headed his Coalition Ministry he was, to all intents and purposes, a Liberal statesman. We are told that at that period there was actually a wholesale conversion of Tories to Liberal principles, the Liberal party having " *gained over nearly all the statesmanship of the Conservative ranks without losing any of its own. Five and twenty years before the foremost men among the Tories had joined Earl Grey, and now again the first

* Erskine May, ' Const. Hist. Eng.,' vol. ii, p. 218.

minds of another generation were won over from the same party to the popular side. A fusion of parties had become the law of our political system." The colour of Lord Aberdeen's political principles may be judged of from the fact of Sir William Molesworth, a Radical, being one of the members of his Ministry.

Lord Clarendon, on succeeding to the earldom on the death of his uncle in 1838, did not think it necessary to change his political creed, as the fourteenth Earl of Derby did. The older the century grows the more solid have the foundations become upon which Liberal principles rest, and consequently a rare fortitude was required, after the middle of the century was passed, to go back to principles which had then become so discredited. The Right Hon. S. H. Walpole was a Liberal convert, at least on the question of Reform. He was at the head of the Home Office in Lord Derby's second Administration in 1858, but resigned owing to differences of opinion with his colleagues on the subject of the Reform Bill. Mr. Walpole's resignation was justified by the Government he deserted being beaten after an appeal to the country on the question of their Reform proposals.

The conversion of Lord Palmerston to Liberal principles was rather slow, but it was complete. He took office in a Tory Administration in 1807, and again in 1809 under Perceval. He commenced his career as a follower of Pitt, but was not very pronounced in his views, as may be judged from the fact that he was at the War Office for about twenty years in the time of Lord Liverpool, of Canning, Lord Goderich, and the Duke of Wellington. He even retained his Tory proclivities at the date when ' The New Whig Guide' appeared, whose satirical thrusts at the Liberal party had the assistance

of his pen. The change, however, that was coming over
the country in favour of Liberal principles during the
latter portion of Lord Liverpool's Premiership evidently
disturbed his faith in the doctrines in which he had
hitherto believed, and he began to follow the example of
Canning in his support of Catholic Emancipation. But
he could not see his way to Parliamentary reform,
except within very narrow limits. He made further
progress towards conversion to Liberal principles while
Wellington was in office, but retired from his Ministry at
the same time as Huskisson, the Duke doing, however,
all he could to prevent him from resigning, but in vain.
In 1830 he openly espoused his new faith, and joined
the Whig Ministry of Earl Grey. From that time, with
a brief interval, when the Duke of Wellington filled the
office, he was Secretary for Foreign Affairs for ten years,
and showed himself to be a master in that department.
From 1841 to 1846 he was in opposition, but again returned to his old post under Lord Russell, which he
held till 1851.

Lord Palmerston's opinion of the Tories, when he
had come really to see and understand the very different
aims of the two parties, may be judged of from the following:—*"Brought up in the school of Canning, and
holding that brilliant Minister's sound and liberal ideas
upon the subjects which then divided the Cabinet, Lord
Palmerston had scant sympathy with the views of those
'old women,' 'spoonies,' and 'stumped-up' Tories who
constituted the majority in the Government of Lord
Liverpool. 'The Government,' he writes to his
brother, 'are as strong as any Government can wish to
be as far as regards those who sit facing them; but, in
truth, the real Opposition of the present day sit *behind*

* Ewald, 'Rep. Statesmen,' vol. ii, p. 311.

the Treasury Bench; and it is by the stupid old Tory party, who bawl out the memory and praises of Pitt while they are opposing all the measures and principles which he held most important; it is by these that the progress of the Government in every improvement which they are attempting is thwarted and impeded. On the Catholic question; on the principles of commerce; on the corn laws; on the settlement of the currency; on the laws regulating the trade in money; on colonial slavery; on the game laws, which are intimately connected with the moral habits of the people—on all these questions, and everything like them, the Government find support from Whigs and resistance from their self-denominated friends.' " He was Prime Minister for a greater number of years than any man, with the exceptions of Lord Liverpool and Mr. Gladstone.

Lord Granville and Sir George Cornewall Lewis, whose names figure prominently in the history of their time, were both possessed of minds which very early in their career perceived which was the right and the just course for those to pursue who were responsible for the government of the country. The latter was, besides being a politician, a philosopher and writer of no mean order. Sir Stafford Northcote seems unaccountably to have been drawn away from his early political love, for it is a little curious that a man who was once Secretary to such a powerful personality as Mr. Gladstone could afterwards adopt political principles diametrically opposed to those of his great teacher. That Sir Stafford Northcote approved of Liberal principles is proved by the fact that he became legal Secretary to the Board of Trade in 1847 when Lord John Russell was Prime Minister. But as in other cases to which we have referred, on succeeding to the family title and estates in 1851, Liberal principles were changed for Conservative, and he took office for the first time under Lord Derby. The change of principles, however, it seems to us was rather one of expediency than a conversion to Conservative principles, for Sir Stafford's attitude has been so unmistakably in favour of measures designed for the benefit of the nation as a whole, and his views are always so mild and generous, that in spite of his vote being given to his party for consistency's sake, if his real convictions could on all occasions have been analysed, we believe he would have been found to be what he was at the beginning, and, but for the estates, would probably be now—a Liberal politician.

A still more curious study from the point of view of principles is the career of Benjamin Disraeli, Earl of Beaconsfield. It is scarcely an exaggeration to say that his principles were of that supple nature, that they yielded very much to circumstances. Beginning at the right end he finished his career at the very apex of the wrong end. While midway in that career, that is the part in which he was a power, he was not content to throw over his own principles, but in order to gain what he wanted he proposed changes in the matter of Parliamentary reform that took away even the breath of the most Radical politicians themselves. Statecraft with him was nothing if not showy and dramatic. He was the very man to have a large following among English men of business of the speculative type. A speculator lays his nets for game that he thinks will in a very short time come into them. A speculator always runs a risk which fidgets and irritates him if the burden of it has to be long endured. Consequently he admires a statesman who is emotional and will respond quickly to any agita-

tion got up in the country and will act with prompti-
tude. Lord Beaconsfield was designed by nature to
revive the hopes of Conservatives in their cause, by the
way in which he won adherents among the class referred
to. Although he could wait with the most exemplary
patience when he was out of office for a chance to get
in—and no one will deny that in that respect he got a
good training — when once in he showed that he intended
to make up for lost time by making one *coup-de-théâtre*
follow another as quickly as possible. Instead, however, of being before his time as some geniuses have
been, he was after it. Statesmen of the Canning type
of brilliancy are no longer wanted. Three-bottle men
and gentlemen pugilists are as much out of date as
emperors of the Bonaparte type, and so also are statesmen of the class who were required to deal with their
machinations. We can all of us easily understand that
Benjamin Disraeli would desert Liberal principles, just
as he would have left the occupation of a market
gardener, for instance, if he had been brought up in that
line, to join a travelling circus. Red breeches, a sky-
blue jacket trimmed with gold lace, and a fez with a
yellow tassel, would correspond much more with his
ideas of life and enjoyment, especially when his appearance on the stage was greeted with the ringing applause
of the admiring spectators, than a career which demanded much self-sacrifice and little reward beyond
that of feeling that he had been unostentatiously useful
in his day and generation.

Disraeli attempted first to enter public life by putting
up for the borough of High Wycombe in Buckinghamshire, and the voucher for the principles on which he
stood is seen in his sponsors, Joseph Hume and Daniel
O'Connell. But a Whig, the Hon. Charles Grey, beat

the Radical Disraeli. This attempt to get into Parliament was during the height of the Reform agitation, which it is necessary to remember because it marks the circumstance of his early and natural sympathies being entirely with that movement. In 1836 he again tried to get in for High Wycombe, but failed, and in the following year tried as a Conservative to get returned for Taunton, but was defeated there; a just penalty, some people would say, for so precipitately turning his political coat. He alluded to his early profession of Liberal principles as the sowing of his political wild oats. This, as we know, was only one of his many inconsistencies. Having, for reasons to which we shall presently refer, decided to throw in his lot with the Tories, he did all he could to persuade himself and his new friends that the Reform Bill which they had opposed with all their might was after all a blessing, and that by extending its operations and organizing societies to promote general registration they would further "three great democratic movements quite in keeping with the original and genuine character of Toryism." He did not explain, however, how it was that the three movements, being in keeping with genuine Toryism, they did not realize that from the first. It would have saved much time and trouble had that view been taken from the beginning. That Lord Beaconsfield was ever a Liberal is, however, stoutly denied by some of his friends, among whom are Mr. Hitchman, who is the author of ' The public Life of the Right Hon. the Earl of Beaconsfield, &c. ; ' but with all due respect for the opinions of his friends, facts are facts, and those we have referred to cannot be ignored. If Disraeli had succeeded at his first attempt to get into Parliament he would undoubtedly have sat and spoken and voted as the Liberal Member for High Wycombe, and it was clearly his intention then to do so. His biographer refers to his pamphlets—among others 'The crisis examined'—and maintains that they give forth the trumpet-note of Toryism. But in the same sentence it is admitted that withal Disraeli is a reformer. He is willing to repeal the malt tax; he is disposed to "improve" the Church of England, and to reform the Irish Church; "he will concede the claims of Dissenters as far as marriage and registration are concerned; and, he will meet them half way in the matter of church rates." What is all this, when viewed in the light of his ultra-Reform efforts in the winter of his career, but proof of the Liberal tendencies of the man; that his early career, before he tried to get a seat in Parliament, had been passed in the atmosphere which teaches every healthy mind that if civilisation in its higher and deeper meaning—in its meaning beyond the mere high cultivation of one plant in the hothouse at the expense of withering and destroying the rest—is to be promoted, it must be on the enduring lines laid down by the Liberal statesmen who have carried all the great reforms and purified the channels through which the revenue flows from the people into the National Treasury? In 1837 he took his seat in the House of Commons. How he coquetted with the principles first of one side and then of the other and was evidently looking to see which offered the best chance of advancing his personal interests is seen from the following. *"The ground he had taken hitherto was one to which he was as little as possible committed, circumscribed, or embarrassed, and any one of three paths lay open to him. He had often held language that might be construed into leaning towards free trade

* 'Times,' April 20th, 1881, "Review of his Life."

in corn and liberty in religion and he might have easily
waived unimportant differences and tendered his support
to Peel.   But such welcome as he might reasonably look
for was hardly likely to tempt him to the sacrifice of
more ambitious hopes.   At best, he must have been
content to remain the lieutenant of a man whose nature
had little in common with his own, while in choosing
differently he might aspire to lead either a Whig or Tory
opposition.   His avowed democratic inclinations might
with slight violence have   softened into decorous
Liberalism and he would have had to step little out of
his way to attach himself to the Whigs.   But, putting
principle out of the question, his objections to that
course sprang from feeling as much as calculation."   We
then come upon the key to the formation of his political
opinions and how it was that from the fluid state to the
hardened block his determination to abandon Liberal
principles and   throw in his lot with the Tories was
fixed.   The bitter fights he had for so many long years
with his greater rival Mr. Gladstone, shows how well
he could hate, and how when once he had a rooted
dislike for a person in his soul he relentlessly nurtured
it.   Detestation of the Whigs had evidently as much if
not more to do with the ultimate choice of principles he
made than any well-grounded belief at that time that
the views of Conservatives were sounder than those of
Liberals.   He looked upon the Whigs as his natural
enemies, and to force his way to the front of that body
he must run the gauntlet of a number of dangerous and
powerful rivals who were notorious for their jealousy
of talented strangers; while on the other hand he
perceived that by throwing in his lot with the Protectionists, who at the time were staggering under the
blows of their successful adversaries, he saw a great

chance of attaining eminence at once. They were longing for vengeance and only lacked a capable leader. Here was just the man for them. He would stick at nothing, as he afterwards amply proved. He was a clever tactician, fertile in resource, and gifted to an extraordinary degree with the power of satirical argument, which caused many a sturdy debater to pause before challenging him to a single combat. But after all, what an exhibition is this, when viewed from the standpoint of a public character who aspires to be a great statesman and the Prime Minister of England. We have the clearest evidence that he started as a Liberal, and that when he perceived that he had a better chance of acquiring fame and Parliamentary honours he flings one set of principles to the winds and adopts another with as little thought or concern as if he were buying a pair of gloves, and threw down his first choice for another simply because a pair of a different colour better suited his purpose. If everyone else formed their political opinions in this fashion what would the world think of them? And yet here is a man worshipped by his party and held up to the gaze of coming generations as a model statesman, compared with whom the quiet, sober, consistent, sound undemonstrative politicians who form the real ballast in the ship of State are held to be nothing at all. Where, indeed, would have been the destinies of the nation if such leaders had not been checked and guided by that sound intellectual section of the people whose collective judgment at all critical periods indicates the course to be pursued, and often saves the nominal leader from committing the nation to irreparable blunders?

The greatest of all Liberal converts is a man of whom everybody who is familiar with the part he has played on the stage of politics during the last fifty years must speak with becoming diffidence. He must be a bold man indeed who ventures to declare that Mr. William Ewart Gladstone is not a patriot and has truckled to foreign Powers. Yet there are such men, and we have heard them revile him and denounce his Government as a cowardly, peace-at-any-price Administration that would lay the honour of the country in the dust. Have such men looked into his face and seen the determination and the conscious power that is resolved not to be moved by the cry of the trader, who would plunge the people into a war any day, if by doing so he could increase his own gains? John Bull is nothing if he is not a fighter. He loves to fight for the sake of fighting. The difference between such a John Bull and a fighting statesman is, that the latter thinks first and, if necessary, fights afterwards; while the former very often fights first and when the damage is done he thinks what a fool he has been. The class of John Bull to which we refer presented their doubled fists to our cousins on the other side of the Atlantic when they made their Alabama claims, and wanted to fight them without thinking. Our Jingo friends were fortunately not in power, or we might have had something very serious to think about after the fight they would no doubt on that occasion have done their best to involve us in. The real general, whether military or political, is not the one who is successful in the greatest number of fights, but the one who is successful the oftenest without fighting. If the last word has been said; the final offer which a country can make without sacrificing its honour, has been made; depend upon it, few Prime Ministers, not even Beaconsfield himself, could fight like Mr. Gladstone. Anyone who has looked him full in the face does not need to be told that. All such random talk, in fact, as Jingoes indulge in about the truckling of the Gladstone Ministries to foreign Powers is nothing better than the blatant rubbish of uninformed mediocrity, which is incapable of arresting attention by any other means than that of abusing men who are as far above some of them both intellectually and morally as the sun is above a pancake. No, we live in an age which is approaching, if it has not already crossed the border line, beyond which the leading nations will, whenever it is possible, substitute moral for material warfare; arbitration for gunpowder. Every period of great change produces the man to bring it about. Mr. Gladstone has been, during his two periods of Prime Ministership, standing at the parting of the ways to direct the stream from the material into the moral channel. With a nation which is a fierce and a fighting nation such a task is no easy one when a large section of the people are awakened by a feeling that their honour is at stake. But he has succeeded in making them think first on more than one occasion, and we venture to think the number is daily diminishing of those who regret they could not overpower him and his party.

Mr. Gladstone was returned to Parliament in December, 1832, in the Conservative interest, for Newark. After studying for the Bar for over six years he petitioned to have his name removed, having decided to enter the arena of politics. From the time of his appointment to a Junior Lordship of the Treasury, in 1834, his mind began gradually to perceive that the cause he had espoused was the wrong one, and that his mission was to carry to the front the banner upon which was inscribed the principles of Liberalism. On one question after the other he found himself opposed to his friends, until in

16

February, 1851, he separated himself from the Conservative party.

The slow conversion of Mr. Gladstone from the principles which he professed when he entered public life is well described in the following extract, which appeared in the 'Fortnightly Review' for November, 1884:

" The contrast between Mr. Gladstone and Mr. Bright is even more strongly marked than that between Mr. Gladstone and Sir Robert Peel. As he now draws towards the end of his career Mr. Bright cannot be charged with having abandoned, violated, or withdrawn a single principle that he ever proclaimed. Not a flaw of inconsistency or blemish of self-contradiction is to be seen in his whole career. Others have come round to him; he has lived to behold the convictions, which he firmly embraced, and which were condemned as extravagant and absurd, incorporated in the accepted doctrines of the Liberal party and of all parties, and into the unquestioned traditions of English policy. But though Mr. Gladstone's record and retrospect are of the most opposite character, his mutations have never had anything in them of vacillation; they have partaken from the first of the nature of a slow growth, and have indicated the successive periods of an intellectual development. Slowly, but with the certainty of daybreak, his horizon has expanded. He has himself told us that when he entered public life he had but an imperfect sense of the ineffable blessings of liberty. This deficiency was not unnatural to one who had been brought up in the straitest school of authority and tradition, and who in early manhood was, in Macaulay's familiar words, 'the rising hope of the stern and unbending Tories.' As men rise on stepping-stones of their dead selves to higher things, so Mr. Gladstone has throughout his whole public life been engaged in bursting, and disentangling himself from the cerements of his dead faiths. Whether he would have been greater or less than he is but for this progressive movement of his mind may be questioned; it is certain that he is indebted to it for much of the power which he exercises over those who are associated with him, however remotely or indirectly, in public life. It is because Mr. Gladstone has been so consistently inconsistent, because the continuity of his views and beliefs has known such decisive, if slowly consummated, solutions, that he has carried with him so large a group of politicians, and so overwhelming a majority of the English people. The process of self-education has enabled him effectually to educate others. Those who have themselves learned slowly, at school or college, were declared by Dr. Arnold to make the best schoolmasters, because they could most easily place themselves in the position of unreceptive schoolboys. The wealth of words which Mr. Gladstone expends upon any proposal he introduces to the House of Commons; the variety of the points of view from which he looks at it; his minute weighing of every sort of counter-consideration; the nice and, as they may seem, the tedious and sophistical distinctions which he draws between shades of thought and forms of words—each of these reflects or suggests some experience of his own mental discipline. There are few objections to any policy or scheme of legislation which he has not appreciated, and which consequently he does not set himself to remove. For this reason he is in his treatment of public topics the least dogmatic of statesmen. Mr. Bright, who has neither receded from nor advanced beyond the tenets with which he first entered public life, cannot avoid a certain autocracy and absolutism in a statement of opinion. He has been troubled with no doubts, and even his fertile imagination can make little allowance for doubters. But it is to the doubters, the most illustrious of whom he himself has been, that Mr. Gladstone chiefly addresses himself. Hence the extraordinary complexity and comprehensiveness of his argumentation; hence what may be called the metaphysical quality in his eloquence, the subtle series of appeals to the consciousness of his hearers, which runs like an undertone through his most splendid orations, and which is perhaps the secret of their occasional verbosity, and even obscurity.

" Whatever history may say of Mr. Gladstone it will not say that he was a perfect leader of the House of Commons. He fails to be this for the very reasons which make him a great popular leader in the country. He understands more of man in the abstract than of man in the concrete ; more of the passions which sway humanity in the bulk than of the motives to which individuals are amenable, and the treatment to be applied to them. He is at his best when he is the exponent not so much of the policy of a party as of the ideas which animate that policy, and which touch the heart of nations. It was not till he had made his famous ' flesh-and-blood ' speech that Mr. Gladstone was really recognised as a great popular leader, and struck a responsive chord that still vibrates in the breasts of the English people. He had hitherto been best known as a financier, as the greatest Chancellor of the Exchequer England ever had, and as somewhat academic, narrow, and exclusive in his sympathies and tastes. But this phrase, to which additional effect was given by the glow of the language and the atmosphere of ideas associated with it, produced an instantaneous and almost electrical result. The place into which he may be then said to have leaped he has continued to hold. Notwithstanding his temporary retirement and the eclipse which, with the metropolitan public, his popularity suffered in the melodramatic days of Jingoism, events have conclusively shown that Mr. Gladstone surpasses all his contemporaries in his power of interpreting and placing himself at the head of public feeling when it is deeply moved. The Bulgarian atrocities supplied him with one of those opportunities exactly congenial to his character and gifts. His two Midlothian campaigns, whether in their oratorical labours or in the results that followed them, form a monument which supplies a fair measure of the greatness of the man. He took his stand upon general principles, upon those elementary ideas of justice, of humanity, which all can understand, and which he had, in his reply to Lord Palmerston thirty years earlier, during the Don Pacifico debate, clearly foreshadowed."

When such a man, without hesitation or faltering step; without turning to look back as if a doubt had entered his mind, continues over a series of years from 1851 to 1884 to march at first in the ranks and then at the head of the Liberal army, what can we think of the opinions of his opponents? What are we to think of the principles of a party who have had as opponents, consistently from the beginning to the end, such men as Bright and Cobden, whose teaching helped to put the great mind of the present Prime Minister from the wrong into the right track?

However much they may admire the man, every Tory and all Tory journals are naturally sore over the series of overwhelming defeats which they have suffered at his hands, and in reviewing, however briefly, his career and achievements his mistakes are sure to be made the most of by them, and many acts referred to as mistakes which were not so at all. On the occasion of Mr. Gladstone's seventy-fifth birthday the ' Standard ' wrote as follows : " Mr. Gladstone has always, in office or in Opposition, played a distinguished part. Of late years, indeed, so conspicuous has been his figure in the eyes of the nation that he has all but effaced his colleagues, and occupied the scene alone. We do not pretend that this is a healthy condition of things for the country, or for the party which Mr. Gladstone's personality holds together. But it is a tribute of no ordinary kind to the character of the leader. Judgments differ, and will differ greatly, as to the worth of the work which Mr. Gladstone has done, but as to the scale and quality of his achievements there can be no manner of dispute. He gives not only coherence but momentum to a combination of essentially discordant political atoms. He is not merely a dictator in the present hour, but he connects us, as no other living statesman does, with the past. It is not the easiest thing in the world to reconcile our present political courses with those even of the last generation ; but the persistence of Mr. Gladstone's influence gives the history of Liberalism whatever continuity it can claim. It is no peculiar reproach to him that he has gone from one party pole to another. Change of this kind is rather the rule than the exception in public life. The whole atmosphere of politics changes from cycle to cycle, and the statesman of delicate mould has often to try a new climate, in order to find free play for his energies. Mr. Gladstone, at any rate, if unfaithful to his earliest party vows, has been singularly true to himself."

We are here told that he gives " coherence and momentum to a combination of essentially discordant

political atoms." How is this statement to be recon-
ciled with the fact that the Liberal party remained in all
respects exactly the same during the period of his
retirement until he resumed his post of leader? What
also is gained by asserting that Mr. Gladstone's " influence gives the history of Liberalism whatever continuity
it can claim ?" This is as much as to say that without
him Liberal principles would cease to be, a statement
which could only be made by a writer who has looked
through his Tory spectacles at Liberalism so long, that
nothing that happens can make him see more than one
colour in politics, and that the colour of his own party.

Then we read in the same leading article the following :—" He will vindicate with all the fire of passion the
memory of his chief and friend, Sir Robert Peel, because
he is not sensible of any essential breach in the sympathies which once drew him to his side."

What he is, on the contrary, really sensible of is, that
Sir Robert Peel did exactly the same thing, after taking
longer to think about it, than he did himself, viz. to
renounce his faith in political principles which he found
out were wrong.

The ' Standard ' writes :—" Again, Mr. Gladstone has
become, step by step, the mainstay of Radical hopes,
without losing at any given time his touch with the
body of Constitutional tradition. This is partly due, no
doubt, to the fact that the Radicals are, for the present,
content to be Opportunists. But the Prime Minister
would not serve their turn if he did not to a very
material extent adopt and give effect to their views. .

" How are we to account for this odd conjunction?
Very simply. ' Greed of power '—the instinct assigned
by people who think crudely and speak uncharitably—
will not explain it. No. The secret of Mr. Gladstone's

adaptability lies in the breadth of his sympathies and the fervour of his belief."

Surely Mr. Gladstone could not be expected to give effect to Tory views and thus help to satisfy a greed for power which was persistently manifested by the Tories themselves, in every form of obstruction until the House of Lords itself was in imminent danger of being disestablished.

The following passage from the same leading article is a thrust at a too powerful opponent under cover of false flattery :—" It is the right road because it is the road on which he has set foot; and so he goes on treading it with the ecstasy and exaltation of a political pilgrim; while thousands of the devout ones, whose only guides are burning tapers, who never dream of looking at the stars, press behind, nothing doubting but that he whom they follow must be marching straight to the shrine. For the very tendencies—be they virtues or failings—which enable Mr. Gladstone to become the instrument of what he deems to be the people's will, make him the very object of their homage and the depository of their superstitious confidence. He sincerely loves his country, and, loving it, clings reverently to its past. But he trusts no less the England of to-day."

If it is " the right road because he has set his foot," why did he not remain on the ground on which he *first* set his foot ? How can he be said to cling " reverently to the past," when we learn from a writer in the ' Fortnightly Review' whom we have quoted, that " as men rise on stepping-stones of their dead selves to higher things, so Mr. Gladstone has *throughout his whole public life* been engaged in bursting and disentangling himself from the cerements of his dead faiths ?"

We make one more extract, to show in our opinion

how prejudiced is the mind of this critic. He says :— " There are in Parliament, and out of it, many who have as profound and as unselfish an enthusiasm for the welfare of men as Mr. Gladstone has, but none surrender themselves to the passing emotions as he does. They have not the magnificent defects of his genius. Their conscience imposes on them limitations where his conscience leaves his hands free. Everyone knows the result. Mr. Gladstone makes all sorts of blunders; but his name is still the one great name in the ear of the people. Others may point out how grievous are his errors; but he remains Mr. Gladstone still."

In our opinion if there *is* a man who has declined to "surrender himself to the passing emotions" it is he. Take the case of the Alabama claims. He and nearly all his supporters stood firm for arbitration, while the Conservatives were boiling over with "emotion" in favour of resistance à *outrance*. When a handful of British soldiers got worsted at Majuba Hill through the incompetency of a general, emotional people were for sending a force to annihilate the Boers; but he "imposed limits on his conscience" and saved the country from an act which would have been looked back upon with regret and shame.

The following from the 'Daily News' is much nearer the truth :

"It has always been an intellectual necessity with Mr. Gladstone, and it is an honorable characteristic of him, to find a basis of principle for the opinions and policy of the moment. Sir Robert Peel's Conservatism, the shifty Conservatism of the hour, the Conservatism of compromises and practical expedients, certainly did not rest on any basis of principle. In trying to find one for it, Mr. Gladstone was of necessity led to formulate those

maxims of government which deceived Macaulay into
the idea that in him stern and unbending Toryism had
its predestined leader. This habit of mind, associated
with a large and variously stored intellect, and with
quick and sympathetic perception, carries with it the
corrective of the casual errors with which tradition,
training, and early association have hampered it."

The following is the testimony of the ' Times ' to Mr.
Gladstone's abilities as a statesman on his attaining his
seventy-fifth year in 1884 :

" To-day Mr. Gladstone completes his seventy-fifth
year, and it may be said without reserve or misgiving
that the anniversary is consecrated by the congratula-
tions and kindly wishes of a whole people. True it is
that few Ministers have aroused in the breasts of opponents so much bitterness of feeling as the present
Premier ; but the very strength of this sentiment is a
testimony to the powers of the man, and, outside of the
arena of political strife, it has, we rejoice to believe, no
prevailing force. Englishmen, we trust, know how to
fight their battles in a manly and loyal spirit without
rancour and without spleen ; they easily forget and forgive defeats of which they have no reason to be ashamed,
and they are always ready to honour the high qualities
of a stout and valiant antagonist. So we are sure the
overwhelming majority of Mr. Gladstone's party foes
will join cordially with his followers in wishing him joy
on the attainment of an almost patriarchal age, not only
without any apparent diminution of his physical and
intellectual energies, but with a positive increase both in
his prescriptive authority and in his active influence over
other minds. There have been Ministers who at as
advanced an age have retained their political ascendency,
and ruled with a sway as unchallenged and overmaster-

ing as that of Mr. Gladstone himself. When Lord
Palmerston came into power for the last time, after the
downfall of the Derby-Disraeli Government in 1859, he
had reached his seventy-fifth year, and, as it proved, he
had still before him a long period of tranquil and uncon-
tested supremacy. But Lord Palmerston, from 1860 to
1865, was content to shape the policy of the empire and
to dominate the House of Commons with a kind of
Olympian *nonchalance*, graceful and genial, but delegat-
ing to younger and more ardent spirits the strenuous
labours of official creativeness and Parliamentary conflict. It may be that this method has its advantages,
and, indeed, Lord Palmerston's reign, calm and un-
eventful as it was, may claim the credit of having
nowhere injured, impaired, or brought into jeopardy the
Imperial interests of England. But for impressive
effect on the popular imagination it cannot be brought
into comparison with Mr. Gladstone's later career. In
spite of his years the Prime Minister is still not only the
mainstay of his party in council; he is their foremost
champion in the political battle. The admiration which
his individuality inspires is the sheet-anchor of Liberal
hopes. At every critical moment, when alarming events
have to be explained away, when dangerous combinations
have to be faced, when formidable arguments have to be
grappled with, it is to the Prime Minister himself, and
to none of his subordinates, able as they may be, that
the Liberal party, the House of Commons, and, we may
add, the country look for the decisive blow.

"It is not uncommon to find in men of Mr. Gladstone's age the mellow and tempered wisdom of Nestor,
but this is not the Prime Minister's peculiar gift. What
is rare is to find a statesman of seventy-five from whom
is expected, not in vain, the sleepless energy of Achilles

and the versatile craft of Ulysses.   Never have Mr.
Gladstone's singular gifts been more strikingly displayed than in the year now drawing to a close.   As a
master of debate for every purpose—for the exposition
of complicated details, for the defence of untenable positions, for averting inconvenient inquiries, for overwhelming criticism, reasonable or unreasonable, in a
torrent of rhetoric, for inexhaustible ingenuities of dia-
lectic—the Prime Minister has during the earlier and the
later session almost surpassed himself.   Mistakes there
have been in his policy—as we have frankly pointed out
—many of them gross enough to have brought a strong
Government to shame and ruin, but Mr. Gladstone has
averted disaster and again and again turned defeat into
victory."

CHAPTER X.

It is held by some authorities that the cultivated but inexperienced members of society find fewer opportunities for employment as servants of the State under the modern representative system than was the case formerly. In support of this view Conservatives maintain that there is less chance now for men like Lord Chatham, William Pitt, Addington, the college friend of the second Pitt, Fox, the third son of the first Lord Holland, Canning, also a friend of the second Pitt, &c., than there was in the days when those men flourished. Such a contention is no doubt correct, and the reason is that, instead of the great families selecting their own friends and dependents as they naturally would when they governed the country, the best men are now appointed without reference to their social position. In other words the system which obtains in the Civil Service is now adopted in respect of nearly all political appointments which the responsible Ministers have to fill up from time to time. It is quite natural that those in power should lean in the direction of asking for lieutenants among their own relations and friends, whereas the interests of the State imperatively demand that the best men should be called into its service, entirely regardless of other considerations than the full qualification to discharge the duties of the office. Whether competitive examination is by itself a sufficient guarantee that the best men are chosen is perhaps an open question; but at all events the physical condition of the candidates being approved of, there can be no question that intellectual ability and experience should be allowed to decide the rest. The next point is, who is to decide which are the best qualified intellectually? Ministers have no time to decide such matters. They should therefore be left to duly constituted and qualified authorities. The following remarks, which are very much to the point, formed part of a leading article in the 'Times' on January 1st, 1885 :

"In its eagerness for legislative changes, some good and some bad, it is earnestly to be hoped that the democracy will not forget the paramount importance of good administration. It is quite possible for a people hailed as sovereign to be at the mercy of a cluster of petty tyrants disguised as its servants, and to find the real business of government mismanaged and neglected while it is devising means for making its will theoretically absolute. Of all the changes that may be signalized as desirable at the present day, none is more urgent than one which shall restore the responsibility of public servants, whether Parliamentary or permanent. That responsibility has dwindled to an empty phrase, and in some important departments of the public service elaborate arrangements exist apparently for no other end than to make it impossible to bring home mismanagement however gross to any man in particular. Under the new arrangements there will probably be a rush of candidates for place and power, some of whom may fail to offer those guarantees for independence and incorruptibility which we have been accustomed to think that we possess at present. But it must be admitted that if such men find their way in considerable numbers into the public service the path will have been opened to them by the failure of the aristocratic system to provide energetic and capable administrators. The virtues of an aristocracy are essentially militant. From it we have a right to expect keen susceptibility to slights upon the national dignity, careful maintenance of the public interests, and anxious vigilance for the public security. These qualities are conspicuously absent from some of the men whom aristocratic traditions place at the head of affairs, and the defence of the country's vast interests and much-coveted position must apparently be undertaken by the democracy for itself. Unless the education of the people is very much more backward than we believe it to be, we do not think that men sprung from the people, reflecting its sympathies and recognising its wants, will approve of the treatment recently accorded to our colonies. To the hardened official or the aristocratic chief the colonies are simply a nuisance to be abated as much as possible. To the people they are their own flesh and blood, Englishmen of like passions with themselves, relatives and friends bound together by ties of interest and affection, customers more steady and faithful than any foreigners, members of an empire which alone redresses the balance of power and dignity sorely depressed by the rise and growth of gigantic rival States. The advent of the democracy to power will, we believe, be marked by a more just, more generous, and more far-seeing policy towards our kin beyond the sea than is embodied in the recent actions of the Colonial Office. Nor are we less hopeful that in our relations with other nations the English democracy will be found more straightforward in its actions, more ready to define its wants, more tenacious of its own dignity, and more mindful of the just claims of others than this country has recently shown itself. Indeed, when we consider how tamely the present Parliament has endured evils which it could at any moment have terminated, and how in Egypt, in the Soudan, in South Africa and in the Pacific it has allowed the country's interests to be neglected, its friends estranged, its money wasted, and its dignity lowered, we cannot but feel that the times are ripe for such change in the governing power as the nation is able to effect."

As regards the Civil Service, candidates for admission are tested by a body of examiners, and candidates for seats in the House of Commons should on the same system be tested, but by a still larger tribunal, that of the nation itself. In a word, a man's ability to occupy a seat in the House of Commons ought absolutely to depend upon his individual ability to force himself into recognition outside the House of Commons. However good a man's judgment may be, however sound may be the formation of his political opinions, he has really no title to sit in the House of Commons unless he can speak; and his ability to speak better, more wisely, and more to the point than other people should be the measure of his title to a seat in that House.

In our day legislators who exercise that function on the ground of hereditary claim do so more by courtesy than because they are duly qualified legislators. This is well understood; but it is no less well understood that the political opinions of those hereditary legislators who do not happen to be men of intellectual distinction carry very little weight in a division, because their opinions are known to be biassed by traditions whose roots are carried back in many cases through a long line of ancestors. In these circumstances, in order to ensure just and impartial legislation, and at the same time preserve a great and noble institution, it has been found necessary to transfer the real legislative power to the Chamber whose members can only have a voice by reason of a qualification which has been duly tested.

In the times in which we live it is more important than it used to be to ensure the House of Commons being recruited from men of worldly experience. When this empire was being formed a young and brilliant but inexperienced statesman had a better chance of succeeding than he would have now. For a man to be of real use in the House of Commons in our day his knowledge and experience of the rights and wants of the people should be great, and the more completely tested his political opinions the better. Without, in fact, wide experience and matured opinions upon the questions of the day, the most brilliant genius is of little use.

Aristotle says : *" Young men understand geometry, &c., but are not wise or prudent, because wisdom is concerned about particulars which are derived from experience, and for experience a lapse of time is requisite." He says that a young man is not able to understand social science, for it relates to human life and conduct, of which he is inexperienced. In Ret. II 12, § 14 he says that " young men always violate the maxim μηδὲν ἄγαν— ne quid nimis. They love in excess and hate in excess, and do everything in excess. For the same reason they think they know everything, and assert it with confidence." Hence the precept of Cicero : " Est igitur adolescentis majores natu vereri, exque his deligere optimos et probatissimos, quorum consilio atque auctori-

* Sir G. C. Lewis, ' Influence of Authority,' &c., p. 79, note.

tate nitatur.   Ineuntis autem ætatis insatia senum
constituenda et regenda prudentia est " (De Off. I, 34).

Legislators who are responsible for the laws of a great
country should be men, all will allow, who devote themselves to the task with an anxious desire to assist in
framing the best laws possible.   Young men, however
clever, will fail in this unless aided by the required experience.   Experience of the world and of the various
requirements of different classes of people are essential
qualifications.   Young hereditary legislators will in very
few cases have had a training which brings them up to that
standard.   On the contrary, they are brought up in many
cases to look upon a life of pleasure and leisure as the chief
object of existence, and when they are old enough to
take their seat in the Upper Chamber they are bored by
debates they do not understand, and vote against all
measures which in the least degree tend to weaken the
political power of the class to which they belong, no
matter how much justice demands it in the interests of
the community as a whole.   There are no doubt some
noteworthy exceptions to this rule, but our contention
is sound enough to justify the conclusion that admission
to the House of Peers on the hereditary principle is a
system hardly likely to be tolerated much longer.   Every
fresh conflict between the two houses, such as that over
the 1884 Reform Bill, is another nail in the coffin of the
hereditary principle.

The mass of the Members of the House of Commons
will, we believe, under a democracy, become more
and more efficient legislators, and in proportion as the
constituencies become enlightened so will they choose
worthier representatives.   As the self-respect of each
elector increases so in proportion should his anxiety increase to be represented by the best man in all respects.

The capricious choice which has now and again brought into the House such men as Kenealy and others of that type must inevitably in time give way to wiser counsels, as the status of the voters improves and their sense of what is fitting, sober, and decent becomes stronger.

There are many rising men at the present time who have the stuff in them of which Prime Ministers are made; but will anyone venture to maintain that had Addington, Spencer Perceval, the Duke of Portland, or Viscount Goderich lived in our time that either would have stood the least chance of becoming Prime Minister? If we look down the list of Prime Ministers who have followed these men we shall see that, with perhaps the exception of the Duke of Wellington, who was a first-rate square man in a round hole from the beginning of his tenure of that office, all, without exception, were well fitted to perform the responsible duties of Prime Minister, their respective fitness only varying in degree.

Mr. T. E. Kebbel in the December, 1884, number of the ' National Review,' has an article upon the " mediocrity " Tory Prime Ministers whose names we have mentioned, and it is worth while to observe how he attempts to throw the blame for some of the Tory blunders which they committed on the Whigs; but those who will take the trouble to examine the facts for themselves will see how little foundation there is for the disparaging statements he makes. The article we refer to is entitled " Tory Prime Ministers: II. The ' mediocrities.' Lord Liverpool, the Duke of Portland, Mr. Perceval." Mr. Addington and Viscount Goderich might well have been added. With the exception of Pitt, in fact, the Tory Prime Ministers of the present century were all more or less incapable down to the time of the passing of the first Reform Bill, and we fully endorse

Mr. Kebbel's views that they were mediocrities. It is
no wonder, with men at the head of affairs whom the
Tories themselves sneer at and call mediocrities, that
the country bestirred itself and took the management of
the Government out of such incapable hands.   One
mediocre Tory Prime Minister following another equally
incapable was enough of itself to precipitate reform
which should put an end to such a miserable state of
things.   With the object of discrediting the Whigs Mr.
T. E. Kebbel endeavours to throw the blame upon them
of not having availed themselves of the opportunity presented by the battle of Eylau to crush the power of
Napoleon.   Now let us see what the Liberals had to do
with the famous but most disastrous military expedition
known to modern warfare.   The only period of Liberal
rule from Pitt's time down to that of Earl Grey, who
took office in 1830, was when Lord Grenville was Prime
Minister, for one year and forty-eight days, from the
11th of February, 1806.   That Government was formed
as is well known by a coalition of "all the talents,"
under Lord Grenville and Mr. Fox, and was held together until the King arbitrarily dismissed Lord Grenville.   While this Ministry were in office there was
obviously no opportunity of crushing Napoleon after the
battle of Eylau, for the simple reason that Eylau was not
fought till February 7th—8th in 1807, immediately after
which the Duke of Portland, was appointed Prime
Minister.   The Duke of Portland being a member of
Pitt's party, and consequently a Tory, the responsibility
of checking Napoleon's career lay with them.   In these
circumstances it is highly entertaining to read in Mr.
Kebbel's article that " they (the Liberals) had been in
long enough to work irreparable mischief.   Bent at once
on reversing the whole policy of their predecessors, they

lost the golden opportunity for destroying the power of Napoleon which presented itself after the battle of Eylau, when, if the 50,000 British troops held in readiness by Lord Castlereagh to be thrown in a body on any point in the enemy's position where their action seemed most likely to be decisive, had been landed in the north of Germany to operate on the French communications, his ruin was apparently inevitable." The real fact is that the Liberals, owing to the interference of the King and his supporters, never had a chance to govern the country on the principles which, when they did get a real hold of power, brought such prosperity and so many blessings to the country. Mr. Kebbel probably holds the Liberals responsible for driving the American colonies into revolt during the Administration of Lord North, a Minister who sought to save himself from impeachment by throwing himself into the arms of the Whigs. No, the real responsibility for the disastrous events following the battle of Eylau lies at the door of the Tories, and to attempt to make it out otherwise is one of the many instances of the way in which Tory writers endeavour to cast discredit upon their opponents and wreak their revenge upon the party whose triumph has for so long excluded them from office and power. Lord Castlereagh did, we admit, arrange what is known as the Walcheren expedition, but how the Liberals can be held responsible for the dilatoriness which resulted in the unprecedented disaster which attended it, few mortal men we should think could imagine. After saddling the Liberals with alienating Russia from Great Britain, with being responsible for the battle of Friedland, the Treaty of Tilsit and the placing of Europe at Napoleon's feet, Mr. Kebbel states that "the Liberal policy at this juncture of our affairs is computed to have cost this

country something like four hundred millions sterling."
There is not a shadow of foundation for this statement.
It is not only wrong, but the reverse is the truth.   Up
to the passing of the first Reform Bill the Liberals
cannot be said to have exercised any real political power
in the country at all, consequently the accumulation of
debt up to that period must have been the work of the
Tories.   During the Administration of Lord North one
hundred and twenty millions of debt were incurred in
the American war, and the additions made during the
French war, which constitute the great bulk of the debt,
were incurred under Tory rule.   The real fact is that—
the question of the value received for that expenditure
apart—the debt has been in the main incurred by the
Tories and in the main paid off so far by the Liberals.
Farther on in Mr. Kebbel's article we come upon the
following amusing statement :—" Toryism, in one form
or another, had now been predominant for exactly forty-
two years.   Within that period the English Tories had
lost America, but they had saved Europe."   We may
here parenthetically remark that Wellington and his
soldiers saved Europe in spite of the blundering of Mr.
Perceval and Lord Liverpool in the matter of supplies,
which as Mr. Kebbel says, the Duke complained of as
the result of the " little dirty feelings in Ministers which
had hitherto impeded the contest."   How far the Tory
party through the medium of their statesmen saved
Europe is further testified to in Mr. Kebbel's article,
where he says that the Duke " adds that he doubts if
they had either the inclination or the nerve to do what
they ought."   Mr. Kebbel continues, " They had stood
forward as the advocates and representatives of Parliamentary Reform, Roman Catholic Emancipation and
Free Trade."   Everyone knows enough of the origin of

all three of these reforms and the means by which they
were carried, to render it necessary again to deal with
them here. We shall content ourselves by remarking
that to put forward such statements is to make a bur-
lesque of history. Pitt, as we have stated elsewhere, no
doubt desired reform in each of these three directions,
but he was met by the violent opposition of the Tories.
He "stood forward as the advocate and representative"
of those reforms, which proves, not that the Tories
desired them, but that he was at heart a Liberal.
Whatever artifices they may resort to to prove the contrary, there can be little doubt in the mind of any man
who knows how obstinate and persistent has been the
opposition of the Tory party to almost every kind of
reform, the end of which has been that the people shall
govern themselves through their own chosen representatives, that the support given by the Tories to the
absolute monarchies was given with the same object and
intention as that which gave rise to the manifestation of
their implacable hostility towards every rising English
statesman who ranged himself on the side of the
Liberals.

What has happened as regards what we may call the
generals of our political army is also to be seen in their
lieutenants down to the rank and file; and further, the
improvement inside the House of Commons has been
much more than surpassed by the improvement outside.
Hence the change in the quality of the Prime Ministers
which has taken place since the government of the
country passed from the Conservatives to the Liberals.
Did the House of Commons presided over by the Duke of
Portland, Henry Addington, Spencer Perceval, and Viscount Goderich, as Prime Ministers, reflect "the express
image of the feelings of the nation?"   No one will ven-

ture for a moment to maintain that it did. It reflected "the express image of the feelings" of the aristocracy who placed them there. Burke said, " The virtue, spirit, and essence of a House of Commons consists in its being the express image of the feelings of a nation." Unhappily what he saw the House of Commons ought to be was unattainable in his day. It has taken eighty years to remove all the obstacles which stood in the way of such a consummation when Henry Addington was elevated to a position for which, had he lived now, he would have acknowledged himself that he was wholly unfitted. In our day the people are so well posted in political affairs, and follow so closely upon the course of events as they happen both at home and abroad, that a candidate for a seat in the House of Commons can no longer aspire to that honour under the impression that he will be admitted without his abilities and his knowledge being duly tested.

When the extension of the franchise has been carried to the limit marked out in the Reform Bill of 1884, the next reform will be in the direction of improving the formation of political opinion ; for it must be admitted by all reasonable people that the methods by which a large proportion of voters arrive at the opinions they hold are even now faulty in the extreme. That an improvement is, however, steadily making headway is conclusively shown by the fact that Prime Ministers of the stamp of the four we have referred to, who filled that office in the first quarter of this century, are as impossible in the present day as Members of the House of Commons who are the mere close-borough nominees of some lord or duke. Whether the Government goes wrong, or individuals even in large numbers vote against measures which ought to be passed, or in favour of measures that ought not to be passed, it is tolerably certain that in a large number of cases, if the right thing is not done, the wrong one is avoided, through the influence of a section of the community—often the least demonstrative, the seldomest seen on platform or in office—who think, but do not talk, until the time comes when the right thing is said in the fewest words. With all his rough cynical uncouthness, such a one was Thomas Carlyle; and there are many in that respect like him who are not so well known, because they are not eminent writers; but when the time does come the greatest of our politicians seek counsel and guidance from such men as these. How many and various are the opinions we hear expressed on the topics of the hour, and how little do those who express them as a rule take the trouble to test and examine the data upon which they are founded !

If the composition of the House of Commons may be looked upon as fairly complete, now that its Members are chosen by the householder in county as well as borough, it furnishes the political student with an interesting subject for reflection. If historical record on the subject can be trusted we, who think ourselves so highly civilised, have only in reality got as far, as regards the principles upon which the political opinions of our people are represented, as the small city republics of antiquity. The only difference would seem to be that the habits and customs of our time are different, as well as the machinery by which the wishes of the represented are made known. But the system is more or less identical. Instead of every citizen attending a local centre as in our time, and his views being represented through a delegate to a grand central Parliament, each one exercised a direct influence in those small commonwealths. The views and desires of each one would naturally under such circumstances have a better chance of being made known and carried into effect; and greater perfection of government would seem therefore to be attainable. But civilization could not reach such a degree of development in all respects as in our day, for the same reason that peasant proprietorship could never make the earth yield so well or on such a proportionate scale as under a system of farming which enables a large and wealthy proprietor to apply the scientific methods of cultivation known in these times.

Now that the representative system has been pushed so far as practically to include all adult males on the register of voters, in what direction is the next improvement of the governing machine to be made? We are accustomed to read in the journals of the day frequent complaints against Ministers presiding at the Foreign Office and at the Colonial Office for alleged negligence, as, for instance, with reference to the late German annexations. Supposing, for the sake of argument, the case is proved against the Minister, and that the interests of the country suffered owing to carelessness or indifference, which is quite possible under the circumstances of a moribund Parliament, of the indisposition of the Minister, or of the possibly peculiar political views of the gentleman entrusted with the Presidency of the Foreign or Colonial Office, there is, we believe, in such a case practically no redress. This has been admitted. Such being the result of mistakes, the obvious remedy seems to be that a permanent Parliamentary Committee should preside over such department, and not one Minister only. The Cabinet is supposed to be responsible for the despatches issuing from each department, and it is understood that no important step is taken without the sanction of the whole Cabinet, but the very German annexations to which we refer prove that the Cabinet cannot possibly meet and discuss every such question which arises ; nor can the vigilance of the permanent officials in each department be expected to be exercised with that watchful care that might be expected from a Member of Parliament who was associated with the Cabinet Minister and upon a Parliamentary level with him, which compelled the nominal chief to listen to and act upon suggestions made by such colleagues. The institution of grand committees of recent years, for example, proves that the Parliamentary machine broke down under the strain, and the German annexations proves that the strain upon the Cabinet Ministers has also caused the system under which they collectively work to break down. Moreover, these are by no means the only instances which show that the head and front of our Parliamentary and representative system needs widening considerably. The empire is for ever enlarging ; the constituencies have been enlarged, perhaps, to their utmost capacity, and it is reasonable to assume that the work demanded of Parliament will grow also, and the number of persons to do the work must therefore likewise be increased. The head of one man, no matter who he is, cannot continuously, day, week, month, and year after year, conduct the business of the Foreign or Colonial Office of an empire like ours without falling into errors which it is not too much to say ought not to be allowed to occur. The necessity for secrecy surely is not so great but that three, four, or, if need be, half a dozen Members of Parliament can be admitted to the counsels of the Cabinet Minister in charge for the time being. If there were, say, six deputy Foreign Ministers meeting twice or three times a week, authorised to read

all despatches and all answers, and to keep a watch over
the business of the department, there is little doubt that
many mistakes would be avoided that now give rise to
much unnecessary trouble and irritation with foreign
Powers.   If any nominal chief of a department objected
to take office under such circumstances someone else
must be found, and there are no doubt plenty of capable
candidates.   When the affairs of an empire like that of
Great Britain are at stake no question of personal sus-
ceptibilities can be entertained.

It has been quite plain and evident on many occasions
for years past that Ministers have fenced with the House
of Commons night after night in order to shield themselves from the consequences of blunders which not
only ought not to have been made, but which when made
should have been rectified at once.   Under the system
we propose, the secrecy which a Cabinet observes to avoid
exposure and possible ejectment from office would be
impossible.   If the deputy Foreign and Colonial Ministers had a mandate from Parliament under authority of
a special law passed for the purpose, they would discharge
their duties under no such fear of losing their places, as
is felt by the Minister under existing circumstances.
On the contrary their reputations would suffer if they
did not bring before the notice of Parliament questions
which were being mismanaged, and there can be no
doubt that the mere knowledge that such would be the inevitable consequence of blundering would go a long way
towards preventing it.   Supposing that the new constituencies are faithfully represented in the House of Commons
and that its composition may thus be considered as fairly
perfect as it can be, short of a selection by *plébiscite*, it
is imperatively necessary that we should devise means for
making that machine do its work more efficiently in the

future than it has in the past. There is the all-important question of liberty of speech. Liberty of speech in Parliament, and freedom in the expression of opinion, are among the grandest achievements of modern civilization. Both for offensive and defensive purposes they may be justly described as the palladium of our liberties. But in the hands of wilful obstructionists and of wrong-headed Socialists, they are weapons whose blows recoil upon the system which has created them with very damaging effect. All who have watched the proceedings of Parliament of late years and have followed the debates must be well aware that much valuable time is wasted that proved mediocrity may have its say, and that the avowed enemies of the empire may obstruct legislation and paralyze the Parliamentary machine. If Members of Parliament of this stamp continue to be returned, the people of this country are surely not so apathetic and blind to their own interests as to permit them to continue to fritter away valuable time with frivolous discussions, or by simply talking against time to wear out, worry, and irritate the real hardworking and efficient Members. If freedom of speech is to be purchased at such a price as we have seen has had occasionally to be paid for it of late years, when the House of Commons has been kept sitting all through the night, then instead of its being the palladium of our liberties we should almost be justified in asserting that it was the palladium of our follies. Not to reform the system on which the debates are thus conducted and controlled, is in fact to connive at the degeneration of liberty of speech and opinion into license. It would be invidious no doubt to classify Members of Parliament according to their rank as debaters, and to allow each class so many minutes in which to deliver what they had to say, but the question

is, should anything at all be allowed to stand in the way
of reforming the present system? We are decidedly of
opinion that it should not. Why then could it not be
agreed that Cabinet and ex-Cabinet Ministers were not to
be limited as to time, but that all other speakers were
to be limited say to twenty minutes, unless the House
signified its assent that the speaker should continue?
What objection can there be to such an innovation any
more than there was to the ballot? For years timid
politicians thought the ballot was going to ruin the
country, and their fears have been shown to have rested
on nothing at all. We venture to predict that many
years will not elapse before the business of the House
of Commons will have fallen into such hopeless arrear
that a bridle, in the sense we have suggested, will have
to be put upon the tongues of speakers who now waste
a great part of the session with irrelevant arguments,
and who have nothing new to say upon any question that
has not already been said before the debate reaches their
level in the House. So far as we are aware all
the foremost Liberal statesmen of our time and of
times gone by, whose position has not warped their
judgment, have aimed at one grand consummation
in their endeavours to perfect the science of government. We cannot expect any progress to be made in
the direction so long pursued by this country, by a nation,
for instance, like Russia. The Government of Russia
has in principle for generations been in a hopeless
state of decay. It is just kept so far from falling into
ruin like the dead body of the king which Tennyson
speaks of in such profoundly suggestive and majestic
lines, because the light of the truth has not been able
to touch it.

> " Like that dead body of the king,
> Found lying with its urns and ornaments,
> Which, at a touch of light an air of heaven,
> Slipped into ashes, and was found no more."

The Russian army may be likened to the coffin in which the dead body of the Russian Government is encased. Nihilism is the corsair, who with other motives than those of plunder, is destined to lift with stealthy hand the lid which stands between the truth and what is false. The touch of light, the air of heaven, is daily eating its way through the Russian army, and when that, the last stronghold of a mephitic despotism, bends and yields, all will disappear for ever—save the urns and ornaments, the stately trappings, and the ghastly memory of a *régime* which eked out its consumptive existence upon steel and ignorance, fear and corruption. The future of the representative body of the foremost civilised nations must be so constituted in the end as that no single individual shall be allowed to exercise his uncontrolled will. Where such a system prevails it can only be during construction. The German empire is a case in point. The founder of an empire is no ordinary person, and while he lives may be entitled to exercise extraordinary powers; but the certain demonstration at some time or other of his fallability is of itself the proof that the only safe and just system of government is that which is founded on the sense and will of the people, duly ascertained by the press and public meetings, and carried into effect by the appointed instruments or Ministers.

The German empire is scarcely out of the builder's hands, and the retention of the architect in his office is therefore considered justifiable. But we have almost daily evidence that, instead of now proceeding to perfect the machine which shall govern his new empire, Prince Bismarck's ambition finds insufficient sustenance by playing such a part. The pleasure and satisfaction in seeing the ship of the State move in obedience to his word of command to the man at the helm is too great to be handed over to the people, and consequently, out of deference to the great services he has rendered, his whim must be indulged, and the political education of the community over which he presides retarded until he disappears from the scene.

We are well aware of the defects of our political machinery, but we are also happy in the knowledge that every day with us sees some change, however trifling, in the direction of improvement. With us the object is that, whoever are the men who rise to the highest places, the machinery of government shall be so perfected that no single individual shall be able, no matter how eminent he is, to carry into effect a policy in any direction that is not fully sanctioned by the people. This is the highest ideal of government, and one to which every nation should aspire.

Since it is recognised on all hands that we should strive for a more perfect government of the country, in accordance with the wishes of the mass of the people, and not in accordance with the views of any one man or set of men, the difficulty of dealing with foreign negotiations involving deliberations in secret might be met by the Executive Government taking the House of Commons into their confidence by holding sittings from which reporters for the press were excluded. The precaution of enlarging the Council Chamber to the limits of the House of Commons itself would reduce to a minimum the possible risks of the country being committed to engagements with foreign Powers which the people might not approve.

It may be a fine stroke of business for Mr. Disraeli to have Cyprus in his pocket as a present for the nation in return for having kept Russia out of Constantinople; but the question is, What does the acceptance of such a gift involve? If it deprives this country of the right to protest against other Powers appropriating to our disadvantage any bits of land about the world they can lay their hands on, instead of such an acquisition being a gain, it may turn out that we have established a precedent of the most damaging description.

CHAPTER XI.

THE question of whether we are to have two Legislative Chambers or one in the future has been so much discussed since the opposition of the House of Lords to the Bill of 1884 for the extension of the franchise to county householders, that it is certain to occupy the serious attention of politicians as time goes on, and may again assume an acute phase any day should the Peers manifest a disposition obstinately to oppose the popular will. This being the case we may usefully anticipate a revival of the strong feeling shown when the last Reform Bill was under discussion, and endeavour to reason out the question whether, as Mr. John Morley said, the House of Lords had better be "mended or ended."

Whether or not the people have degenerated since the time of the Greeks is a question about which different opinions are no doubt entertained; but the history of those times, at all events, furnishes us with some examples which are worth recalling for the information of some at least of our legislators of the present day. One of the principles of action with the Greeks was for the minority when once outvoted to co-operate with the majority in carrying out in practice a measure on which they had been defeated. The aims of those who advocate what is known as proportional representation are at variance with what the Greeks looked upon as just in principle, for the simple reason no doubt that the Greeks did not consider that minorities had any rights. By submitting a question to the test of a division, all concerned agree to abide by the decision. Once that division is taken, all should co-operate in giving effect to the decision of the majority. Mr. Grote, for example, in his ' History of Greece,' vol. iv, refers to the conduct of the five dissentient generals who, when outvoted by the decision of the polemarch, regarding the policy to be pursued at Marathon, heartily co-operated in carrying out measures of which they disapproved. Mr. Spurgeon is reported to have once said, " If you resist the devil he flies from you ; but if you resist a deacon he flies at you." The parallel is not complete, since we cannot liken the dissenting Greek generals to the devil, nor modern political minorities to a deacon ; but we do know that modern minorities are very apt to develop a tendency to fly at the majorities who overrule them. Tories, for example, seem to be, as a rule, in the minority on most questions which have been brought forward for many years past in the House of Commons to improve the condition of the people. The Liberals generally propose the measures and the Tories resist, or, as Mr. Spurgeon said of his deacon, fly at them. Now, it may with some show of reason be said that the country has no right to complain of the minority not heartily co-operating in carrying out the measures of the majority in the House of Commons, because the Liberals, who are always in a minority on questions of Reform in the Upper House, act in the same way. This we cannot deny ; but there are widely different reasons for the Liberal minority resisting the will of the Conservative majority in the House of Lords. The majority in the House of Lords does not represent the opinions of the

people, whereas that of the House of Commons, as a
rule, does. Consequently it would appear that it may
with justice be maintained that the minority in the one
case is justified in resisting the will of the majority,
while in the other it is not. The proof of this justification lies in the fact that the resistance of the majority
in the House of Lords nearly always has to give way
to the minority, through the pressure brought to bear
by the majority in the other House. Whether this be
always the case or only occasionally so, it occurs often
enough to justify the question being raised : Is not the
fact of the two branches of the Legislature continually
falling to loggerheads, an outward and visible sign that
there is something very wrong about the constitution of
one of them which loudly demands investigation with a
view to rectifying what is wrong? We are aware that
this view is held by many, and if it were not for the
traditions and for the lustre which a Chamber of Peers
may be said to lend to the corpus of the Constitution,
which in a measure satisfies a feeling of pride among the
people, who in all ages and climes have had a weakness
for their ancient lines of nobles, we fear there would ere
this have been a rather dangerous movement in favour
of getting rid of this somewhat obstructive part of our
political machinery. What, however, is now a theoretical
discussion might very easily become a practical one, if a
great Liberal majority in the House of Commons was
headed by a Prime Minister of strong Radical proclivities.

But our more immediate object is to endeavour to
reason out the question, what are the advantages to be
derived from having two separate Chambers, supposing
they resembled each other in most respects? As far as
we are able to judge, we are of opinion that two

legislative bodies are better than one, for the following reasons. In the first place, as we have said before, there is greater safety in many counsellors than in a few, and, secondly, there is still greater safety if a detached body discusses and amends a measure which has been discussed in the heat of the incubating assembly. There is, in fact, the same advantage to be derived from one assembly revising and examining the work of another, as there is in the editor of a newspaper bringing his cool and if possible unbiased and mature judgment to bear upon the leading article of a member of his staff. For one Legislative Chamber to be able to bring its unbiased judgment to bear upon the proposals of another, is, we admit, more easily imagined than realised, as we see from the position of our two Chambers at the present day.

But it cannot be said that we do not find parallels in other branches which have to deal with the affairs of the nation. In law, for instance, we could not go on without Courts of Appeal. In nearly all large institutions it is the practice for the proposals of the executive to be considered by a Board of Directors. There are cases, it is true, such as the command of an army or a fleet, in which the responsibility of acting must be placed upon the shoulders of one man, because occasions are sure to arise in which there is not time to consult other authorities. In such cases the commander who makes the fewer mistakes is considered the best, and history records, we know well enough, only too many mistakes from the extreme difficulty of finding one head sufficiently capable of doing the right thing at the right moment. The avoidance of such mistakes is the great object to be aimed at by the Government of a nation. It may be said that in the affairs of a nation there is

not always time to take all opinions and select the right
one.   We cannot conceive that such an argument would
hold good of a great Power of the present day, governed
on the most scientific principles.   People are very fond
of pointing to Germany and its great Chancellor as the
ne plus ultra of scientific government.   Our opinion may
be worth very little on such a point, but it most certainly
is, that the one-man system of government in Germany
belongs to a period of development from which this
country has long since emerged.   France will probably
never return permanently to a system which has cost her
people so much useless suffering and such grievous
burdens, which at this hour weigh down the backs of
that high-spirited and intelligent people till they are
near breaking.

Since legislation as a rule is initiated by the popular
Chamber, the second Chamber's functions come to be, as
a rule, those of a reviser.   The House of Lords should,
in fact, be so constituted as to be able dispassionately to
review and weigh the measures sent up to it, entirely
uninfluenced in its judgment by a spirit of antagonism.
In other words, if the work of reviewing and revising is
to be done effectually there must be no conflict of interests.   This is the real key to the differences which
have always arisen between the two Houses, and the
proposition which is before the country, and which
must be solved if the two branches of the Legislature
are to work usefully and harmoniously in the future, is,
how is the source of this conflict to be rooted out and
removed ?   The answer seems to us to be a plain one.
The Upper House must be recruited on a different
principle from that which has hitherto prevailed ; while
the elements which keep the House of Lords in conflict
with the spirit which, as a rule, animates the House of

Commons, continue to be renewed, bicamerism, as we have it at present, is a form of political machinery which will now and again come to a dead lock.

So much has been now done in the direction of giving the people a voice in the government of the country that the House of Peers is, comparatively speaking, harmless as an obstructive element in the Constitution. In these circumstances it is perhaps better to allow time to attenuate and deprive of its evil influence the antagonistic feeling which Conservative Peers entertain towards their political opponents, than by violent measures to seek to remove an element which all sound thinking men know to be a political relic which must loosen its hold upon the Constitution as every year goes by. Bit by bit other reforms have been carried, and there is good reason to hope that this further change of a gradually remodelled second Chamber, representing the feelings and interests, and expressing the sentiments of the great majority of the people, will be brought about by the peaceful means which have been found sufficient to compel the Lords and their unennobled friends and adherents to give way before the overwhelming but withal peaceful coercion which have given us the invaluable reforms which have been touched upon in the foregoing pages. We can afford, now that so much has been done, to write up over the entrance to that great hereditary Chamber "Paulatim." But there is much yet to be done, and the Peers themselves should, in the face of the two millions who are just about to exercise their rights as electors, tread warily lest they give cause for a cry which shall make the people unwilling to allow the reform of their body to proceed any longer on the *Paulatim* principle.

CHAPTER XII.

THE difficulties into which England drifted with Egypt after the suppression of Arabi's rebellion have been used by Conservative statesmen and politicians as an argument against the system of government as practised on what we may call Liberal principles, as opposed to the principles which guided the Government of Lord Beaconsfield. It is argued by many who are in a position to gain a hearing that a country cannot be safely governed unless at the same time that treaties are made with foreign Powers, measures are always adopted to enforce them, and that, before the ink is dry, preparations should be made to that end. The difficulties which arose with Russia on the Afghan frontier question are pointed to by Conservatives as justifying Lord Beaconsfield's action, which resulted in the death of Cavagnari. The 'Observer' adopted that line of argument on March 8th, 1885, when it said :—" We are suffering now from the loss of that prestige the worthlessness of which has been a favourite dogma of latter-day Liberalism. Russia will always argue that the Power which annexed the Transvaal and then surrendered it after her defeat by the Boers; which first deposed Cetewayo, and then reinstated him; which cannot make up its own mind either to take Egypt or to leave it; which allowed Gordon to be sacrificed; and

not; which shrinks from all extension of her responsibilities, and invariably yields to external pressure, is not
a Power which is likely to engage in grim earnest in a
remote and arduous war for such an object as the re-
covery of Herat. If war is to be averted, it can only
be by England showing that she has abandoned the
policy which has paralysed her strength abroad, and
that she is at length prepared to assert her own power
and defend her own interests." This, to say the least,
is a curious statement. Do English people as a rule
believe that because a handful of British troops were
worsted in a position to which they had been led by a
rash general that England, out of fear of the Boers, gave
up what they rightfully claimed as their own? To think
of avenging what we may really call a deserved defeat
would be to emulate in a higher sphere the undignified
course pursued in many of the small squabbles in
private life which arise between unduly sensitive people.
It will be remembered that impartial continental statesmen approved of the attitude of the British Government on that occasion, and thought they set a wise and
high-minded example in considering it quite beneath
their dignity to take measures to restore what only
foolish people looked upon as injured prestige. Many
of the terrible and useless wars that have been waged
in the world have had their origin in such encounters
as that at Majuba Hill; and it would be difficult perhaps
to cite another instance in which so righteous and noble
an example was set as that by the Government of Great
Britain. Strong Powers with a high sense of morality
to guide the Government in power, can afford to take up
such an attitude. It is the small State that fears being
laughed at on account of its real weakness, and feels bound

by a false necessity of repairing its wounded prestige, that gives the trouble and causes the bloodshed when it happens to be placed in a similar position. Parallels used often to be met with in private life in this country, but they have gone out of fashion. There are countries still, unfortunately, where people feel in honour bound to draw blood before full amends are considered to have been made for an insult, often only a fancied insult; but it is a barbarous practice, and signifies really that the young gentlemen who thus give way to their feelings are not in the true sense courageous, but that they are fools sacrificing themselves to an idiotic sense of honour.

Then with reference to not being able to make up their minds, as the 'Observer' says, "either to take Egypt or to leave it," there has been no question of doing either from the beginning of the Gladstone Government's administration of that country to the present time. We happen to have before us 'Blackwood's Magazine' for March, 1885, which, in the later stages of its career at least, cannot be accused of favouring a Liberal Government. On page 318, in an article entitled "Our Egyptian Atrocities," we read, "With the accession of Tewfik Pasha, however, an undeniably abnormal state of affairs begins. From that date, a state of foreign intervention existed on the Nile. *Egypt was placed under a moral protectorate by the European Powers, with England and France at their head.*" The 'Observer' ridicules that "moral protectorate" by implication, and believes that Russia took advantage of England refusing to break its pledges. So much the more to the credit of the English Government, which apparently declines also to be drawn from the path of virtue by the German Chancellor. The Conservatives are not likely to improve their position with the English people by encouraging the formation of such political opinion as that. The next indictment of the 'Observer' is that the British Government "allowed Gordon to be sacrificed." That question was raised in the House of Commons, and disposed of there in favour of the Government. As Lord Aberdare said, with his accustomed shrewdness, if Khartoum had held out two days longer, the nation would have flung their caps up and have proclaimed the Government to be a successful and satisfactory one. Political opinion thus formed is grown in an emotional soil which depends for its fertilizing powers upon its coming under a particular set of influences. All the other collateral circumstances necessary to the formation of sound opinion upon that question are forgotten and lost sight of by the politician who waits to make his effects till he can pounce upon just what supports his views. Again we read in the same columns, "And which cannot determine whether to go to Khartoum or not." This is a charge for which there is no foundation at all. It was determined at once, so far as existing circumstances enabled a judgment to be formed, to go to Khartoum, a good part of the railway necessary for the purpose being already at Suakin before that sentence was in type at the office of the ' Observer.' It was decided subsequently to postpone opening up the Soudan to civilisation owing to the difficulties with Russia. Then we read, " Which shrinks from all extension of her responsibilities, and invariably yields to external pressure." The difficulties the country now finds itself in is owing to the Government having been forced by circumstances to extend its responsibilities. The breakdown of the Egyptian Government left the British Government no option in the matter, as is well known. From the present standpoint we may ask: would the writer of the above sentence have willingly extended the responsibilities of this country to the extent of the present position we occupy in Egypt? The difficulties of that position will, we believe, sober his judgment on that point. This is another instance of how irresponsible people form their political opinions. Lastly, we are accused of "invariably yielding to external pressure." That is perhaps the hardest cut of all, and one which would be the most fiercely resented if the gentleman occupying the editorial chair had been removed from that to a seat in the Cabinet, when we consider that in the very midst of our difficulties our Foreign Minister and also our Prime Minister were in the black books of the Iron Chancellor because they are well known and amply proved to have steadily declined to yield to the pressure he put upon them. Moreover, if there is a nation in the world that does not yield to any other when it has right on its side, it is the British. Any schoolboy historian knows that; and we are surprised that any journal could lend itself to such statements. We refer to them seriatim in all good humour because the explosion of such fallacies is part of our scheme, and moreover, it is impossible to resist the inclination to bombard a fortress of indictments constructed of such very easily demolished materials. It will, no doubt, not have escaped attention how immediately advantage was taken by other Powers of the British Government being engaged in Egypt, to try and forward their own interests. "Now the great European policeman," they said to themselves, " has been called from his beat to quell some disturbance, this is our chance, and we will see how we can profit by his absence." No greater compliment could have been paid to this country. The Czar of Russia proceeds at once to pounce upon Afghanistan. No matter what the Afghans think; that was also the opinion of the Tories. Lord Beaconsfield pounced upon it, and, as might be expected, they pounced upon his Envoy in return and destroyed him. There is the difference between a Conservative and a Liberal Government. The former appropriates other nations' territory without their consent; the latter distinctly declines to do that sort of thing, and is in consequence accused of " shrinking from an extension of its responsibilities."

We often hear it said by the shallow political thinker, " See, now if you had only left Lord Beaconsfield's work alone, what an advantageous position we should now be in for the encounter with Russia." Among other pieces of evidence which attest the unsoundness of that view, we quote the following from the ' Pall Mall Gazette,' which quotes from a native journal which is in a position to know the real facts of the case :—

" The rage professed by many Primrose Leaguers at what they describe as our impotence on the Afghan frontier is natural enough. But although they do well to be angry, they should remember that the cause of our impotence is the policy of Lord Beaconsfield. It was his fatal invasion of Afghanistan in 1878 that has rendered it impossible for us to send an army across the country to defend Herat in 1885. Referring to this subject, the ' Indian Statesman ' (March 24) says :—

" ' We have done everything that one people can do to another to earn the active and undying hatred of every Afghan. A burning desire is felt throughout Afghanistan to retaliate upon ourselves the sufferings and wrong to which we have twice over subjected the

Afghan people without provocation. At this moment, any Russian subject may enter Afghanistan where he pleases, and traverse every part with nothing but hospitality and welcome, from all classes of the people; while no Englishman dare cross the border anywhere but at peril of his life. When the Boundary Commission was proposed, Lord Ripon's Government affected strong indignation when told plainly by the Ameer that it was impossible for the Mission to travel either through the Hazara country or by Candahar, because of the deadly hatred with which the English name is regarded in the country. The extraordinary route that was finally adopted was the humiliating one of avoiding Afghanistan altogether, and marching through the desert tract that divides the Persian border from the Ameer's territory. It was even then put under the charge of an Afghan officer, Mir Sad-u-deen Khan, with instructions to avoid every inhabited village and tract of country. We have done what we cannot undo. The crime we committed against the people by the invasion of 1839 we repeated in 1878, and our imagination unfortunately is too sluggish to permit us to realize what these invasions meant to the unhappy people who suffered under them. They have made us an abhorrence to the Afghan people, and no Englishman dare cross the Afghan border. Afghanistan is practically Russianized at this moment by our own conduct, while we stupidly ascribe it to Russian emissaries and Russian trickery. The Afghan people have no more desire to see Russia occupying Afghanistan than ourselves. They have learned to fear both nations, but they know well the service which Russia has done throughout the Khanates to the world and to themselves, and individual Russian subjects are received in Afghanistan with as cordial a friendship as Englishmen are with detestation.' Curses like chickens come home to roost, and it is not surprising that the Primrose Leaguers dislike the returning brood."

Prince Bismarck is a Conservative, and very naturally tried to dislodge a Liberal Government that would not set an example, which on his *do ut des* principle would afford him a colourable pretext for appropriating other people's property. We hope the Conservative politicians do not lose sight of the fact that if Lord Beaconsfield had succeeded in annexing Afghanistan, when we really required their aid and co-operation in 1885, instead of being friends as they are now they would have been enemies. That little fact shows the soundness and justice of the Liberal policy, and the unsoundness and injustice of that of the Conservatives.

The conviction is slowly working to the front, even among moderate Conservatives, that the general principles which guided the Gladstone Administration were sound principles. There is a ring of endurance about them which gradually brings in converts from the opposite ranks. The fabric of Liberal principles, notwithstanding mistakes—and mistakes there will always be, temporarily reducing the Liberal majority of voters, where all sorts of people's opinions must from the necessities of the case be taken—is always growing, while that of the Conservatives is always diminishing. Very strong interests bind people for a time to express certain opinions and take a certain course of action; but as those interests decline they become gradually converted. Such a process is going on at the present time upon a scale which overshadows everything of the kind that has been witnessed during this century. The great depression in profits, which some people have called a depression in trade, has carried down with it, like a huge avalanche, a mass of commercial middlemen, who, in their privileged positions, were Tories to the backbone. The City proper of London is full of them, and they have been for years past abusing the Liberal Government. The trade channels have shifted; the mode of doing business has changed by which many of them have been left as superfluities with little or nothing to do, and they visit all their misfortunes on the Liberal Government. But the natural selection of processes, both commercial and political, goes on. All the ravings of those who declare that the country is going to the dogs, and that the late Liberal Government was what Lord Salisbury calls "imbecile," avail nothing. A power that no man or combination of men can withstand keeps hard at work forging new links to the chain which is drawing the Truth up against an opposing stream of Error. Men may raise their voices in Parliament and out of it against what they proclaimed to be a policy of vacillation and weakness, but the sound portion of the country sees through these arguments, and knows that while all Governments make mistakes, the worst blunders are invariably made in the long run by statesmen who are too precipitate in their action. Showy statesmanship is like destructive literary criticism. It delights the ignorant, and satisfies an untaught brute instinct; but there is reaction as well as action in all mundane affairs, and the farseeing politician is the one who, when planning his action, thinks at the same time of the reaction.

The British Liberal Government of our day is a type of Government which rises to a higher moral standard than has ever been reached before. The men who thus govern seek a reward which consists solely of the approval of the sound thinkers of the nation. No titles, no money, is anything to them. A Peerage is to the laurels worn by plain Mr. Gladstone as the tinsel finery of human ingenuity compared with the glory of the summer sun. They can get no higher as far as place is concerned. They sit on a level which is above any throne, even that of the country which they govern, and when the people whose servants they are see and feel, as they do, that their actions are guided by disinterested motives, it is no matter for surprise that one vote of censure followed another without materially disturbing the foundations of their power. Those supporters who fell away from the Liberal Government of Mr. Gladstone during the months which preceded their fall in June, 1885, did so quite as much through a defective understanding of the merits of the case as they did from a well-grounded belief that the Government had committed blunders which ought to have been foreseen. No people know so well as sober men of business—that class of undemonstrative successful English traders—how many and intricate are the difficulties which an English Cabinet of to-day has to deal with. Amidst the storm of partisan feeling, the abuse of foiled opponents, the screaming of ignorant thousands who have their little axe to grind and do not care for anything else but to get it ground and pocket the benefit, this sober middle class of educated men of sound calculating judgment perceive that on the whole the Liberal Government does by far the best for the country in the long run, and makes the fewest mistakes.

Dr. Johnson in his preface to Shakespeare says that authors are judged by their worst works while they are alive, and by their best when they are dead. This is very much the principle on which the Opposition judges the party in power. Everything that appears in print against the Government is referred to in all Opposition speeches with a view to discrediting them, while no single success is ever mentioned.

We end this short inquiry into the formation of political opinion from the reign of the great families to the advent of democracy by reminding the Conservatives that their principles have in these pages been proved, on the whole, to be wrong principles; that such proof is established by the fact that their endeavours to prevent the Liberal reforms from being carried has been on nearly all occasions defeated; that the nation has in consequence withdrawn from them their confidence, comparatively speaking, as shown in the diagram of the duration of Governments since the passing of the 1832 Reform Bill at the beginning of the book; and that under the most difficult and trying circumstances which probably any British Government has had to encounter, their opponents failed to carry, as we have before remarked, one vote of censure after another against the policy of the Gladstone Ministry. The unfortunate and unlucky events in the Soudan in the years 1884 and 1885 would have been enough to shipwreck any but the strongest of Governments; and the reason why the Gladstone Ministry survived events which caused the nation to weep and mourn not only for its own heroes, but for those whom they attempted in vain to rescue, was that the sober judgment of the sound thinking portion of the Empire were fully satisfied that Mr. Gladstone and his colleagues had availed themselves of the best advice they could obtain on all questions outside the strictly political problem which they themselves had to deal with, and that they decided upon action, or decided not to act, with one sole object before them at all times, and that was to do the best in their power and judgment to discharge faithfully the duties entrusted to them by the people of this Empire.

PRINTED BY J. E. ADLARD, BARTHOLOMEW CLOSE.

www.ingramcontent.com/pod-product-compliance
Lightning Source LLC
Chambersburg PA
CBHW020457270326
41926CB00008B/637